American
Writers and Compilers
of
Sacred Music

The earliest music printed in America, from the ninth edition
of the Bay Psalm Book, 1698.   Massachusetts
Historical Society

American
Writers and Compilers
of
Sacred Music

By
Frank J. Metcalf

NEW YORK / RUSSELL & RUSSELL

CONTENTS

TUNE COMPOSERS

ARRANGED BY DATES

PART I

PART III

6 CONTENTS

PART V

LIST OF ILLUSTRATIONS

PREFACE

THE following pages are the results of ten years of research into the history of the writers of sacred music. For at least an equal period prior to that the writer had been studying the history of hymns, and had written much concerning them, when suddenly he discovered that very little had been written up to that time about the tune composers. When he sought information he found few sources. Encouraged by Mr. Edmund S. Lorenz, he began to collect facts about the development of church music, and the results were published in the Choir Herald, and other publications of the Lorenz Company. By the courtesy of Mr. Lorenz, permission has been granted to use those articles which appeared from time to time in his magazines. The other articles appear for the first time and afford some information regarding nearly every one of the composers whose work was done before the year 1800, and it has been thought advisable to include also some matter of a miscellaneous character which has from time to time been gathered for various occasions.

The printed periodicals relating to sacred music, or containing information about American composers of tunes, begin with the Euterpiad, edited by John R. Parker in Boston, 1820 to 1823, but it furnished very little about the early writers. Nearly every such periodical printed up to 1900, and many of those printed since that date which might prob-

9

ably add any items of interest, have been read, and other sources of information have been sought. Much of the record here preserved has been obtained from relatives of the composers through private correspondence. Genealogies and biographies have furnished much of value, and many of the music books themselves contain facts that cannot be obtained elsewhere. It would be impossible to give credit to every source from which facts have been extracted. The Library of Congress, the Boston Public Library, and that of the American Antiquarian Society in Worcester, Massachusetts, have been those whose contents have been most thoroughly explored, and the thanks of the writer are hereby extended to the librarians and attendants of those institutions for the many courtesies extended.

FRANK J. METCALF.

Washington, D. C.

PART I

1689–1757

THE REV. JOHN TUFTS AND THE FIRST AMERICAN TUNE BOOK[1]

1689–1750

FOR one hundred years after the landing of the Pilgrims and the founding of the towns in eastern Massachusetts the communities had to rely upon the music which they had brought with them from England. Most of the singing was by rote, and books which contained the tunes were very scarce; in fact, they were not desired, for in most churches it was preferred that the lines should be read one at a time, and the congregation should sing them after the reading. In 1708, John Tufts graduated from Harvard College, a youth still in his teens. He had some knowledge of music, had some ideas as to how he would like to hear it sung, and was soon to become the first compiler of a tune book in the colonies. He had studied theology, and in 1713 was a candidate for pastor of the church in Charlestown, receiving eight votes out of the one hundred and fifty-nine cast. It was not long after this that he secured a church in Newbury, the second parish. Their pastor was getting old and an assistant was desired. The parish records show that on

January 15, 1713-4, voted to give Rev. John Tufts £70 a year so long as Mr. Samuel Belcher lives, and the use of the whole parsonage, and after the decease of Mr. Belcher £80 a year, provided the said Mr. Tufts accepts the call to the ministry in the parish and preacheth a monthly lecture.

[1] From The Choir Herald.

13

He was ordained June 13, 1714, and a few months later published a small book of church hymns and psalm tunes with instructions for singing by note. This was the first publication of its kind in America, and was considered by many as a daring innovation. Before the appearance of this book the number of tunes known and used in the ordinary congregation could be counted upon the fingers of one hand. This new collection contained thirty-seven tunes, arranged for the several meters that were needed. At least eleven editions of this little book were issued during the next twenty-five years. The date of the first edition is given by different writers as between 1714 and 1721. The earliest which I have seen is the fifth, dated 1726, in the Boston Public Library. Its title page is as follows:

AN
INTRODUCTION
To the Singing
of
PSALM TUNES
In a plain and easy method

with
A collection of tunes
In Three Parts
By the Rev. Mr. Tufts.
The Fifth Edition
Printed from Copper Plates

Neatly Engraved
BOSTON in N. E.
Printed for Samuel Gerrish
At the Lower End of Corn-
Hill, 1726.

The copy of the tenth edition in the New York Public Library has a modern binding, but the partial covers which are included indicate that the original was a pamphlet bound in marbled-paper covers. There were twenty-three pages. It is not strange, therefore, that most of the copies of so small a book should have been lost during the nearly two hundred years that have elapsed since it was first issued, and that only a few are to be found at this day. Again, as the new book of Thomas Walter came out with notes instead of letters, as Tufts' book had, the old was doubtless discarded and not valued as the remaining copies of it are at the present time. An interesting incident in point is told of an experience of the Bodleian Library, which possessed a copy of the First Folio of Shakespeare's works when it was first issued. But when the Second Folio came out the First was disposed of as a duplicate of less value. The strangest part of the story is that three hundred years later, after such a high value had been placed upon first editions, this very volume was offered for sale on the market, and the Bodleian Library placed it again upon its shelves, but at a cost of £3,000.

Some of the rules of Tufts' book are as follows:

The tunes are set down in such a plain and easy method that a few rules may suffice for direction in singing. The letters F S L M marked on the several lines and spaces in the following tunes, stand for these syllables: that is, Fa. Sol. La. Mi. Mi. is the principal note, and the notes rising gradually above Mi. are Fa. Sol. La. Fa. Sol. La., and then Mi. again; and the notes falling gradually below Mi. are La. Sol. Fa. La. Sol. Fa., and then comes Mi. again in every eighth. For as every eighth note gives the same sound, so it has the same letter and name. The place of Mi. is altered by flats and sharps put at the beginning of the five lines on which the tune is prick'd.

The length of the tone is not indicated by different kinds of notes as it is in present-day music, for there were no notes used. But, for instance, the letter F indicated a quarter; F. (followed by a period) was equal to a half; and F: (followed by a colon) was equal to a whole note. The thirty-seven tunes are printed on twelve pages, and, as has been implied, the letters took the place of notes upon the lines. The tunes in this book were set in three parts called cantus, medius, and bassus.

Biography

John Tufts was born in Medford, Massachusetts, May 5, 1689, and was the son of Captain Peter Tufts and Mercy Cotton. His maternal grandmother was Dorothy Bradstreet, the oldest daughter of Simon and Anne Bradstreet, the latter being the first female poet in America. Through his mother he could also trace his ancestry to the Rev. Seaborn Cotton and the Rev. John Cotton, the latter of whom was frequently referred to as the patriarch of New England. Because of these ministerial ancestors it was but natural that he should follow the same profession after his graduation from Harvard in 1708. One of the earliest references to him after he had settled in Newbury is found in a curious contract dated May 13, 1718, by which a few persons were given permission to use certain lands in that town on condition that they give one salmon per year to the pastor of the First Church, and one to the Rev. John Tufts, pastor of the Second Church in Newbury "if they catch them." It was in 1731, while he was still pastor of the Second

Church, that a petition was presented to the General Court of Massachusetts for a division of the parish; and the Fourth Church of Newbury was organized. The third parish had been formed in 1725, now the First Church in Newburyport, and the dedication sermon had been preached by Mr. Tufts on June 25, 1725. Two of his sermons have been printed and may be seen in the library of the Massachusetts Historical Society. One of them, "The Duties of Ministers," was printed in 1725; the other was preached at the ordination of the Rev. Benjamin Bradstreet at Gloucester, September 18, 1728. After more than twenty years of service in the Newbury church, Mr. Tufts was in 1737 accused of immorality and unchristian behavior by some of the women of his parish, and in February a council of ten ministers was called to consider "the distressed state and condition of ye Second Church of Christ in Newbury." Mr. Tufts strenuously opposed the investigation and declined to cooperate with the council or to question the witnesses called to testify against him. On March 2, 1738, "in consequence of the unhappy differences prevailing in the parish," he asked to be released from the duties of pastor. The church voted to grant his request and the council with only one dissenting voice consented to the separation, "hoping thereby to restore harmony to the church." During the first year of his pastorate Mr. Tufts had married, December 9, 1714, Sarah Bradstreet, a daughter of Dr. Humphrey Bradstreet and Sarah Pierce. There were four children, the second of whom, Joshua, graduated from Harvard in 1736, and became minister in Litchfield in 1741. After leaving Newbury Mr. Tufts went to Amesbury, where he died in August, 1750. His "easy method of singing by letters instead of notes," as one of his title pages reads, was not a success, in the sense of being permanently adopted, though his book passed through at least ten editions in twenty-five years. Much opposition followed the attempt to teach the congregation to sing by note, instead of the old way of having the tunes taught by rote. But Mr. Tufts' book was the entering wedge for the new way, and it was only a short time before his ideas, if not his methods, were adopted.

EDITIONS

The date of the first edition of Tufts' "Plain and Easy Introduction to the Art of Singing" is given as 1714[1] and 1721. I am inclined to think that the latter date is the correct one. The Brinley library had a copy of this year, "Printed by J. F(ranklin) for S. Gerrish," which sold for ten dollars. It was a small pamphlet of sixteen pages, and was of such a size that it could be laid in or bound in with the psalm books in use at that date. Charles Evans in his *American Bibliography* gives the title page of a copy printed in Boston in 1723, but does not locate it. The earliest copy that I have seen is in the Boston Public Library. It is the fifth edition, printed in Boston for Samuel Gerrish, 1726. A news note states that the sixth edition bears date of 1728. The seventh edition is in the library of the American Antiquarian Society, Worcester, Massa-

---

[1] George Hood, in his *History of Music in New England*, says that he has "the word of a gentleman, who is always correct in dates of olden time, that he has seen a copy of it dated 1714."

"Oxford" and Others

A page from John Tufts' Introduction, fifth edition, 1726.
Boston Public Library. The first American compilation

chusetts, bound at the end of a book of Psalms. It has 2, 10, 12p. The eighth edition, Boston, 1731, in Massachusetts Historical Society. The ninth edition, Boston, 1736, in Essex Institute, Salem, Massachusetts, bound at the end of what appears to be the Bay Psalm Book. The tenth edition, Boston, 1738, in the New York Public Library. The eleventh edition, Boston, 1744, noted by Evans, but not located.

THOMAS WALTER[1]

1696–1725

THE second book of psalm tunes, set to English words and printed in this country, was larger than that of John Tufts and was more extensively used. Its compiler, the Rev. Thomas Walter, was only twenty-five years old when the first edition of his *Grounds and Rules of Musick* was published. Tufts had used letters on the staff in his book, but Walter's book had notes, though they were diamond shaped instead of the round ones with which we are so familiar.

Thomas Walter was born in Boston, December 7, 1696, and was the son of the Rev. Nehemiah Walter and Sarah Mather. Through his mother he was the grandson of Increase Mather and Maria Cotton, and a great-grandson of the Rev. John Cotton. He graduated from Harvard in 1713 at the age of seventeen. He was not a hard student, but was fond of society in his youth, yet "so retentive was his memory that he easily made himself master of almost all the

---

[1] From The Choir Herald.

learning of his uncle Cotton Mather by frequent conversations with him. In this way he acquired more knowledge than most others could have gained by a whole life's diligent study."

In regard to his call to the Roxbury Church the records show that "at a church meeting of the east end of Roxbury in the old meetinghouse, the first day of March, 1717-18, it was unanimously agreed and voted as follows:

1. That it was necessary to choose some meet person for an assistant to our reverend pastor.

2. It was agreed and voted to choose such an assistant at the present meeting. Accordingly the votes being brought in and counted, every vote was for Thomas Walter, son of the reverend pastor.

3. The said church chose and appointed the deacons a committee to acquaint Mr. Walter herewith, and inform the inhabitants of the town in their next meeting with the church's doings, in order for their future proceedings.

On the 13th day of May of the same year

The town met to consider of a settlement of Mr. Walter. . . . Voted that there should be five hundred pounds raised for Mr. Walter, as encouragement for his settling among us.

This call was accepted and he was ordained as colleague with his father on October 29, 1718, the ordination sermon being preached by his grandfather, the Rev. Increase Mather. On the Christmas Day following he was married to Rebecca Belcher, daughter of the Rev. Joseph Belcher, of Dedham. Among the names of the fifteen ministers who signed the preface of his book, recommending his *Rules of Musick*, are the names of his father-in-law, Joseph Belcher; his father, the Rev. Nehemiah Walter, and also Cotton Mather and Increase Mather. Thomas

Walter had one daughter, Rebecca, born in 1722, who died unmarried January 11, 1780, at the age of fifty-eight, the last of the Walter family. In a letter written in 1768 by the Rev. Doctor Chauncey to Doctor Stiles he says:

Dr. Jeremiah Dummer, Mr. John Bulkley, and Mr. Thomas Walter I reckon the first three clergymen for extent and strength of genius and powers New England has yet produced. I was acquainted with the latter, and often had occasion to admire the superlative excellence of his natural and acquired accomplishments. His genius was universal, yet surprisingly strong. He seemed to have almost an intuitive knowledge of everything. There was no subject but he was acquainted with, and such was the power he had over his thoughts and words that he could readily and without any pains write or speak just what he would.

Surely this was high praise for a man who died before he was thirty years old. He was a popular preacher and a keen disputant. His sermons and writings that may be consulted in some of the larger libraries are the following: "Faustus and Jack Tory," "Essay on Infallibility," "The Scripture Rule of Faith," and "The Sweet Singer of Israel." In 1722 he preached a sermon on "Regular Singing," in the preface to which in the printed copy it is stated that it "is the first fruits of your young minister's, who claims a pastoral care for you, though of a different kind." It was dedicated to "Honorable Paul Dudley, esq. one of his Majesty's Council for the province of Massachusetts Bay in New England and one of the Justices of the Superior Court."

The Rev. Thomas Walter died on Sunday, January 10, 1725, of pneumonia, near the close of the afternoon. He was buried in the parish tomb in Roxbury, where the Rev. John Eliot, the Apostle to the Indians, had been buried thirty-five years before, and where his own father was laid a few years later. The funeral bill for the burial of Mr. Walter is an interesting paper which includes items for gloves, rings, a barrel of wine, pipes and tobacco, and a box to put the bones of old Mr. Eliot and others in. The funeral sermon was preached by his uncle, the Rev. Cotton Mather, and was printed soon afterward under the name of "Christodulus: A Good Reward of a Good Servant."

Editions

There were at least eight editions of Walter's book. One of them was not dated, but the several issues may be identified by the names of the printers. The first edition was printed in 1721 and the title page reads as follows:

The Ground and Rules of Musick Explained, or An Introduction to the Art of Singing by Note. Fitted to the meanest capacities, By Thomas Walter, M.A. Recommended by several Ministers. Boston. Printed by J. Franklin, for S. Gerrish near the Brick Church in Cornhill. 1721.

A copy of this edition is in the New York Public Library and was purchased by its original owner the year of its publication. It is oblong in form and has sixteen pages of engraved music. George Hood, in his *History of Music*, tells us that this book "was noticed in the Boston Gazette of May 8, 1721, and duly announced and advertised in the same periodical on the 17th of July."

In April, 1723, the second edition of the work,

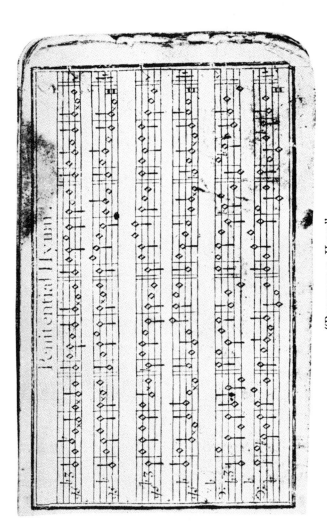

"Penitential Hymn"

Thomas Walter's Introduction, 1721. Massachusetts Historical Society

"Enlarged, corrected and Beautified," was advertised in the Gazette. This shows upon the title page
that it was "The Second Edition," and was Printed
by B. Green for S. Gerrish. I have seen a photostat
title in the Library of Congress.

The next (third) edition appears to have been
printed in 1737. There is a copy in the Lowell
Mason collection in Yale Library, which has no title
page, but has a note by the one who presented it to
Mr. Mason as follows:

STOCKBRIDGE, MASS., April 11/38.

Sir:
   This had a title page which bore the date of 1737, if it is
too old as to be new to you it may amuse you, if not, it may
at least serve to mark the improvements of a Century of
Music—to which you have contributed a full share, accept it
with sincere regards of   S. ROCKWELL.

The next edition was printed in 1740 for S.
Gerrish, and in 1746 another edition was issued for
Samuel Gerrish. In 1760 Benjamin Mecom was
printing in Boston, and he printed Walter's Introduction for Thomas Johnston. The last edition of
this book was printed for and sold by Thomas Johnston in Brattle Street, over against the Rev. Mr.
Cooper's meetinghouse, in 1764. For forty years it
held its place as the sole American tune book, but it
soon gave way to the compilations of Daniel Bayley.

DANIEL BAYLEY

1725(?)-1799

DANIEL BAYLEY was an organist and a printer,
rather than a composer of music. No record has

been found of any musical pieces of his composition, but his services as organist of Saint Paul's Episcopal Church in Newburyport and his published books of music are well known to students of psalmody. The date of his birth and the date when he went to Newburyport have not as yet been discovered, but the latter must have been previous to 1764, for in that year he signed the petition for the separation of what is now the city of Newburyport from the original town of Newbury.

He was probably born in West Newbury about 1725. He married first Elizabeth Deneen, of Gloucester, who bore him two children; and second Sarah Stone, who became the mother of five children. He lived at the corner of High and Summer Streets, directly opposite Saint Paul's Church, where he conducted a small printing and engraving establishment, and engaged in the trade of a coppersmith. He also no doubt gave instruction in music to the young people of the town, and served as organist for many years in the church which became in 1797 the cathedral of the diocese over which Bishop Bass presided. Edward Bass was the rector of this church from 1752 for fifty years, the last five of which he was a bishop, though still continuing to perform the duties of a parish priest.

The organ upon which Daniel Bayley played was the first pipe organ introduced into America. It had been imported by Thomas Brattle of Boston, and at his death was bequeathed to the Brattle Street Church. Not being accepted by this church, it went to King's Chapel, where it remained for forty years. Then, in 1756, when another organ was imported from England, the Brattle organ was sold to the parish of Saint Paul's in Newburyport, where it remained for eighty years. It was during this period that Daniel Bayley was organist here. In 1836 the Brattle organ was purchased by the parish of Saint John's Chapel at Portsmouth, New Hampshire, and there this old organ is at the present day still in service after over two hundred years. Its tone is still agreeable and sweet, but its volume is not so great as in some of the smaller organs of the present day.

Mr. Bayley died February 22, 1799, but where he was buried I have been unable to determine. One would expect to find a monument to his memory in the churchyard of Saint Paul's Church, with which he had been so long and so closely associated, but a personal search has failed to reveal any such marker. There is, however, a stone over the grave of his son Nathaniel, who died May 3, 1849, at the age of seventy-eight, and of whom it was written, "His friends knew his worth." Nathaniel's wife, Abigail, who died June 24, 1856, aged eighty-four, is buried beside him, and near by is the grave of Elizabeth Bayley, a daughter of Nathaniel and granddaughter of Daniel, who married James Cheney, and died April 10, 1858. The son of James Cheney and Elizabeth Bayley was named James William Cheney. He was a musician, and lived in Washington for many years where he was librarian of the War Department. He played the organs in a number of churches, and was organist of a Masonic lodge. He used to tell that at least four in direct line beginning with Daniel Bayley had played the organ in

Saint Paul's church, he himself having played one
Sunday while he was on a vacation in the town of
Newburyport.

Books

Besides his work as an organist Daniel Bayley
kept a bookstore next door to the church, and about
1770 set up a printing press, from which he issued a
number of music books. He had begun to compile
books before this date, and the method he followed
was to reprint selected portions of English works,
taking those parts which suited his purpose and
omitting the rest.

His first book was *A New and Complete Introduction to the Grounds and Rules of Music*, 1764.
For this book he took the title and introduction from
the most popular work of that day—that of Thomas
Walter—the last edition of which had just made its
appearance in Boston, while the second part was
from William Tans'ur's *Royal Melody*, which had
been published in London in 1754. This composite
book was doubtless issued from Boston, for it was
"Printed for and Sold by Bulkly Emerson and
Daniel Bayley in Newburyport." Another edition
was printed this same year "for and Sold by Bulkly
Emerson of Newbury Port, 1764." It appears to
have been printed from the same plates, but there
were several more pages of engraved music than in
the other imprint. George Hood tells us that there
was also a third printing in 1764 "at Salem, Mass.,
for Mascholl Williams." Two years later an edition was "Printed and Sold by Thomas Johnston in
Brattle Street, Boston, 1766," and a new edition was

"Printed in Boston for the author at Newburyport, 1768."

By 1770 Bayley had established his press in Newburyport, for when he issued his *Essex Harmony*, it was printed and sold by the author at Newburyport. This was a small book of tunes prepared to be bound with the Psalms or other hymn books. Several editions of this were issued up to 1785.

In 1775 he issued his *New Universal Harmony, or Compendium of Church Music*, a book of 105 pages, at a price of six shillings. In his preface he says:

I have been advised with a number of friends of music about the choice of pieces that would be agreeable, and I flatter myself I shall have the approbation of the most of those that are judges of the Noble Art. And as I have determined to publish two or three more volumes in case I meet with encouragement in the sale of this, I would signify to my friends and customers that they may depend upon my sparing no pains in procuring such pieces as shall be agreeable to those lovers of church music. I expect I shall be able to procure some curious pieces that are productions of America by some masterly hands who have not yet permitted any of their work to be made public.

In 1784 he issued *A Collection of Anthems and Hymn Tunes*, and the following year, 1785, *The Psalm Singer's Assistant*. The latter was a small pamphlet of sixteen pages, and was intended, like *The Essex Harmony*, to be bound with the collections of hymns.

The New Harmony of Zion, or Complete Melody, was compiled in 1788 by Daniel Bayley, senior, thus indicating a son of the same name. This was a book of 112 pages.

We have left to the last two books which were

more or less reprints from English sources. One of these was *The Royal Melody Complete or the New Harmony of Zion,* by William Tans'ur, and the date given by Evans is 1761, but this is doubtless too early. Tans'ur's *Royal Melody Complete* was advertised in the Boston Evening Post of October 27, 1766, as "On the press, and soon to be published," while in the issue for January 12, 1767, appears the advertisement:

> This day published Tans'ur's Royal Melody Complete, containing his preface on the excellency of church music, an introduction concerning all that is necessary for the Introduction of Learners with all his Psalm tunes, choruses, hymns and anthems, with several canons and ten of the most approved tunes from Williams' Psalmody. The plates are neatly engraved upon copper and printed upon a superfine writing paper on each side.

This was the third edition and was printed at Boston by W. McAlpine for Daniel Bayley in Newburyport. As no first or second edition has been found printed in America, it appears that this third followed the numbering of the English edition which had been issued in London in 1764-65. The control of the fourth and subsequent American editions would seem to have passed to Daniel Bayley, Newburyport.

In 1769 Bayley printed Aaron Williams' *The Universal Psalmist* as *The American Harmony or Universal Psalmodist,* and he prefaced the publication under date of Newbury-Port, January 5, 1769, with the remarks to his friends and customers:

> And I would inform them that I have now added the chief of Mr. Williams' Universal Psalmody, and as I expect they will be bound mostly with the Royal Melody (of Tans'ur) I have therefore left out the tunes which were in it, and as Mr.

Tans'ur's Introduction to Musick is universally approved, I
have not added Mr. Williams's, which is very lengthy.

The seventh edition of this double book was dated
1771, and the ninth, 1774.

ANDREW ADGATE

–1793

ANDREW ADGATE was one of the earliest of the
musical company in Philadelphia whose influence was
exerted for the improvement of sacred music. The
date of his birth has not been found, nor has much
information been obtained in regard to his public
activities in other lines than that of music. We do
know, however, from the title page of his Philadelphia Harmony that in 1790 he was in company with
Westcott conducting a card factory on Front Street,
seven doors below Arch Street, and opposite the
Bunch of Grapes Tavern.

The earliest reference to his Institute for Vocal
Music appeared on a sheet dated Philadelphia, June
1, 1785. He proposed for diffusing more generally
a knowledge of vocal music to teach music to persons of every denomination gratis, and advertised
for contributions of eight dollars each, promising
to every subscriber twelve concerts during the year,
for which three tickets would be issued to admit one
gentleman and two ladies. His plan was completed
during the summer, the institution began on the
first of October, and the first concert was given on
October 19, 1785.

Some idea of his school, and also the slur cast upon

his methods, may be obtained from Andrew Law's reference to him in the preface of his Musical Magazine in 1791:

> Mr. Adgate has taught a common singing school in Philadelphia where schools of every kind frequently obtain the name of academies. Mr. Adgate called his the Uranian Academy, himself the President of the Uranian Academy. His school was never incorporated and there are a thousand schools of equal importance in the United States.

The criticisms of rival teachers seem to have been as sharp a century or more ago as they are to-day, but the good influence of Mr. Adgate's work was appreciated by those who knew him best. The Rev. Samuel Blair, who had been pastor of the Old South Church in Boston for three years, but was now living in Germantown, preached a "Discourse on Psalmody" in the Presbyterian church in Neshaminy, at a public concert given by Mr. Spicer, master in sacred music, in which he paid a high tribute to the benevolence, assiduity, and success of Mr. Adgate's work in behalf of better singing, and rejoiced in the improvement he had effected in music.

In 1787 Young and McCulloch, of Philadelphia, printed a book of "Select Psalms and Hymns for the use of Mr. Adgate's pupils and proper for all singing schools." The next year, 1788, the first issue of his *Rudiments of Music* was printed, containing twenty pages. A third edition, on a new and improved plan, appeared in 1790, printed by John McCulloch on Third Street, near Market Street, and sold by the author opposite the Bunch of Grapes Tavern, between Market and Arch Streets. An eighth edition was issued in 1803. Mr. Law in-sisted that this new method had been tried and rejected in England long before.

His next compilation was

A Selection of Sacred Harmony, containing lessons explaining the gamut, keys, and other characters used in vocal music, also a rich variety of tunes approved by the most eminent teachers of church music in the United States.

This book had eighty-four pages of engraved music, and was printed in 1788, the same year as his *Rudiments of Music*, and contained twelve pages of Uranian Instructions. He proposed, if suitable encouragement offered, to print a collection of the most celebrated anthems. This object was carried out in his next book, *The Philadelphia Harmony*, which was a "Collection of Psalm Tunes, Hymns and Anthems," 1790. In a later edition the name of Mr. Spicer appears as a collaborateur, and in another issue there was an improved mode of teaching music to facilitate the progress of the learner by John Jenkins Husband. All of these books were in the usual oblong form.

In 1793 an epidemic of malignant, or yellow, fever broke out in Philadelphia and a committee was appointed by the citizens of that city to attend to and alleviate the sufferings of the afflicted. The committee was named on September 14, 1793, and included among others Stephen Girard and Andrew Adgate. Four of the committee succumbed to the plague. Mr. Adgate was last present at the meeting of September 24, and his death was reported on September 30. On the list of those who fell victims to the disease were the widow Adgate and her two children.

ANTHONY ARMBRUSTER

ANTHONY ARMBRUSTER was a printer in Philadelphia from 1751 to 1768; during the years 1754 to 1756 he was associated with Benjamin Franklin, and in 1762 he had N. Hasselbach as a partner. He began the publication of a German newspaper in 1762 and continued its weekly issues for several years. A book of "Tunes in three parts for the several meters of Doctor Watts' version of the Psalms, some of which tunes are new," was printed by him in 1763; this was a small collection of forty-four pages. The next year he issued a second edition from his office in Arch Street, and described it with the following title: "Tunes in three parts for the several meters of Doctor Watts' version of the Psalms, some of which tunes are new. This collection of tunes is made from the works of eminent masters, consisting of six tunes for short meter, eight for common meter, seven for long meter and a tune for each special meter, to which are added the gamut with directions to learners of music." This was a stitched pamphlet of fifty-two pages, and sold for one shilling six pence. Nothing of his personal history has been discovered.

JAMES LYON AND HIS "URANIA"

1735–1790[1]

URANIA was the muse of astronomy in Grecian legend. In the history of American psalmody it is

[1] From The Choir Herald.

the name of the first collection of psalm tunes, compiled and partly composed by a native musician. The works of John Tufts and Thomas Walter had been merely compilations; these men did not write any of the tunes which they put into their books. They were taken from English sources and were few in number, yet they added very materially to those that were generally known and used in the churches before that time. Mr. Walter writes in the introduction to his book:

At present we are confined to eight or ten tunes, and in some congregations to little more than half that number, which, being so often sung over, are too apt, if not to create a distaste, yet at least mightily to lessen the relish of them.

Tufts' collection had only thirty-nine tunes and Walter's only forty-three. Both were published in Boston, the last edition of Walter being issued in 1764.

"URANIA"

In 1759 a young man named James Lyon graduated from the College of New Jersey, now known as Princeton University, and two years later—that is, in 1761—his *Urania* was published in Philadelphia. Its title is as follows: *Urania*, "or a choice collection of Psalm-tunes, anthems, and hymns, from the most approved authors, with some entirely new: in two, three and four parts. The whole peculiarly adapted to the use of churches and private families. To which are prefixed the plainest and most necessary rules of psalmody. By James Lyon, A.B." This book was printed in Philadelphia by William Bradford in 1761. According to an advance advertisement, the work was to be published by subscription and to contain about 210 pages. Each subscription was to be accompanied with one dollar, and the remainder, not to exceed one dollar more, when the book was delivered. The author agreed to begin the work as soon as four hundred subscriptions should be received. The list of subscribers as printed in the first edition numbered 141 names, and, including those who took more than one copy, 199 copies were disposed of. Fifty of these were taken by the officers and students of his Alma Mater, the College of New Jersey.

JAMES LYON

A few facts concerning the life of James Lyon have been gathered. He was the son of Zopher Lyon and Mary Lyon, and was born in Newark, East New Jersey, July 1, 1735. Nothing has been found about his early school life, but while he was yet a boy the College of New Jersey was founded in his native town, and its first commencement was held there in November, 1747, when he was only twelve years old. The presence of this institution of higher learning may have interested him to enter its doors, and he may have been one of its students when it was removed in 1756 to Princeton. Its thirteenth commencement was held September 26, 1759, when James Lyon received his first degree of A.B., and (the program states) "The whole ceremony concluded with the following ode, set to music by Mr. James Lyon, one of the students." No copy of this music has been found, but it certainly was an early, if not the first, specimen of the commencement ode by an American. The next year we find Mr. Lyon in Philadelphia, though still continuing his studies, and on September 29, 1762, he took his second degree, A.M., at Princeton, at which time he delivered an English oration.

As Minister

In 1764 James Lyon was licensed by the Presbytery of New Brunswick and ordained to preach. The following year he went to Nova Scotia. He was married February 18, 1768, to Martha Holden, daughter of Daniel Holden, of Cape May in West New Jersey, and returned to Nova Scotia, settling in Onslow, where his first two children were born.

In July, 1771, the proprietors of Machias, Maine, in compliance with the terms of the grant of their township by the General Court, agreed to settle a Protestant minister, and voted to hire one to preach the gospel in that place. Eighty-four pounds were raised for the purpose. In August, 1771, Judge Stephen Jones, of the committee to employ the minister, being in Boston, found Mr. Lyon who had left Nova Scotia. Judge Jones induced Lyon to go to Machias on trial. He went there with his family, and began to preach December 5, 1771. In the spring of 1772 the people invited him to remain on a salary of eighty-four pounds yearly, and one hundred pounds as a settlement.

Mr. Lyon during the Revolutionary War was an ardent patriot, fighting as well as preaching. During this period he and his family suffered great hardships, in common with the people of the congregation, because the lumber interests, upon which they depended very largely for their supply of provisions, were almost stopped. In the intervals between preaching and writing sermons the minister fished and dug clams to provide food for his family. The war passed away, and brighter days dawned for the people of Machias. New settlers came in, many of whom, with some of those already there, were of a character superior to those generally found in new settlements. September 12, 1782, a Congregational church

was organized and Mr. Lyon became the minister. As no
other pastors were near, Mr. Lyon was probably installed by
the church and town of Machias, a proceeding not new in those
days.

Seven other children were born to him in Machias,
and he continued to reside and preach there until
his death, December 25, 1794, at the age of fifty-
nine years.

"WHITEFIELD'S" TUNE

It would be interesting to know the sources from
which Mr. Lyon derived the tunes which he gathered
into his *Urania*. Mr. O. G. Sonneck, former chief
of the Music Division of the Library of Congress,
whose monograph has left little to be investigated,
has come to the conclusion that he copied from the
English collections of Arnold, Green, Knapp, and
Evison, but not from Tans'ur. This omission is
significant, for Tans'ur's *Royal Melody* was largely
used in the colonies, especially in New England,
where it was frequently reprinted, first in Boston,
and then in Newburyport. The tunes in the last
part of *Urania* are from *The Divine Musical
Miscellany*, printed in London in 1754. This is
one of the earliest Methodist tune books, and Lyon's
book has at least three tunes from it. Much interest attaches to the tune called "Whitefield's" because it is the one we know as "America," but used
in England with their national hymn, "God Save
the King." In this book it is set to the hymn "Come,
Thou Almighty King."

"COME, THOU ALMIGHTY KING"

The authorship of this hymn has been one of the

"WHITFIELD'S TUNE"
From James Lyons' "Urania," 1761. Library of Congress

problems of hymnology for years. It is frequently credited to Charles Wesley, but of late has been printed as anonymous. The facts regarding its first appearance in type may help us to come to some conclusion about its origin, even if we are unable to discover its author. A four-paged tract, without date, contains not only this hymn, but one known to have been written by Wesley, beginning, "Jesus, let thy pitying eye." This fact led to both hymns being attributed to Charles Wesley, though "Come, Thou Almighty King" is not found in any of his printed works, and was never claimed by him. This tract is found bound up with the British Museum copy of the sixth edition of Whitefield's collection of hymns, dated 1757. It is also bound in with the eighth edition, 1759, and the ninth edition, 1760, both of which are also in the British Museum. It is embodied in the text of the tenth edition, dated 1761. These facts make it safe to assume that this hymn was a favorite one with Mr. Whitefield and those who used his collection of hymns. We may also be sure that it was used by him in his missionary work in this country. It is well to repeat that *Urania* was published in Philadelphia in 1761, the same year that the tenth edition of Whitefield's collection was printed in London, and the incorporation of this hymn in a book on each side of the Atlantic in the same year is an event of significant coincidence. But where did James Lyon find it for use in his book?

George Whitefield

George Whitefield made seven visits to America, arriving first on these shores in 1738, and traveled up and down the coast from Georgia to New England. He died in Newburyport in 1770. On each of these visits as he passed Philadelphia and its vicinity, he stopped to see the Reverend Gilbert Tennant, "who kept an academy which subsequently became the celebrated New Jersey College."[1]   In 1754 he was granted the degree of A.M. by the College of New Jersey, and he writes: "Such a number of simple-hearted, united ministers, I never saw before. I preached to them several times, and the great Master of Assemblies was in the midst of us." While in this district he was the guest and traveling companion of Aaron Burr, the president of the college. On the occasion of his next visit in November, 1763, he writes, "A blessed nursery, one of the purest in the universe, where the worthy president and three tutors are all bent upon making the students both saints and scholars."

For the eight years between 1754 and 1763 Whitefield was not in America, having been detained by his work in England. It was during this period that Lyon was busy compiling his *Urania*. The melody of "God Save the King" came into popularity through its performance at Drury Lane Theater in 1745 and its publication the same year in the Gentleman's Magazine. Did the tune come to Philadelphia in the Gentleman's Magazine, or did George Whitefield bring it with him?[2]   Intercourse between the colonies and the mother country was close and continuous, and books published in London appeared in this country within a few months, or as soon as

[1] See page 85 in J. R. Brooks' *Life of George Whitefield*.
[2] See this suggested inquiry in the Penn-Germania, 1912, p. 630, by James Warrington.

sailing vessels could bring them over. At the time
Urania was published, 1761, Whitefield had made
five visits to America. His visit in 1763 was his
sixth. His influence had been unquestionably impressed upon the people to whom he had preached,
and his favorite hymns and tunes would be well-
known among them. This would be especially true
in the case of Princeton, and the students in the
College of New Jersey, for here he had been entertained by its president. Lyon would, therefore,
have a splendid opportunity for knowing the music
which the Methodists used. This will probably account for the Methodist tunes that he introduced
into his collection. In noticing that some of the
tunes in *The Divine Musical Miscellany* bear such
names as Boston, New York, Philadelphia, Maryland, and Virginia, Mr. Sonneck asks this pertinent
question, "Should this anonymous collection be the
work of an American Methodist?"

Editions

After a careful study of the thirteen copies of
Urania which he found, the author of the monograph has concluded that there were three, and
probably four, editions of the book issued, in all of
which some slight changes may be noted. Of the
copy in the Library of Congress he says, "Best
copy I have seen." And of the one once owned by
Samuel W. Pennypacker, a recent governor of
Pennsylvania, he adds, "Seemingly perfect." The
library of the latter was disposed of in 1906, and
I do not know where this copy of *Urania* went. In
the catalogue of sale appears this notice of it:

The first music book published in America, and of the most extreme rarity. Only two complete copies known. The work was engraved by Daniel Dawkins, and the engraved title presents no mean example of the noted engraver's work, who ranked the highest in America at that time.

This copy of the book is really a composite, having been made up of pages from two different editions, the remaining pages from one forming the very imperfect copy in the Library of the Pennsylvania Historical Society.

Use

The use of this book in the colonies must have been extensive, for a second edition was published in 1767, a third in 1773 in New York, and there is some evidence pointing to a fourth edition printed perhaps in New England. It would satisfy one's curiosity to know to what extent this book drifted into the field hitherto occupied by the works of Tufts and Walter. *Urania* certainly was taken beyond the limits of the Middle States, for we find among the number of its subscribers John Lathrop, who became pastor of the Old North Church in Boston, and lived in that city for nearly fifty years; James Manning, who became a Baptist minister and settled in Rhode Island; Obadiah Noble, pastor of the Congregational Church in Orford, New Hampshire; Thaddeus Burr, a merchant in Connecticut; Josiah Thatcher, who lived in Gorham, Maine, for over thirty years; and James Huntington, a native of Norwich, Connecticut, and pastor of the Congregational church in Salem for three years. These men were in college with James Lyon, encouraged him by taking copies of his book, and doubtless carried it with them into their new homes in New England. Those who were ministers may have introduced it into their churches and thus its influence widened.

COPIES

We cannot close this account of the pioneer music book without naming the places where copies of it may be seen. Only a few copies of it have survived the ravages of time, but their value, as showing the first step in the growth of musical composition in this country, cannot be overestimated. There are two copies each in the possession of the Pennsylvania Historical Society, Yale University, and the Massachusetts Historical Society and the Western Theological Seminary, Pittsburgh, which bought the library of the late James Warrington of Philadelphia. There is one copy each in the New York Public Library, the New York Historical Society, the Library of Congress, and the Boston Public Library, and Mr. Sonneck has one. The location of Judge Pennypacker's copy is not known to the writer.

JOHN STICKNEY

1744–1827[1]

THE life of John Stickney, from 1744 to 1827, covers the period of the lives of both Andrew Law and William Billings. The tunes of Stickney have almost entirely passed out of modern hymn books.

John Stickney, fourth in descent from Samuel,

[1] From The Choir Herald.

the English immigrant who settled in America, was born at Stoughton, Massachusetts, March 31, 1744. When about seven years of age he was apprenticed to Isaac Davenport, a shoemaker and butcher, who lived in the neighboring town of Milton. At fifteen he went to Roxbury and then to Newbury, and returning to Stoughton, learned from William Dunbar, a lawyer and justice of the peace, the new style of music just being introduced by William Billings, who was also a resident of Stoughton. Stickney was a member of one of the singing schools organized by Billings in that town. Some time after, when Jesse Billings, perhaps a relative of William Billings, went from Hadley to secure a teacher for the people of that place, Stickney went to their assistance, and continued teaching in other towns of the Connecticut Valley, Northampton, Wethersfield, Hartford, and New Haven. This was before the time of music type and cheap printing, so it was his custom to write the music for his scholars, often sixty copies a day, with a pen or, more likely, a goose quill. His efforts to displace the old method of singing by rote met with considerable opposition, but he succeeded in teaching many in the towns which he visited to read and sing by note. He was married December 26, 1765, to Elizabeth Howard, of Stoughton. She also was musical and traveled about with him from place to place. Both were members of the Congregational Church in South Hadley. His home in this town was on a farm near the Connecticut River, where he cultivated the soil during the summer, while in winter he often accommodated the lumbermen and fishermen of that vicinity with board. This too was the time for sing-ing schools, and he continued to conduct them until he was about sixty-five years old. His second mar-riage occurred in South Hadley, October 31, 1813, to Lucy N., widow of Azariah Alvord, whom she had married in 1789. Mr. Stickney had six children, the youngest of whom, Walter by name, born August 10, 1790, was a dentist, but he inherited his father's musical talents, and taught music for ten or fifteen years, and was at one time leader of the First Brigade Band Massachusetts Militia under General Bliss. The father died and was buried in South Hadley and much of the family his-tory is shown upon the monument. The inscrip-tion reads:

John Stickney, Doctor Sacrae Musicae, died April 23, 1827, aged 83 years. Elizabeth H., his wife, died May 28, 1813, aged 68 years. Lucy N., his second wife, died December 24, 1836, aged 86 years.

We must not omit his Revolutionary War record which is given as follows:

John Stickney of South Hadley enlisted January 13, 1776, as a private in Captain James Hendricks' company in camp at Castleton, was adjutant August 25 to December 2, 1777, was at the taking of Burgoyne, October 17, 1777, in Colonel Woodbridge's regiment, Captain Moses Harvey's company.

Mr. Stickney published in 1774 *The Gentleman and Lady's Musical Companion*, "containing a variety of excellent anthems, hymns, etc., collected from the best authors; with a short explanation of the rules of music. The whole corrected and rendered plain. Printed and sold by Daniel Bayley,

Newburyport, and by most booksellers in New England."

Specific mention is made of certain dealers in Boston, in Salem and in Hartford. The price was eight shillings. The preface is dated at South Hadley, June 4, 1774, thus fixing the date of his removal to that town between his marriage in 1765 and the year 1774. The music in this volume is engraved and is written in four clefs. Like most of the music books of that period it had several blank pages bound in at the end, upon which the owner could copy additional music to suit his tastes. After giving eight rules as instructive to the learner, he concludes as follows:

> Singing is an act of religious worship; while persons are learning the art, indeed, they can scarce be considered in a devout exercise. If, therefore, they choose to sing in the words of a psalm, it is most proper to choose those that are not peculiarly devotional. But when it is performed as a part of worship, the utmost care should be taken not only to avoid all levities and indecencies of carriage, which are intolerable, but to adopt no expressions which we cannot conscientiously use, to enter thoroughly into the sentiments of the psalm, and to have the heart affected with them; thus singing with the understanding and the affections, we make melody in our hearts unto the Lord; but if otherwise, whatever harmony our voices may make, we affront and provoke Almighty God. Happy will it be if this hint is attended to whatever else is overlooked or forgotten.

A new edition was issued in 1783 by Daniel Bayley, in Newburyport, Massachusetts, from which "a considerable part of the old music was left out, forty pages added chiefly from Harmonia Sacra and Law with some new pieces never before published." This last statement sounds very much like

EASTER HYMN

From the first edition of "A Compilation of the Litanies and Vespers, * * *" by John Aitken, Philadelphia, 1787.
American Antiquarian Society

Daniel Bayley, an organist and printer of music in Newburyport, who frequently took the main portion of a book, adding and omitting from it, and calling the result a new edition. Whether this edition of 1783 was really compiled by Stickney or by Bayley we cannot determine, but we suspect that Bayley may have done part of the selecting. None of his tunes have been found in recent hymnals.

JOHN AITKEN

1745(?)–1831

A FEW years before the epidemic that carried off Andrew Adgate John Aitken arrived in Philadelphia where he appears as a music engraver as early as 1787. In that year he published

A Compilation of the Litanies and Vespers, Hymns and Anthems as they are sung in the Catholic Church adapted to the Voice or Organ. By John Aitken, Philadelphia, 1787.

It was approved by the Rev. John Carroll, later appointed the first archbishop of Baltimore, by the Rev. Robert Molyneux, the Rev. Francis Beeston and the Rev. Lawrence Graessl; this approbation was signed in Philadelphia November 28, 1787, and was reprinted in German on the same page. This book was entirely engraved, contained 136 pages, and was probably not issued until 1788, as the certificate of the clerk of the court who issued the State copyright is not dated until April, 1788. A copy of this first edition is in the library of the American Antiquarian Society in Worcester, Massachusetts.

A second edition with slightly different title page was "Printed and Sold by John Aitken, 1791," at Philadelphia, and contained 181 pages. It was copyrighted November 25, 1791, under the laws of the United States. A copy of this edition is possessed by the John Carter Brown Library in Providence, Rhode Island.

John Aitken was a native of Dulkeath, Scotland, opened his Musical Repository at 96 North Second Street, in Philadelphia, as early as 1807, as is shown by the *Directory* of that year, and he died September 8, 1831, at the age of eighty-six years, and was buried in Christ Church yard.

DR. GEORGE K. JACKSON

1745–1823

Dr. George K. Jackson was one of the earliest organists and music teachers of Boston. He was an Englishman by birth, born in Oxford in 1745; and was a schoolmate of Raynor Taylor, another English musician, who came to America and settled in Philadelphia. When eleven years old he was a choir boy in the Chapel Royal. He was a pupil of the celebrated Dr. James Nares, and he received his diploma from Saint Andrews College in 1791. Five years later he emigrated to America by way of Norfolk, stopping for varying periods of time in Alexandria, Baltimore, Philadelphia, Elizabeth, New Jersey, and New York, reaching Boston in 1812. Here he began to teach and conduct concerts. He arranged a series of oratorios which

were given with the assistance of Gottlieb Graupner
and Francis Mallet in Boston, and some of them
were repeated in Salem, where the people seemed to
be very fond of this class of music. One of these
concerts was given on October 29, 1812, at the Stone
Chapel in Salem, and the program was as follows.
It was advertised as under the direction of Dr. G.
K. Jackson, assisted by the Theatrical Band and
many respectable Vocal and Instrumental Amateurs
of this town.

Leader of the Band, Mr. Graupner.

Part I

Overture	Occasional Oratorio.
Recitative, Comfort Ye, Messiah.	Mrs. Graupner.
Air, Every Valley, Messiah.	Mrs. Graupner.
Chorus, And the Glory,	Messiah.
Duetts, O Lovely Peace, Judas Maccabeas,	By Amateurs.
Song, Why do the Nations, Messiah.	Mr. Mallett.
Chorus, Lift up your heads,	Messiah.
Song, Arm, arm, ye brave, Judas Maccabeas.	By an Amateur.
Chorus, Break forth into joy,	Messiah.

Part II.

Overture,	Sampson.
Song, Angels ever bright and fair, Jepths—Mrs. Graupner.	
Voluntary on the organ,	Dr. Jackson.
Celebrated Bell Chorus { Welcome, mighty king, Accompanied on the Carilons by Dr. Jackson.	Saul
Song. Honor and Arms, Sampson,	Mr. Mallett.
Chorus, Happy we the Star, &c.	
Song, O, Thou tellest,	Messiah.
Song, The trumpet shall sound, Messiah.	Mr. Stockwell.
Chorus, Hallelujah, (with Trumpet and Kettle Drums)	Messiah.

Doors to be opened at half past four—Performance to commence precisely at half past five o'clock.

A single ticket, $1—A Ticket to admit a lady and gentleman $1.50—Children's Tickets, 50 cents each; to be had at Dr. Jackson's, No. 18 Pinkney Street, and at Messrs Graupner & Mallett's Music-stores, the bar of the Exchange Coffee House.

A later concert in Salem was heard by Dr. William Bentley, pastor of the Second Church in that town, who records his impressions in his diary, December 1, 1812, as follows:

This evening we heard, as it was called, an Oratorio of Sacred Music. The organ of the First Church was preferred to that of the North Church, because of its tones. The celebrated Dr. Jackson, an Englishman, performed on the organ with great power and pure touch. Mr. Graupner led the violins, Mrs. Graupner was at the head of the female singers, which were seven in number. Mr. Jackson's voluntaries were beyond anything I had heard and the best music was before the second chorus when the organ was accompanied only with the violins.

Doctor Jackson, after his location in Boston, was the organist in various churches including the Brattle Street Church, King's Chapel, Trinity on Summer Street, and Saint Paul's on Common Street. At the latter church he was engaged at a salary extraordinarily high for that time, and he held this position until his death. During a part of the period of the war with England he retired to Northampton to avoid the excitement caused by the military measures in the city, but returned and resumed his musical activities when the war was over. Before leaving England he had married, in 1787, the eldest daughter of Dr. Samuel Rogers, a physician of London, by whom he had eleven children. Two of his sons had a music store on Market Street in Boston about 1800. Doctor Jackson died in Boston in 1823, probably in July or August, for on August 19, 1823, the Probate Court of Suffolk County appointed his son Charles as executor of his estate. The total inventory amounted to only $98.86, and among the items were 129 volumes of old music books appraised at six cents apiece.

Before leaving England Doctor Jackson had published *A Treatise on Practical Thorough Bass*, and a number of songs, and upon his arrival in America he began to teach the English manner of chanting. In 1804, when he was organist in Saint George's Chapel, New York, he copyrighted a book of sixty engraved pages called *David's Psalms* "set to music expressly for the use of Churches, Chapels, Meetings and Private Families. New and selected from the best Ancient and Modern Authors." The copy of this book in the Library of Congress was probably Doctor Jackson's own, for the label on it reads "St. George's Chapel, Organ I."

Another book, copyrighted March 29, 1816, was *A Choice Collection of Chants* "for four Voices with a Gloria Patria and Sanctus, the whole figured with a Thorough Bass for the organ as used in Cathedrals, Churches and Chapels." This was an engraved volume, and sold in that day for one dollar. Some of his music was used in the early collections, but none has survived in present hymnals. John Weeks Moore tells us in his *Dictionary of Musical Information* that there has come down to us a manuscript book containing 310 pages of miscellaneous works for instruments, and singing books of harmony, and a system of tuning used in his school. There is also a bound volume of his separate works preserved in the library of the Harvard Musical Association in Boston. There seem to have been at least three musicians and composers in the Jackson family, for we find in this book "A Pastoral Drama," 1753, set to music by Joseph Jackson, and several compositions by a George Jackson, dated 1755. These are of a date too early for Dr. George K. Jackson, and one may have been his father, or both his brothers.

With regard to his business connections, Dr. Henry K. Oliver, in his remarks at the centenary of the North Church in Salem, said:

Monsieur Mallett was a French gentleman of much respectability who came to this country with Lafayette, and served in the army of the Revolution to the end of the war. He then settled in Boston as a teacher of music declining to receive any pension. He was among the earliest publishers of music in Boston, the friend and business partner of the celebrated Dr. G. K. Jackson, the predecessor of Graupner, whose music store was in Franklin Street. In 1812 Dr. Jackson was located at No. 18 Pinkney Street, and Mallett had joined himself as a partner to Gottlieb Graupner, and they were located in business at the Bar of the Exchange Coffee House.

In the Memorial History of Boston John S. Dwight referred to Doctor Jackson as the Gilmore of his day. To this statement General Henry K. Oliver made reply and gives a vivid picture of his friend. He wrote:

Mr. Dwight speaks in a way that neither earlier nor later readers can understand of Dr. G. K. Jackson, a thoroughly well-educated English organist, designating him as "the Gilmore of his day." Knowing both Dr. Jackson and Mr. Gilmore, I fail to see the similarity. With the exception of unquestionable musical endowments, though to each in diversity of directions, they were noticeably unlike in mind, temperament, education, methods, and personal appearance. Dr.

Jackson was somewhat tardigrade and undemonstrative; of a measurably lethargic nature, yet without mental obtuseness. Mr. Gilmore is nervously active, energetic, full of earnest zeal and push, with vivacious mental intelligence. Educationally each was thoroughly trained in his specialty—the one for the church and cathedral, the other for the band and orchestra—each using his best effort in his several specialty. In person they may be classed as antipodal. Dr. Jackson was of vast ponderosity, and like Falstaff, "larded the lean earth as he walked along." He was a very incarnation of obesity. Gilmore is thin, wiry, and, as is written of a Duke of Alva, "of lean body and visage, as though his eager soul desired to fret a passage through it."

WILLIAM BILLINGS

1746–1800[1]

WILLIAM BILLINGS was a giant among the group of composers of church music who flourished in New England during the period of the Revolutionary War. He towered above those around him, and planted the impress of his power upon those who attempted to follow in his footsteps. His style of music has been called Yankee music, and has often been held up to ridicule. Few of his pieces are now in common use, but this is only another instance of the constant change in musical taste, and a desire for new compositions which displace the old. He was self-educated in his art, yet his genius dominated the singing of his age, and he introduced a new style of so-called fuguing pieces which held sway among the leaders of church music for many years. He was not the inventor of this new class, it having been used in England for a few years be-

[1] From The Choir Herald.

fore his time, but in Puritan New England the churches hesitated to depart from their long-established ways till the energy of Billings compelled a change. He was a master of self-praise, and this had much to do in pushing his music to the front and making it popular. His compositions were in many ways far in advance of those which he found in the churches, and we are led to wonder what changes he would have wrought could he have had the training of some of the masters in England. Still, we must grant him high honor in accomplishing such improvements in church singing and in arousing the public mind to the importance of music in the sanctuary.

Biography

Most sketches of William Billings state that he was born in Boston, October 7, 1746. In one of his books he writes that he is a native of Boston. There has been some doubt as to his parents, and the correct date of his birth, as there does not seem to be any record of a birth in the published records of Boston that can be taken as referring to him. The Thayer Memorial, printed in 1835, intimates that the record of birth of a William to William and Mary (Badlam) on November 14, 1742, refers to the musician, and Colonel Pope, who married the daughter of William Billings, follows this statement in his genealogy. In the article which the present writer furnished to the Choir Herald in August, 1914, reasons were given for believing that 1742 was the correct date; but since then it has been found that the evidence on which these conclusions were based was incorrect, and they are therefore untenable. The family Bible of William Billings has now been located, and its records supposed to be in his own handwriting, must be taken as correct. From this record we learn that the musician was the son of William and Elizabeth, and was born in Boston, October 7, 1746. The maiden name of Elizabeth is not stated, but we find in the records of Boston that one William Billings was married to Elizabeth Clark August 6, 1736, by the Rev. Charles Chauncey, and that this Elizabeth was the daughter of William and Rebecca Clark, and was born March 7, 1706. It may be that she was the mother of the William in whom we are interested.

William Billings was a tanner by trade, but could not resist the drawings of his art and devoted much of his time to teaching music and directing singing schools. Some years ago an interesting paper was found among the effects of one of the old residents of Stoughton, giving the names of those who attended one of his singing schools kept in that town in the year 1774. This group of people was the germ of the oldest musical association in the United States, the Stoughton Musical Society. It was on the seventh of November, 1786, that a number of the persons whose names appear upon the list formed the society which is still in existence and which has done so much to keep alive an interest in the old hymns and songs so dear to our New England ancestors in Colonial times. This society published a collection of old church tunes in 1829 called the Stoughton Collection. Among the names on the list of that old singing school of 1774 Lucy Swan heads

the singers of the treble. She was the daughter of
Major Robert Swan and Rachel Swan, of Stoughton, and became the second wife of William Billings,
July 26, 1774. William Billings had married Mary
Leonard on December 13, 1764, and was married
to Lucy Swan at Stoughton by the Rev. Jedediah
Adams. This record appears both in the records
of Boston and those of Stoughton. His children
were

Abigail Adams,	born April 27, 1777.
Elizabeth Adams,	born February 11, 1779.
Sarah,	born August 30, 1783.
William,	born February 7, 1786.
Peggy,	born March 6, 1788.
Lucy,	born October 18, 1792.

Abigail married Amos Penniman, who settled the
estate of his father-in-law. Peggy, who was also
known as Margaret D. Billings, married Colonel
William Pope, who was then living in Boston, but
later they went to Machias, Maine. The youngest
daughter, Lucy, married Levi Scott, and the
family Bible is now in the possession of her
granddaughter, Minnie Fowler Scott in Boston,
Massachusetts. The Rev. George Wallace Penniman, grandson of the oldest daughter Abigail,
is pastor of the Universalist Church in Monson,
Massachusetts.

Although William Billings was such an active
leader in church music, the notice accorded him by
the newspapers of the day at his death was very
meager. The Columbian Centinel, for September
27, 1800, has the following:

DIED. William Billings, age 60, the celebrated music com-

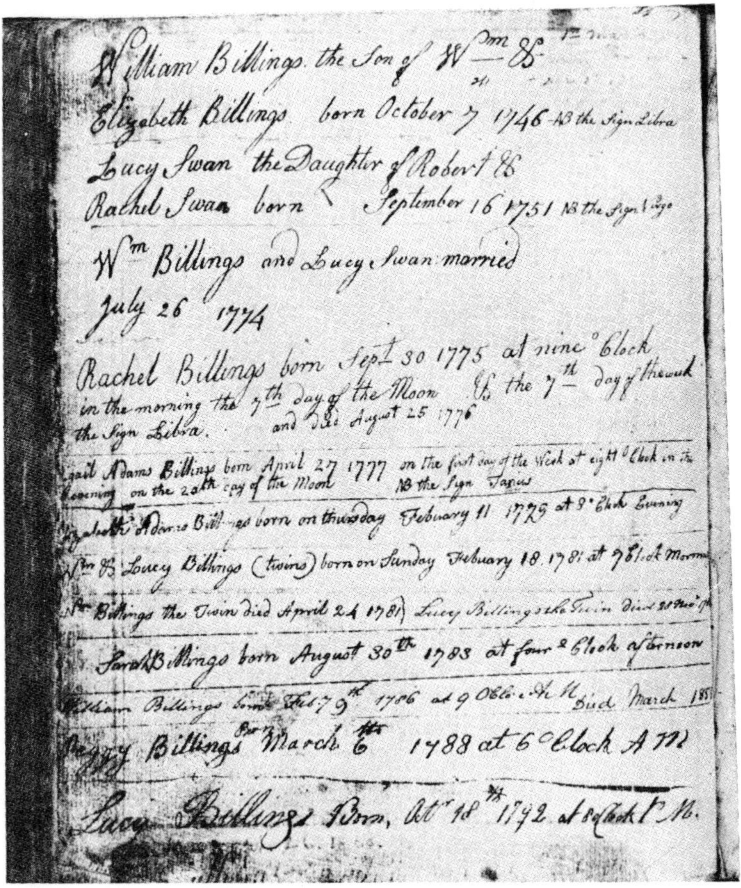
William Billings the Son of Wm &
Elizabeth Billings born October 7 1746 NB the Sign Libra
Lucy Swan the Daughter of Robert &
Rachel Swan born September 16 1751 NB the Sign Virgo
Wm Billings and Lucy Swan married
July 26 1774
Rachel Billings born Sept 30 1775 at nine o Clock
in the morning the 7th day of the Moon & the 7th day of the week
the Sign Libra. and died August 25 1776
[Abi]gail Adams Billings born April 27 1777 on the first day of the Week at eight o Clock in the
Evening on the 20th day of the Moon NB the Sign Taurus
[E]lizabeth Adams Billings born on thursday February 11 1779 at 8 o Clock Evening
Wm & Lucy Billings (twins) born on Sunday February 18 1781 at 7 o Clock Morn[ing]
[W]m Billings the Twin died April 24 1781) Lucy Billings the Twin died [illegible]
Sarah Billings born August 30th 1783 at four o Clock afternoon
William Billings born Feb 7 9th 1786 at 9 o Clock A M Died March 18[illegible]
Peggy Billings born March 6th 1788 at 6 o Clock A M
Lucy Billings Born, Oct 18th 1792 at 8 o Clock P M.

William Billings' Family Record

poser. His funeral will be held to-morrow, [Sunday, September 29], at 4 p. m. from the home of Mr. Amos Penniman, in Chamber Street, West Boston.

The date of his death is not given, but it was September 26. He was buried in the inclosure on the common in an unmarked, and now unknown grave.

He taught the singers of the Brattle Street Church in 1778 with great approbation, and in 1785 he was interested in the music in the Old South Church. The following notice appeared in the Boston Centinel for November 26, 1785:

Singers of every denomination, both male and female, are desired to attend and give their assistance at the Old South on the first Lord's Day in December. The intent of said meeting is for the purpose of relieving the distressed. Your compliance with this will oblige many. But none more than your humble servant,

WILLIAM BILLINGS.

The distress which this charity was to relieve was very great among the poorer classes, and was due chiefly to the depreciation of the continental currency. Billings was an intimate friend of Samuel Adams, the patriot, and together they liked to sing the 137th psalm, which had been put into political paraphrase. The Revolutionary War gave opportunity to express in music his feelings toward the mother country, and the tune "Chester" was called his patriotic song. The words set to it were also of his composition, and the first stanza will indicate his patriotism:

> "Let tyrants shake their iron rod,
>   And slavery clank her galling chains;
> We fear them not, we trust in God.
>   New England's God forever reigns."

An item in the Musical Herald for 1890 states that at the time of the Revolutionary War:

Billings was a member of Brown University. The college was for awhile abandoned by the students and occupied by soldiers for barracks. Billings retired to Wrentham, Massachusetts, seventeen miles from Providence, where he spent some time in teaching and composing music.

In reply to a letter of inquiry to the secretary of Brown University the following was received:

Upon investigation we find that no William Billings was attending Brown University at the time of the Revolutionary War. Apparently, no man of that name has ever attended the institution. We regret, of course, not being able to couple the name of the university with the gentleman in question.

It appears, however, that he was in Rhode Island at that time, for the town clerk of Stoughton recorded on June 4, 1774, the marriage intention of William Billings, of Providence, to Lucy Swan, of Stoughton, but the marriage record shows Billings was of Boston.

With these few personal facts we pass to a consideration of his music books, and from his own writings we will learn much more about him and his work.

MUSIC BOOKS

His first book was published in 1770 and was *The New England Psalm-Singer, or American Chorister*, "containing a number of psalm-tunes, anthems and canons, in four and five parts never before published. Composed by William Billings, a native of Boston in New England." The copy in the Library of Congress was "Bought of Mr. Billings, June 12, 1770; cost 9 shillings," and belonged to William Holdroyd, of Providence. The frontispiece is an engraved oval of music inclosing a view of a room in which seven men are sitting around a table and singing. The preface is so interesting that it may be quoted entire:

Although this composition has cost me much time and pains, yet I little thought of exposing it to public view, but being repeatedly importuned by my friends I was at last prevailed upon to commit it to the press. And, such as it is, I now offer it to the public, from whom, should it meet with a favorable reception, it would compensate for all the trouble I have been at and the time I have spent in the prosecution of it. Perhaps there may appear in the eyes of the accurate much incorrectness that I was not able to discern; therefore, would beg the critic to be tender and rectify those errors, which through inexperience may happen to have escaped the notice of a youth in the course of so large a volume.[1] I would here take occasion to return my thanks to those gentlemen who have put so much confidence in this performance as to promote and encourage it by subscription, before they could have an opportunity of examining it, and I would acknowledge myself in a particular manner obligated to that gentleman who has honored me and this book with his learned philosophical essay on Sound. Yet, at the same time I can't but be sorry that I am not allowed to give the public the satisfaction of knowing his name. For, somewhat contrary to nature, modesty in this gentleman has so far gained the ascendency over ambition, that the world must remain deprived of the knowledge of him, 'til his name shall shine on the page of some future work.[2] It would be needless for me to attempt to set forth the usefulness and importance of psalm singing which is so universally known and acknowledged and on which depends no inconsiderable part of the divine worship of our churches. But this much I would say: that he who finds himself gifted with a tunable voice and yet neglects to cultivate it, not only hides in the earth a talent of the highest value, but robs himself of that peculiar pleasure of which they only are conscious who exercise that faculty.

Authors in general, upon subjects of this nature, abound

---

[1] He was only twenty-four years old when this book was issued, and probably some of the music, at least, had been written some time before.
[2] Probably Dr. Charles Stockbridge of Scituate.

mostly in tunes of Common Meter, but in this respect I have deviated from them, endeavoring to have a sufficiency in each measure. In the composition I have been as plain and concise as possible; and yet have tried to the utmost of my power to preserve the modern air and manner of singing, and should it, upon proof, be found equal to the attempt, I hope it will be as well an inducement to the unskilled in the art to prosecute the study of it as an entertainment to the more experienced in it.

This is dated at Boston, October 7, 1770.

Many of the tunes have no words set to them, and on the first page he explains that "No doubt the reader will excuse my not adapting words to all the tunes, as it is attended with great inconvenience." This book has more than one hundred pages of music, engraved on copper by Paul Revere. The last page contains a hymn of twelve four-line stanzas "Composed by the Rev. Mr. Whitefield with design to be sung at his own funeral, and here inserted at the request of a number of his friends." Upon investigation, however, it is found that this hymn was not written by Whitefield, but was one of John Wesley's. In the advertisement of this his first venture Mr. Billings says: "If this work should meet with encouragement, it may be an inducement to the author to publish another volume, which he has in possession, consisting chiefly of anthems, fuges (sic), and choruses of his own composition." This volume is now very rare, one volume some years ago having brought eighty-five dollars at auction, while a sale made in 1920 brought two hundred and ten dollars. If he could have received this amount from his own sales, he would not have hesitated to issue his second volume.

The Singing Master's Assistant

It was eight years before another book was put forth. In the meantime he kept on writing more music and teaching singing schools. *The Singing Master's Assistant or, Key to Practical Music,* was an abridgment from *The New England Psalm Singer,* together with several other tunes never before published, composed by William Billings. It was engraved by Benjamin Pierpont, Junior, of Roxbury, and printed in Boston in 1778. This book has sixty tunes, and to many of them are set words taken from the versions of the psalms made by Doctor Watts and by Brady and Tate; but "Where no credit is given," he says, "the words are written by the author." Thus we learn that besides being a composer, he was a writer of rime. It is in the preface of this book that he shows his enthusiasm for music. He writes:

Perhaps some of my grave readers may conclude I am possessed with a musical enthusiasm if I insist too much on the marvelous. That I am a musical enthusiast I readily grant, and I think it impossible for the votaries to be otherwise, for when we consider the many wonderful effects which music has on the animal spirit, and upon the nervous system, we are ready to cry out in a fit of enthusiam, "Great art thou, O Music."

In the eight years between these books he had learned much regarding music, and his experience led him to write in the preface of his second volume:

Kind Reader: No doubt you will remember that about ten years ago I published a book entitled *The New England Psalm Singer;* and truly a most masterful performance I then thought it to be. How lavish was I of encomium on this my infant production! "Welcome thrice welcome, thou legitimate offspring of my brain. Go forth, little book, go forth and immortalize the name of your author; may your sale be rapid and may you speedily run through ten thousand editions." But to my great mortification I soon discovered that many pieces were never worth my printing or your inspection.

This was his most popular production, was called *Billings' Best*, was issued in a second edition in the following year, and again in 1780, all by the same publisher.

Music in Miniature

His next venture was *Music in Miniature*, containing a collection of psalm tunes of various meters set in score. It was engraved by B. Johnson and printed in Boston for the author in 1779. There were seventy-four tunes, thirty-one new and original, thirty-two from his former books, and eleven old standard European tunes. There were no words printed.

The Psalm Singer's Amusement

The Psalm Singers' Amusement, 1781, contained a number of fuguing pieces and anthems, twenty pieces in all, and was printed and sold by the author in Boston. His apology for such a small book throws an interesting side light on the price of copper and paper in the colonies during the Revolutionary War. He writes:

This work is a part of the book of anthems which I have so long promised. My reasons for not publishing the whole in one volume must be obvious to all who consider the present extravagant price of copper-plate and paper—the copper in special is so scarce that I don't think it possible to procure enough to contain the whole at any price; besides, if I was able to publish the whole, but few would become purchasers, and I believe that most will be of my opinion when I inform them that the book could not be afforded for less than ten dollars. However, I hope that notwithstanding the present difficulties, I shall shortly be able to publish the remainder at a much lower price.

One of the pieces has the following directions: "After the audience are seated and the performers have taken the pitch slyly from the leader, the song begins." This is the first stanza:

> "We've met for a concert of modern invention;
> To tickle the ear is our present intention.
> The audience seated, expect to be treated
> With a piece of the best."

THE SUFFOLK HARMONY

The Suffolk Harmony consisted of psalm tunes, fugues, and anthems, and was printed in Boston in 1786. This was a book of fifty-six pages, and has sold in recent years for as high as fifty dollars. The five books already mentioned were printed from engraved plates.

His next publication was *The Continental Harmony*, printed "typographically," that is, from music type, by Isaiah Thomas in Boston in 1794. Besides anthems and fugues it contained a number of choruses in several parts. As fugues were the distinguishing style of Billings' compositions, it will be interesting to know his own opinion of them. This he tells us is as follows:

It has more than twenty times the power of the old slow tunes; each part straining for mastery and victory. The audience entertained and delighted, their minds surpassingly agitated and extremely fluctuated, sometimes declaring for one part and sometimes for another. Now the solemn bass demands their attention; next the manly tenor, now the volatile treble. Now here, now there, now here again. O ecstatis! Rush on, you sons of harmony.

One more book must be mentioned, *The Massachusetts Harmony*, which Charles Evans, in his *American Bibliography*, attributes to Billings, but with an interrogation after his name. It was published in Boston prior to 1785, for a second edition was issued in that year, and the first is not dated. It is stated in the chapter on Andrew Law that this may have been the pirated edition of one of Law's books to which he refers in his *Rudiments of Music* in 1783. We cannot think that William Billings, who was so fond of self-praise, would allow any of his own productions to go forth without his name upon the title page. We doubt therefore that *The Massachusetts Harmony* could be his, as it is signed only "By a Lover of Harmony."

The music of Billings' style has passed, and it is rare to find any of his pieces in modern collections. His tune "Majesty" appeared in the Baptist book, *Sursum Corda*, published so late as 1898, and the editor has added the following note: "This favorite among the early American psalm tunes ought not to be forgotten. Some of its quaintness has been sacrificed in correcting it, but in a certain joyous stateliness it remains unsurpassed." The tune also appeared in the Methodist Hymnal of 1878, and was included in both the collections made for old folks concerts by Father Kemp and Brother Cheney. In the latter book it stands first, indicating the popularity it attained as a representative of the music of Revolutionary times; for this piece was

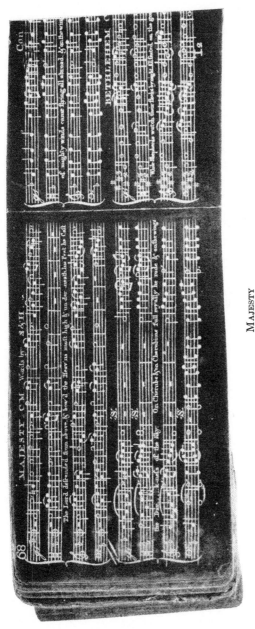

MAJESTY

William Billings, Singing Master's Assistant, 1778. Library of Congress

published in the author's second book, *The Singing Master's Assistant*, printed in 1778.

The following contemporary estimate of Billings is quoted from the diary of William Bentley, for many years an editor and a pastor in Salem, Massachusetts. The entry was written on Sunday, September 28, 1800, two days after the death of the musician, and is as follows:

William Billings, ae. 60, died in Boston. This self-taught man thirty years ago had the direction of all the music of our churches. His "Reuben," [The Singing Master's Assistant] as he whimsically called it, with all its great imperfections, had great fame and he may justly be considered as the father of our New England music. Many who have imitated have excelled him, but none of them had better original power. His late attempts, and without a proper education, were the true cause of his inferior excellence. He taught the singers at the Brattle Street Church in 1778 with great approbation, and his fame was great in the churches. He was a singular man, of moderate size, short of one leg, with one eye, without any address, and with an uncommon negligence of person. Still he spake and sang and thought as a man above the common abilities. He died poor and neglected and perhaps did too much neglect himself.

A recent writer has said that "Billings was an uncouth but forceful personality, and neglected his tanning to lead choirs with a voice that drowned all others; to publish psalm books that had a wide sale, and to compose music that had a certain crude worth." Ritter says of him: "Billings taught his choir, so far as he could, to sing musically, that is, in time and with a certain swing and warm expression. He gave it in the best way he was able and he gave his own. He was an honest though poor composer." He did not adapt other writers' tunes, but all his publications were original. Whatever may be said of the style that he adopted, especially the fuguing pieces which had been recently introduced from England, this style captured the hearts of the people of his day, and drew them away from the solemn and unmusical tunes then in use. Musical taste has changed during the last century, and new composers have arisen to crowd out the old, but it cannot be denied that musical development was given an important start by the energy and persistence of William Billings.

SIMEON JOCELYN

1746–1823

SIMEON JOCELYN was not a composer of music, but he compiled and published a number of books, which were sold by him in New Haven, and his work as an engraver of some of them is of interest. He was born at Branford, Connecticut, October 22, 1746, and was the son of Nathaniel and Elizabeth Jocelyn. Simeon established himself in business in New Haven as early as 1782, when he was in company with Amos Doolittle.

His first music book was *The Chorister's Companion,* which contained the usual rules of psalmody, a choice and valuable collection of psalm tunes, hymns, and anthems, as well as several tunes never before published. Later editions contained additional music which was also published separately. These were printed by T. and S. Green for Simeon Jocelyn. In 1787 there was printed by Thomas and Samuel Green and sold by Simeon Jocelyn in

ZION'S HARP, 1824
Title page and Sicilian Hymn.   A fine example of engraving.
From the author's collection

New Haven a collection (sixteen pages) of favorite psalm tunes from late and approved British authors, the whole never before printed in America. He died in New Haven June 5, 1823.

OLIVER BROWNSON

Oliver Brownson, of Connecticut, was the compiler of two collections of sacred music. In 1783 his *Select Harmony,* containing eighty-four pages of engraved music, was printed in New Haven, by Thomas and Samuel Green. The American compositions in this book have their authors' names set over the tunes, and it appears that many of the compositions were original with the compiler, while others were by such authors as were then well known—Edson, Billings, and Swan. There was another edition printed in 1791, containing the same music, but the preface and introduction are in a smaller type.

His second book appears to be very rare. It was *A New Collection of Sacred Harmony,* and was printed at Simsbury, Connecticut, in 1797, and was sold by the author at his dwelling house. It had fifty-six pages, and, like the other, was oblong in shape.

In 1775 Oliver King, of Bolton, Connecticut, advertised for subscriptions to his *Universal Harmony,* and added that they would be received, among others, by Oliver Brunson (or Brownson), singing master, Litchfield.

JUSTIN MORGAN

1747–1798

JUSTIN MORGAN was born in 1747 at West Springfield, Massachusetts. Besides being a musician, he is known as the breeder of the Morgan horse. The following items are taken from advertisements in various papers. For the season of 1778 he advertised Sportsman at his home in West Springfield, Massachusetts. In 1783 he kept Diamond and advertised him in the Massachusetts Gazette of April 29 as follows:

> Will cover the season at the stable of Mr. Justin Morgan in West Springfield, the horse called Diamond, who sprang from a good mare, and from the horse formerly owned by Mr. Church of Springfield.

The season of 1783 he kept the stallion, True Briton. This is the last season Mr. Morgan is known to have kept the stallion before his removal to Vermont in 1788. He moved to Randolph, Vermont, between June 20 and September 3, 1788. His health was delicate, and he was unable to do any hard work after he was twenty years old. He taught writing schools, singing schools and the common district schools for many years, the proceeds of which, together with the money from his horses—when he had them—and from his little tavern constituted his means of livelihood.

As a teacher he seems to have been successful, and was greatly liked wherever he went on account of his urbane manners and upright character. He was married at the age of about thirty, and four daugh-

ters and one son were born to him.   His second
daughter, Emily, afterward Mrs. Edgerton, was
born in February, 1786; Justin, March 15, 1788;
Nancy, September 3, 1788, at Randolph, Vermont;
Polly, March 10, 1791, at Randolph.   Ten days
after the birth of this last child Mrs. Martha Morgan, the wife and mother, died at Randolph.   These
last three dates appear on the records of Randolph.
The date September 3, 1788, indicates the approxi-
mate date of the removal of the family to Vermont.
Mr. Morgan was chosen lister in Randolph March
19, 1789, and town clerk March 9, 1790, and held
the latter office until March 18, 1793.   In the spring
of that year the family was broken up, and the
children found homes in the families of different
neighbors, the son, Justin, then seven years old,
together with his sister Emily, going to live with
Daniel Carpenter, by whom they were brought up.
Mr. Morgan never had his little family together
again.   He survived only five years, and died at
Randolph on the second of March, 1798, in his fifty-
first year.   The little property that he left was
appraised at only $160.13, as appears from the pro-
bate records, where the different articles are enu-
merated.   There is no horse or livestock in the
appraisal.   It is therefore apparent that he had
parted with his famous horse some time before his
death, and there is no evidence that he ever owned
any other horse in Vermont than the one known as
the Morgan horse.   On the 17th of November, 1800,
a dividend of thirteen cents was ordered paid to the
creditors.   Thus closes the short and simple annals
of the man who brought into the then young and

growing Green Mountain State a most interesting and important element of its prosperity.

Mahlon Cottrell, who drove the stage from Royalton to Montpelier, states that he often met Mr. Morgan on the original Morgan horse going to his singing schools.

Mr. Morgan composed many tunes, a remarkable anthem called "Judgement Anthem," and left a book of manuscript music. One of his tunes, "Montgomery," was introduced into *The Antiquarian*, by Leonard Marshall as late as 1849, but his music has now passed entirely out of use, and is of interest only to the historian.

ANDREW LAW

1748–1821[1]

A musical magazine, a new form of musical notation, and several compilations of tunes, original and selected, are the additions made by Andrew Law to the literature of American psalmody, which in his day was extremely meager. The period, however, during which his pen was productive, saw the rise of many native musicians, and music books increased rapidly in numbers. William Billings, of Boston, was perhaps the most influential of the new writers, and he had many followers. The music of Mr. Law did not prove lasting and none of his pieces are to be found in modern collections.

A large part of the life of Andrew Law was

---

[1] From The Choir Herald.

devoted to the teaching of music, so that the account
of his activities is to be obtained from his music
books, but these facts indicate his preparation. He
was born in Milford, Connecticut, in March, 1748,
was the oldest son of Jahleel Law and Ann Baldwin,
and the grandson of Governor Law, of that State.
When he was five years old the family removed to
Cheshire, and with that town he was more or less
closely connected the rest of his life. He joined
the church there in 1769. He graduated from
Brown University in 1775, and received his master's
degree from the same institution three years later.
In the meantime he had been studying divinity,
according to the custom of that day when there
were no theological schools, with the Rev. Levi Hart,
of Preston, Connecticut, and in 1777 we find him
preaching in Chesterfield, that State. Yale conferred upon him the degree of A.M. in 1786, and
Allegheny College of Meadville, Pennsylvania, then
in its infancy, honored him with LL.D. in 1821.
He was ordained as a minister September 8, 1787,
at Hartford, by a Congregational council, and on
the 18th of October following he was recommended
by the Philadelphia Presbytery to preach in the
South. Mr. John W. Moore, a prolific writer
about musicians, states that "as late as 1820 Mr.
Law resided in Newark and from thence wrote letters
for publication, recommending his system of notation." In another place he notes that "he died in
New Haven, Connecticut, 1824," though "it had
been stated by Allibone that he died in Cheshire in
1821." Evidently, Moore did not have access to
papers that would verify his statements, for we may

read in the Connecticut Courant, printed in Hartford, July 17, 1821:

Died, at the house of William Law, Esqr., of Cheshire, on the 13th, inst., the Rev. Andrew Law, in the 73d. year of his age. For the last forty years Mr. Law has been an assiduous cultivator and teacher of sacred music.

Mr. Law never married.

In an advertisement in the last part of one of his musical magazines is the following notice referring to works of his:

Also by the same author, and to be sold by William Law at the press, a small number of the Select Harmony, and also a collection of Hymns and Tunes; likewise, upon short notice, at the press and very cheap, any number of a collection of fifty-four Psalm Tunes, designed to be bound in with editions of psalm books.

This last-named collection doubtless refers to his first publication of *Plain Tunes*, issued at Boston in 1767, and followed by other editions in 1772, 1781, and 1785. Sixteen pages of plain tunes engraved by Joel Allen, are found in a copy of Tate and Brady's *Psalms* of 1774 in the Boston Public Library, but there are fifty-five tunes instead of fifty-four. Twelve of these tunes had been used by Lyon in his *Urania* in 1761, and one, called "Mear," is still in common use in the hymnals of the present day.

His next book was the *Select Harmony*, containing, in plain and concise manner, the rules of singing, together with a complete collection of psalm tunes, hymns, and anthems. New Haven. Printed by Thomas and Samuel Green, 1779. There were one hundred pages of music engraved by J. Allen, of Farmington, and the first part of fifty pages may have been published in advance of the entire work as an advertisement; on the title is dated Cheshire, December 10, 1778 (so says Charles Evans in his *American Bibliography*). The copy of the *Select Harmony* in the Library of Congress was "Prudence Minor's and Sally's book, bought October, 1787, giving (sic) by their brother, Andrew Minor." The index of this book shows the names of the composers, but there do not appear to be any of Law's own tunes in it. Another edition of a *Select Harmony*, "containing in a plain and concise manner the rules of singing, chiefly by Andrew Law, A.B., to which is added a number of psalm tunes, hymns and anthems from the best authors, with some never before published" was "printed and sold by Daniel Bayley at his house in Newburyport, 1784."

In 1780 the first edition of his *Musical Primer* was issued by Mr. Law from New Haven, in the common round notes; but the fourth edition printed in Cambridge, Massachusetts, by W. Hillard in 1803, appears to have been the first one to contain his new system of notation, for he says:

This book exhibits a new plan of printing music. Four kinds of characters are used, and are situated between the single bars that divide the time, in the same manner as if they were on lines, and in every instance where two characters of the same figure occur their situations mark perfectly the height and distance of their sounds, and every purpose is effected without the assistance of lines. These four kinds of characters also denote the four syllables, mi, faw, sol, law, which are used in singing. The diamond has the name of mi; the square of faw; the round of sol; and the quarter of a diamond of law.

As he had been a teacher of music for over twenty years, he had felt the need of some musical notation that would be easily read by the learner. This notation, however, did not become popular and was used in only a few of his books.

The *Christian Harmony*, which was a collection of sixty-five psalm and hymn tunes, was printed in 1805 at Windsor, Vermont. In 1792 Mr. Law had projected a musical magazine which he hoped to make a periodical publication, and the first number of it was issued from Cheshire, Connecticut in that year. A second number followed in 1793. This was not such a magazine as is now published under that name, but merely contained a few tunes without reading matter. I have not seen a copy of the contents of the first number, but the second contains eight tunes, had covers of coarse paper, and in advertising it he says:

This is a periodical publication and is designed to contain several new and a number of celebrated pieces of American and European composition. Numbers 1 and 2 are already out. Price of each number by the dozen, one-eighth of a dollar, and singly, one-sixth of a dollar. Printed and sold by William Law, Cheshire, Conn.

Later we read: "Additional numbers may be printed upon this plan and published as frequently as the public mind shall be prepared to receive them." The sixth number was "published as the law directs, November, 1801." and contained eight pieces set from type.

In the year 1800 he had proposed to issue *The Art of Singing*, in three parts, to contain in one volume his *Musical Primer, The Christian Harmony,*

and *The Musical Magazine*.   A volume was printed
with Parts One and Three in 1801 with the common
style of round notes.   Then in 1805 he put forth
the completed book with music in his new notation.
It is of interest to observe that the three parts
which go to make up this volume were printed in
three different places.   Part One was printed in
Cambridge, Massachusetts, by W. Hilliard in 1803;
Part Two at Windsor, Vermont, by Nahum Mower
in 1805, and Part Three at "Boston, for the author,
by E. Lincoln," in 1805.   This last part is desig-
nated as a fourth edition with additions and improvements, so it is evident that three editions were
printed in the years from 1801 to 1804.   "The plan
of printing music," he says, "with four kinds of
characters and the method of teaching by characters
are explained in the fourth edition of the Musical
Primer."   The first imprint of this latter title bears
date 1780, but the copy which I have examined in
the Library of Congress is "newly improved and
revised, designed especially for the use of learners,
by Andrew Law," and the plate printing was "done
by William Law in Cheshire, Conn." in 1793.   A
third edition, which is not dated, was published in
Philadelphia "upon the author's new plan."   The
date is penciled in some copies as 1812.   It could
not have been earlier than that year for the reason
that some of the recommendations are dated as late
as June 13, 1811.   One was from the pen of the
Rev. William Staughton, then pastor of a Baptist
church in Philadelphia, and later president of what
is now called the George Washington University,
located in Washington, D. C.   Another letter,

approving his new system, was written by John Hubbard, professor of music in Dartmouth College, a man well versed in music, who later wrote and published an essay upon that subject. At the April session of the Philadelphia Methodist Conference a committee to whom had been referred the matter of introducing Mr. Law's book into the churches, reported favorably. His new form of musical notation had been invented several years before this, in 1803, and in his advertisement to his *Musical Primer*, he says:

A book that might be obtained at little expense and be suitable for learners at their first setting out has been frequently called for. Such a one is the following. The rules comprised in it are explained with the utmost conciseness and simplicity. If the learner, upon perusing them and practicing upon the additional lessons and tunes, finds that he is likely to succeed as a singer, he may safely venture to purchase other music; if not, he may relinquish this book and his undertaking together without much loss of time or money.

He then compares the new plan with the old and concludes that the characters and their locations compare as seven to twenty-eight, so that the advantages which are gained by the new plan are very great and of vast importance. To the objection that it is new and not in general use he adds that upon this ground every improvement in the arts must be rejected. Nevertheless, the new notation did not last long, though it may have obtained some vogue, and he himself, as well as later composers, went back to the common round notes that are now almost universally used.

A Collection of the Best and Most Approved

Tunes and Anthems for the Promotion of Psalmody
was printed in New Haven by Thomas and Samuel
Green, in 1779, and what was perhaps the third edition with this title, *A Collection of the Best and
Most Approved Tunes and Anthems Known to
Exist*, was issued from the printing office of William
Law at Cheshire in 1782. In the meantime, 1781,
a second edition had been printed by the Greens at
New Haven, and for it he had procured protection
by what was the second copyright given by special
legislative enactment in the United States. For in
October, 1781, the General Assembly of Connecticut
by special act granted the author the exclusive
patent for imprinting and vending his collection for
five years and imposed a fine of five pounds and
payment of damages for every infringement of his
right. He was led to take this action by an experience with his Select Harmony, for he says in the
introduction to his *Rudiments of Music* that he
hopes this "will not be pirated as the other was by
those who look, not to the public good, but to their
own private emolument."

This statement raises a very interesting question
and one that we would be glad to solve. The question is this: Under what title did the pirate edition
appear? In 1784 there was a *Select Harmony*
printed and sold by Daniel Bayley at his house in
Newburyport, containing in a plain and concise
manner the rules of singing, chiefly by Andrew Law,
A.B., to which are added a number of psalm tunes,
hymns, and anthems from the best authors, with
some never before published. This could not have
been the edition referred to, for the reason that it

was not issued until the year following his remark.
There is no doubt, however, that so much of it as
was taken from Andrew Law was pirated, by which
we mean that it was printed without his consent,
for Daniel Bayley was not a composer, but merely
a compiler who took what he chose from the books
that came in his way, leaving out what he did not
care to reprint. In one of his reprints of the English Collection of Aaron Williams he plainly states
that he has left out some of the pieces, and it will
be noted that in the title of his *Select Harmony*
the rules are taken chiefly from Andrew Law, but
some of the hymns, etc., have never before been published.

The *Massachusetts Harmony* presents a more
promising field for speculation. The editor is not
named in this book and it is not dated. In a recent
letter from Mr. Hubert P. Main, he writes: "I am
very certain that Billings was not the editor of the
Massachusetts Harmony from evidence I have."
And in Warrington's *Short Titles* he is quoted as
saying that this is printed from plates that are
identical with one of Law's books. It was presumably attributed to Billings because it was printed in
Boston, which was his home. Mr. Evans, in his bibliography, puts it in the list for 1784, and questions
Billings as its editor. The book itself is undated,
and 1784 was probably given to it because a second
edition was issued in 1785. It is rather improbable
that the two editions should follow each other so
closely, and therefore two or three years earlier may
be nearer the correct date. This would take it back
to a time when reference to it could be made in a

OLD HUNDRED

In Andrew Law's New Notation. From The Harmonic Companion, 1819. In the author's collection

book printed in 1783. As to its editor it may be said that Billings was not at all backward in acknowledging the work of his genius, and it is not conceivable that he should have been the editor of the *Massachusetts Harmony*, and let it go forth signed only "By a Lover of Harmony," withholding his own name. On the other hand, we cannot think of any motive which would cause Law to omit his name from the title page, if it were really his book printed with his consent. But if it is true, as Mr. Main writes, that *"The Massachusetts Harmony* was printed from plates that are identical with one of Law's books," and if we are right in assuming that this is the pirated edition referred to by Mr. Law, then we discover a reason for omitting the name of the real author and for not having any name appear upon its pages.

In 1782 he issued *A Collection of Hymns for. Social Worship*, in forty-eight pages. This collection and his book of tunes were frequently bound together.

His *Rudiments of Music* was "A short treatise on the rules of psalmody, to which are annexed a number of plain tunes and chants, by Andrew Law, A.M., in 1783." This was entered for State copyright December 3, 1783. A second edition was printed two years later. A fourth edition was printed and sold by William Law in 1792, with the addition of a number of pieces never before published. This too was entered according to the laws of the United States. There were eighty-seven pages of engraved music as compared with the twenty in the first edition, and the common notation of round notes was used. The purchaser of the book which is now in the Library of Congress has written the price as six shillings. The copy of *Law's Rudiments of Music*, which is in the library of the Harvard Musical Association, was presented to it by Timothy Swan, a contemporary composer and recognized as the author of the minor tune "China," which is still in common use.

Two other publications of his are *The Harmonic Companion* and *The Art of Playing the Organ*. Copies of these may be seen in the Essex Institute, Salem, Massachusetts. The former is thus described in an advertisement:

The first and second parts of the Art of Singing are comprised in the Harmonic Companion, which is a volume of 120 pages. It contains the rules of psalmody, 145 psalm and hymn tunes and eight set pieces.

It was first issued in 1807 and reprinted in four editions. *The Art of Playing the Organ* was a small pamphlet of eight pages, printed in 1807 also and reprinted twice.

In 1814 Mr. Law began a series of *Essays on Music*. They were copyrighted August 24 and printed at Philadelphia for the author. Two numbers were issued. The first was on the general subject of music and in his second essay he says, "One object of these essays will be to notice the musical publications of this country." He then proceeds to discuss critically one of the recent books of church music.

An idea of the esteem in which Andrew Law was held by his contemporaries may be had in a sen-

tence taken from the notice of his death in a newspaper of 1821:

> To his correct taste and scientific improvements may be
> ascribed much of that decent, solemn and chaste style of
> singing so noticeable in so many of the American churches.
> He led a life of exemplary obedience to religious impression
> and has doubtless entered "into that rest which remaineth to
> the people of God."

Though he may have improved upon the manner of
singing, his style of composition did not abide, and
his tunes have passed from the hymnals. Dr. F. L.
Ritter, in his *History of Music in America,* says of
him:

> Law was more thorough in his musical knowledge than
> many of his contemporaries. The different collections of
> church music he published prove him to have been a singing
> teacher of comparatively good taste and judgment. Billings
> and his style seem not to have had much attraction for him.
> His aim was more serious. He selected his tunes with more
> care, and the harmonic arrangement of his pieces is simple
> and correct, and more in accordance with the spirit of church
> music. He did not indulge in much "fuguing." He does
> not seem to have been very popular as a compiler or as a
> composer. Only one of his original tunes, "Archdale,"
> acquired great popularity. It was for a long time reprinted
> in almost every book of church music. Law's most efficient
> work was that of a singing teacher. He did good pioneer
> work in the New England States and in the South.

THE REV. SOLOMON HOWE

1750–1835

Solomon Howe was a native of Massachusetts,
born in North Brookfield, September 14, 1750. At
the age of twenty-seven he graduated from Dart-

mouth College, 1777, and started on a career which was rather eccentric and desultory at times. Part of the time he was a preacher, then a teacher, then he practiced the art of printing, and when not otherwise engaged he turned his energies to farming. He was living in Greenwich, in the western part of Massachusetts, when his three music books were published, and he had attained to the age of eighty-five years when he died November 18, 1935, at New Salem.

His first music book was called *The Worshiper's Assistant* and contained, besides the rules of music, which at that time were usually introduced into every singing book, "a variety of easy and plain Psalm Tunes adapted to the weakest capacities and designed for extensive utility as an introduction to more critical and curious music." This was printed from music type by Andrew Wright at Northampton for the author in 1799. "The author has put his own hymns to the following tunes and has in manuscript five hundred more which he intends to publish in the future."

His second book was *The Farmers' Evening Entertainment*, was printed by the same firm in Northampton in 1804, and contained new hymns and a number of new tunes of as various airs and meters as the compass of the book will admit. An interesting side light on the time for which a copyright was issued is found in the statement that the copyright was secured to the author for fourteen years, one half the period of a copyright at the present time, or one third if a renewal is made. The next year, 1805, he issued a collection of 92 pages, *Divine*

Hymns on the Sufferings of Christ, "for the use of religious assemblies." None of his hymns are now in use.

ELIAS MANN

1750–1825

ELIAS MANN was born in Weymouth, Massachusetts, in 1750, but most of his life was spent in Northampton, where he taught music during the week, and led the singing in the Congregational church on Sunday. The time of his removal to Northampton is approximated by the date on which he and his wife joined the First Congregational Church there, which was in 1796. Here in the town made famous by the long pastorate of the Rev. Jonathan Edwards, he taught singing and printed books. At one time he was employed by the town to teach singing school on Thursday, Friday, and Saturday evenings during the months of December and January. He was paid twenty-six dollars for this service, and was to lead the singing on the Sabbath. He was again hired to conduct the singing school for two days a week from November to May, for which he was to be paid fifty dollars. The years during which these schools were to be held are not stated. He was one of the fifteen who met in Boston in June, 1807, to organize the Massachusetts Musical Society, from which sprang the Handel and Haydn Society, which was founded in 1815. He appears to have stopped in Worcester before settling in Northampton, for in the Massachusetts Magazine, printed in 1789 and 1790, we find that there were several pieces of music credited to E. Mann, of Worcester.

His earliest compilation was *The Northampton Collection of Sacred Harmony*, printed in that town by Daniel Wright and Company in 1797, and a second edition in 1802. He next issued *The Massachusetts Collection of Sacred Harmony*, a book of 200 pages, printed in 1807 by Manning and Loring in Boston. The first tune in this book is "Confidence," by Oliver Holden, and the copy of this book in the Library of Congress is the presentation copy from the compiler to Mr. Holden. On one of his visits to Boston he was asked to write a recommendation to *The Psalmodist's Assistant*, which Abijah Forbush had compiled in 1803.

Elias Mann died in Northampton, May 12, 1825, and was buried there with five of his children, and his widow, who survived him till April 22, 1842.

Herman Mann

Herman Mann, whose work as a printer of music may be considered with that of his relative, was born in Walpole, Mass., November 10, 1771. During his young manhood he taught school, but after he had removed to Dedham, in 1797, he engaged in printing. For a year he lived in Providence, Rhode Island, but most of his days were spent in Dedham. From 1797 to 1804 he published a newspaper called The Minerva, but it was not a profitable business, and it was discontinued. From 1804 to 1815 he printed a number of music books compiled by Daniel

Read, Walter Janes, Stephen Jenks, Amos Albee,
D. L. Peck, and Oliver Shaw. The last named was
a Providence musician whom he had met during his
stay in that city.

SUPPLY BELCHER

1751–1836

SUPPLY BELCHER, whose name is sometimes incor-
rectly given as Samuel Belcher, was associated with
William Billings in the early development of music
in Massachusetts, though his maturer years were
spent in Maine, and his musical career should be
credited to that State. References to him, however, are found on the records of Massachusetts, of
which the District of Maine formed a part up to
1820, when it became a separate State. Supply
Belcher was born in Stoughton, March 29, 1751.
As this was the year when the change from old to
new style was effected, and eleven days were
dropped, according to an act of Parliament, it may
be that the date of his birth, which is sometimes
stated as occurring on April 10, 1752, may be
accounted for by this means. For eleven days added
to March 29 would give April 10, and throw the
date into the following year. Mr. Belcher kept a
tavern in his native town, which was the favorite
resort for the musicians of that vicinity, and he
was a member of the famous Stoughton Musical
Society.

In 1785 he removed to Hallowell, Maine, and in

1791 to Farmington, where he became one of its best-known citizens. When the town sought incorporation from the Massachusetts Legislature, he was the agent sent to Boston on that mission. At home he was a justice of the peace, even as late as 1815, as appears from a copy of the Massachusetts Register for that year, which happens to be at hand. He was the principal magistrate of his adopted town until near the end of his life, and repeatedly represented that town in the Legislature of Massachusetts. He also taught the first school in the town.

He was the first choir leader in Farmington, and for many years led the music in the old church. The Rev. Paul Coffin in his journal refers to "Squire Belcher's singers, who were called together and gave him an evening of sweet music." In 1792, accompanied by another member of the Stoughton Musical Society, he visited the commencement exercises at Harvard for the purpose of enjoying the musical program, and in 1796, when Hallowell Academy gave an exhibition near the close of its first year, Squire Belcher was called from Farmington to conduct the music. In the language of the Tocsin, a paper then printed in Hallowell, "The exercises were enlivened by vocal and instrumental music under the direction of Mr. Belcher, 'The Handel of Maine.' " As a composer of music and as a performer on the violin he displayed far greater abilities than as a singer.

After Mr. Belcher had settled in Farmington, he prepared *The Harmony of Maine*, which was published in 1794 by Isaiah Thomas and Ebenezer T.

Andrews in Boston. The title page shows that the compiler was of Farmington, County of Lincoln, District of Maine, and that the book was an original composition of psalm and hymn tunes of various meters suitable for divine worship, also a number of fuguing pieces and anthems, and a concise introduction to the grounds of music, and rules for learners. Two of his pieces were included in the *Centennial Collection* of the Stoughton Musical Society, and a third was used in Holyoke's *Columbian Repository*, 1802.

Mr. Belcher was married March 2, 1775, to Margaret More, a native of Boston, and they had ten children. He died June 9, 1836, in Farmington, Maine, at the age of eighty-five.

ABRAHAM WOOD

1752–1804

The Columbian Harmony was the joint compilation of Abraham Wood and Joseph Stone. It contained, besides the rules of psalmody, "a collection of Sacred Music designed for the use of worshiping assemblies and singing societies." It was an oblong book of 112 pages, engraved partly by Joel Allen, and the last few pages by E. Ruggles, Jr. The pieces were mostly by American composers, Mr. Stone contributing forty-two tunes, and Wood twenty-six. Mr. John W. Moore, who wrote so much about the early music of this country, tells us that Joseph Stone was from the town of Ward, Massachusetts. This town, near Worcester, was named for General Artemas Ward, of Shrewsbury, a town on the other side of Worcester, and in 1837 its name was changed to Auburn, later to be made famous as the home of Clara Barton, the founder of The American Red Cross. From the records of this town we gather that Joseph Stone was born about 1758; was married there and raised a large family, that he died February 22, 1837, at the age of seventy-nine, and is buried in one of its cemeteries.

Abraham Wood was a native of Northboro, Massachusetts, spent his whole life there, and became one of its prominent citizens and officials. He was the youngest son of his parents, was born July 30, 1752, married April 1, 1773, Lydia Johnson, and had a large family. Military duties and music occupied much of his time. He was clerk of a militia company of which his brother was the captain, and on the Lexington alarm he marched with his company to Cambridge, the headquarters of the army, where he served as a drummer.

As an example of the interest the women took in the great struggle for independence, it is recorded that his young wife sat up the entire night previous to the departure of his company and melted her pewter ware into bullets to be fired at the British. The soapstone molds used on that occasion are still in the possession of the family. General Artemas Ward, who was in command of the Provincials around Boston before the arrival of General Washington, was in command of his regiment, and his brother Samuel Wood was captain of the company; this service was for twenty-two days. He also served in the Revolutionary War from July 27 to August

29, 1777, and from July 31 to September 1, 1778. During the war he was also one of the Committee of Correspondence in 1777 and 1780, and was one of the assessors of the towns in 1781-82 and 1795. For many years·after the war he was captain of a company of militia. His private business was that of a fuller or dresser of cloth. He was chorister of the church in Northboro, and a musician of considerable note for those days. Besides *The Columbian Harmony*, already mentioned, he published in 1784 a "Hymn of Peace"; in 1789, a book of *Divine Songs*, and shortly after the death of George Washington, a "Funeral Elegy," 1800. The latter was republished in 1840 at the time of President Harrison's death for use on that occasion.

Abraham Wood died suddenly of an apoplectic fit at his home in Northboro, August 6, 1804.

JOEL READ

1753–1837

The Reads were a musical family. Daniel's older brother, Joel, born August 16, 1753, was a choir leader, and organized and conducted singing schools in the towns around his native Attleborough. He was also a teacher in the common public schools and took an active part in the affairs of the town. He was selectman, assessor, and treasurer, represented the town in the State Legislature for a number of years, and was a surveyor and conveyancer. In his journal Daniel Read notes on Sunday, January 8, 1797, "Brother Joel arrived last eve in a sleigh from Attleborough," and on January 11, "Brother Joel set out to return home." He compiled and published a music book, *The New England Selection, or Plain Psalmodist,* in 1808. The preface of the second edition is dated at Attleborough, June 20, 1812. Forty-three composers contributed to this volume, and there are also twenty-seven tunes which are anonymous. This book was in common use in Massachusetts for over thirty years. It has fifteen tunes attributed to "Read," but as no given name is mentioned it cannot be stated whether any of them are by Joel. The list includes a number which are known to have been composed by his brother Daniel. It is said that one of Joel's tunes was called "Consolation." None of his are found in use at the present time. He died in his native town, January 27, 1837, upward of eighty-four years of age.

There was a third brother, William, who was a teacher of psalmody, and a composer of music, but not to such an extent as the others.

JACOB FRENCH

1754–

JACOB FRENCH was the second child of his parents, who were Jacob French and Miriam Downs. He was born in Stoughton July 15, 1754, and probably lived there at least till his marriage May 26, 1779, to Esther Neale, who was also of that town. We have not discovered where he died, but he may have removed to Northampton, where his last book was issued, and may have died there.

His first music book was *The New American Melody*, printed in 1789, and sold by Jacob French in Medway, Massachusetts. His stay in Medway must have been short, for his name has not been recorded in the history of that town. His second book was *The Psalmodist's Companion*, and was printed in Worcester by Isaiah Thomas in 1793. In this book he states that he has been a teacher of music for many years. His third book was *The Harmony of Harmony*, and was printed in Northampton for the compiler in 1802.

Music seemed to run in the family. A younger brother, Edward (1761–1845), was a very good singer, and composed at least one tune called "New Bethlehem."

"The Heavenly Vision," the most widely known of all anthems of Jacob French, is not in any one of his books, for the reason that he sold the copyright to Isaiah Thomas, who used it in an edition of the Worcester Collection in 1791, but it is not there credited to anyone.

AMOS DOOLITTLE

1754–1832

His partner, Amos Doolittle, was a native also of Connecticut, having been born May 8, 1754, at Wallingford, and he died in New Haven, January 31, 1832. He learned the trade of a silver smith, and was the first engraver on copper in America. Perhaps his most noted work was his illustrations of the battles of Concord and Lexington. He went to these towns with the military company of Benedict Arnold, and with the help of eye-witnesses he made sketches of the battle, and afterward engraved four views of the battle of Lexington on copper which were printed and sold for six shillings per set.

Nathaniel Jocelyn (1796–1881) was the son of Simeon, began engraving in 1818, and with S. S. Jocelyn (1799–1879) continued the business of engraving and printing music books. One of the most interesting of the music books issued by this firm is a little book called

ZION'S HARP: or a new collection of music intended as a companion to "Village Hymns for Social Worship, by the Rev'd Asahel Nettleton"; also adapted to other hymn books and to be used in Conference Meetings & Revivals of Religion. Engraved by N & S S Jocelyn, 1824.

This book is frequently attributed to Asahel Nettleton, but it is probably the work of the engravers, as the quotation marks indicate that it was the Village Hymns that were by Mr. Nettleton. This book was until a few years ago almost unknown to the large libraries, but now copies may be seen in the Boston Public Library, the New York Public Library, the Library of Congress, and the library at Oberlin; and there are several in private collections.

ASAHEL BENHAM

1757–1805

Most of the information for this sketch is taken from The Musical Herald of September, 1882, to which it was contributed by the Rev. George Hood, who had written a *History of Music in New England*. Asahel Benham, he tells us, was a teacher and compiler of music, who was born in New Hartford, Connecticut, in the year 1757. He was one of the few who, having no craft, devoted themselves to teaching. Like many others he went from place to place, living on the avails of his schools, and finding them wherever he could. He taught mostly in the New England and Middle States. His education in early life was small, even for that day, but a good mind and diligent reading supplied in part the defect and placed him far above mediocrity.

His personal appearance was remarkably prepossessing. Above the average height, with a noble face and fine address, he commanded the respect of the stranger, and with good sense and intelligence, correct morals and a kind heart, he retained the respect and love of his acquaintances. He died in 1805 at the age of forty-eight years.

Music

Mr. Benham wrote many pieces, but in the loose style of his contemporaries, and his compositions have long ago fallen into disuse. There were two books published over the name of Asahel Benham. His *Federal Harmony* first appeared in 1790 at New Haven, and was a small oblong of fifty-eight pages of engraved music and sixteen pages of introduction to music. His first book has the following title:

THE FEDERAL HARMONY, containing in a familiar manner the rudiments of psalmody with a collection of sacred

music most of which are entirely new. New Haven, printed
and sold by Abel Morse, 1790.

It was a small oblong book of engraved music, had
twelve pages of introduction, and thirty-six pages
of music. A second edition appeared in 1792 with
fifty-eight pages. Of the third and fourth editions
I have found no trace, but the fifth was issued at
Middletown in 1794, and the sixth at the same place
by Moses H. Woodward, but is not dated. When
the Hartford Collection was issued in 1812, Mr.
Benham was one of the subscribers, and gave his
residence as Wallingford, Connecticut. The first
hymn in the sixth edition of his *Federal Harmony* is
a "Hymn for Wallingford" and a tune by that name
is the first one printed in the book. This book has
sixteen pages of introduction, and fifty-eight pages
of engraved music. There are forty-six tunes, and
two anthems, and besides the music of the compiler
it contained tunes by the popular writers of that
day—Daniel Read, Justin Morgan, Oliver Brownson, Timothy Swan, and Lewis Edson.

The publisher cheerfully presents the following collection of
music (without either gloss or comment) to the inspection of
the public, and if it meets with their approbation, his most
sanguine wishes are answered; if not the consequence is
obvious.

His *Federal Harmony* must not be confused with
another book of that name which was issued from
Boston in various editions, without name of compiler, but has been attributed to Timothy Swan.
That was a larger book of 100 pages or more.

About 1800 there appeared a collection of music

called *Devotional Harmony*, a posthumous work by Merit N. Woodruff, late of Watertown, Connecticut, deceased, published under the inspection of Asahel Benham. There were eight pages of introduction, followed by engraved music, nine to sixty.

AMOS BULL

Amos Bull was apparently another Connecticut man who made a collection of church music, *The Responsary*, which was set with second trebles instead of counters, and peculiarly adapted to the use of New England churches. It was printed in Worcester, Massachusetts, by Isaiah Thomas, in 1795, and was sold by the editor in Hartford, Connecticut. It had one hundred pages, and about half of the music was new. Mr. Bull was born about 1744. The date is taken from an advertisement printed in a New Haven paper in 1766, when he stated that he was twenty-two years old. He wanted subscribers for a new book that he was about to publish, but whether the book ever saw the light of print has not been discovered. In 1775, when Oliver King advertised for subscribers to his *Universal Harmony*, he refers to a Mr. Bull, singing master in New York. Perhaps this is the same Bull. By 1805 Amos Bull had located in Hartford, and July 5, 1805, advertised that he

continues to receive constant supplies of goods. Among those lately come to hand are Clock and Watch files. He proposes to open a school for Reading, Writing and Arithmetick, with other learning, useful and necessary in common life. The price will be only two dollars per quarter for each scholar; so that none who wish to have the benefit of his instructions, need be excluded on account of price. The school to begin as soon as six scholars shall have entered their names for one quarter.

Nothing further has been found about him or his work in music.

DANIEL READ

1757–1836[1]

ONE of the early composers whose tunes have been retained in the hymnals of the present day is Daniel Read—Masachusetts-born, but most of whose business activities were carried on in the Nutmeg State. He was born November 16, 1757, in Rehoboth, Massachusetts, the son of Daniel and Mary Read. He had hardly reached his majority when he was called out as a soldier in 1777 and 1778 during the Revolutionary War in three short expeditions into Rhode Island. Each of these services lasted about a month. Before the close of the war he had removed to New Haven and entered into a partnership with Amos Doolittle, an engraver, and engaged in the business of book publishing and selling. About 1785 he married Jerusha Sherman in New Haven, and four children were born to them. Their second son was a graduate of Yale, class of 1811, and was a clergyman. He died at sea near Cape Cod in August, 1821, and was buried at Edgartown, Martha's Vineyard. A daughter, Mary White Read, married Jonathan Nicholson, lived in New Haven, and is buried there. After her death the oil portraits of Daniel and Jerusha Read were pre-

[1] From The Choir Herald.

sented to the New Haven Colony Historical Society. This society also possesses a volume of manuscript music which belonged to "Daniel Read. Saturday, July 9, 1777." This was indorsed by his son, George Frederick Handel Read, whose name suggests the famous composer, as follows: "Whether any of the tunes were of his composition I do not know. February 9, 1855." One of Mr. Read's journals, or letter-books, also belongs to this society. It contains items covering the period from 1796 to 1812, and indicates that he took an active part in public affairs. Besides his book business, he was a manufacturer of ivory combs, was a stockholder in one of the New Haven banks, a director of the Library, and he assisted Elisha Munson in the preparation of the catalogue of the Mechanic Library.

Upon the death of his wife's father he writes, "Her father would not consent to her marriage with me, because I was guilty of the unpardonable crime of poverty." On January 15, 1797, he "attended singing meeting in the State House, it being the second time of meeting there for the purpose of singing this season." In March, 1793, he wrote to Oliver Holden subscribing for the periodical issues of music that might be made by the latter.

Daniel Read's first book was called *The American Singing Book*. This was intended as a new and easy guide to the art of psalmody, designed for the use of singing schools in America, and it was printed in New Haven in 1785. It had seventy-three pages, and the contents were composed by "Daniel Read. Philo Musico." The copy of this book in the

Library of Congress was Silas Hough's book, bought February 7, 1789, for seven shillings six pence. So extensive was the sale in New England that a fourth edition was issued in January, 1792. A copy of this edition is in the library of the Massachusetts Historical Society. It has a supplement containing five tunes that were not in the original work, which had forty-seven. A supplement to *The American Singing Book* was issued separately in 1787 containing twenty-five tunes from different composers. About the time that the fourth edition was issued he wrote in his journal under date of January 9, 1793, that he was proposing to Richard Atwell, of Huntington, that he go to Alexandria as agent for his books. For he says: "A young man made in six months by one school only $300," and that "books of the size of *The American Singing Book*, without the Supplement, sell for one dollar per piece," and advises sending ten or twelve books to Alexandria immediately. The cost of binding his books he states in 1798 as "nine pence each."

In 1786 he began to publish *The American Musical Magazine* monthly. In the first volume (Yale Library) he says it is "intended to contain a great variety of approved music carefully selected from the works of the best American and European masters." This contained both sacred and secular music and was published and sold by Amos Doolittle and Daniel Read in New Haven.

INTRODUCTION TO PSALMODY

His next book was

An Introduction to Psalmody, or, The Childs Instructor in

vocal music, containing a series of familiar heads, viz: Psalm-ody in general, stave, musical letters and cliffs, an exercise for the bass, an exercise for the tenor or treble, an exercise for the counter, tones, semitones, flats, sharps and natural, sol-fa-ing transposition, &c. the several notes and rests, and their proportion, the several moods of time, several other characters used in music, key-notes, &c., graces, illustrated with copper plates by D. Read, Printed . . . in New Haven, 1790.

This was followed in 1793 by *The Columbian Harmonist*, which reached its fourth edition in 1810. There were three numbers which were issued sep-arately, and also bound together in a single volume of 112 pages. The author explains the three parts by saying that "those who object to purchasing this book (No. 2) because it contains tunes before pub-lished, are requested to make use of the First Num-ber, which contains a collection of tunes never before published. And those who think anthems a necessary part of a collection of music are desired to peruse the Third Number, which contains anthems and set pieces, suitable for Christmas, Good Friday, Easter, Fasts, Thanksgiving, Funerals, &c."

In 1817, in connection with Eleazer T. Fitch, pro-fessor of divinity at Yale, and other men of musical taste and ability, he was requested to compile and arrange a collection of music for the use of the United Society of New Haven. In this work the labor of arranging and preparing for the press devolved entirely on Mr. Read; and he entered into it with his usual zeal and success. This was his last published work. It met with favor, and was used in that society for many years, and was also used in many other churches in different parts of the country.

The book referred to in the preceding paragraph was called

THE NEW HAVEN COLLECTION OF SACRED MUSIC, containing a set of tunes adapted to the metres and subjects of the Psalms and Hymns in general use, selected principally from the works of the most eminent authors, by an Association of Gentlemen for the promotion of Classical Sacred Music in the United Society in New Haven; to which is prefixed a concise introduction to psalmody for the use of Singing Schools. Dedham. Printed typographically by Daniel Mann, 1818.

There is no name in the book to indicate who the gentlemen were who prepared the book, but the Rev. George Hood gives us the information above. The book is a narrow oblong, and contained 149 pages.

His last work, which occupied his attention for some years, was completed in 1832, when he was in his seventy-fifth year, but was never published. It is neat in execution, methodical in arrangement, and well exhibits the character of the man. It contains nearly three hundred pages and over four hundred tunes. The manuscript he presented to the American Home Missionary Society, for them to publish, with the request that the avails which may arise from its publication be applied, under their direction, to the cause of missions in the United States. This donation, under the request to publish the work, was declined by the Board, feeling they were not authorized to take such a responsibility.

Some of Mr. Read's tunes have been in common use in the hymnals of this country down to the present time. "Lisbon" and "Windham" are the most popular, and have been found in seven of the recent books examined. One book contained three of his tunes, and *The Methodist Hymnal* of 1878 has no less than five—one of them, "Sherburne," belonging to that class so frequently used years ago known as fugue tunes. His "Windham" bears a strong resemblance to a German choral, and Charles Zeuner in his *Ancient Lyre* calls it a choral by Martin Luther arranged by Read. When we realize the change in sentiment regarding church music during the more than one hundred years since Read wrote, it is surprising that any of his compositions should have any vogue at the present time.

PART II

1758–1772

TIMOTHY SWAN

1758–1842[1]

"All records agree that July twenty three
Was my birthday a long time ago;
  'An' I will engage, ye'll ken my auld age
If yee'll read the four lines just below.

Twice twenty yars an haf a skore
An' ye mayn ad jist ten yars more,
Noo join eight yars twa times an then
  Cast a' thegither my age ye'll ken."

THESE lines were written by Timothy Swan at
Northfield, July 23, 1834, and signed by him upon a
slip of paper which is pasted inside the front cover
of his *New England Harmony*, 1801, in the library
of the American Antiquarian Society in Worcester,
Massachusetts.   The place of his birth is stated
in some histories as Suffield, Connecticut, while in
others it is given as Worcester, Massachusetts.
From the printed records of that city we verify
the statement that he was born in Worcester, July
23, 1758, and learn that he was the son of William
and Lavina Swan.   The following information is
taken from a magazine printed in 1853, and is said
to have been revised by the daughter of Mr. Swan,
so that it may be relied upon as correct: There
were thirteen in the Swan family, Timothy being the
eighth.   After the death of his father he was placed
under the care of a Mr. Barnes, of Marlboro, Massachusetts, an English gentleman, who was a merchant there, and whom young Swan was to serve

[1] From The Choir Herald.

103

till of age. When the difficulties between Great Britain and the colonies arose, Mr. Barnes, who was intensely loyal, was induced to return to England, and Timothy, now sixteen years of age, went to live with his brother, who was a merchant in Groton. It was while here that he obtained his musical education by attending singing school for three weeks. Soon after this he began to compose airs, but being completely ignorant of the rules, both of musical composition and harmony, his work was uncouth and unpolished. In the same year he joined the army at Cambridge and attained considerable efficiency in playing the fife under the tuition of an English fifer. At seventeen he began to learn a trade by apprenticing himself to a brother-in-law, who was a hatter in Northfield. He now commenced to compose hymn tunes, "Montague" being the first. These were done mostly while he was at work. He was accustomed to write the melody first, and then the other parts, jotting down a few notes at a time until the piece was complete. During his apprenticeship he composed "Poland" and many other church tunes, which were copied and used in manuscript form over a considerable part of New England. When he heard of William Billings he was exceedingly anxious to see the man, who, strange as it may seem to modern musicians, for a long time gave direction to the music of New England. This desire was not gratified, however, until some years afterward, when Mr. Swan met him in Boston.

At the termination of his apprenticeship he went to Suffield, Connecticut, where at the age of twenty-

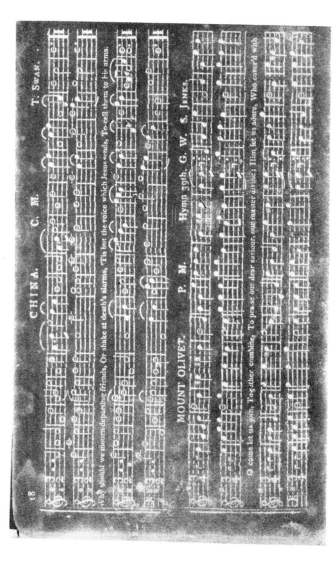

CHINA, TIMOTHY SWAN

Jenks' Delights of Harmony, 1804.   Library of Congress

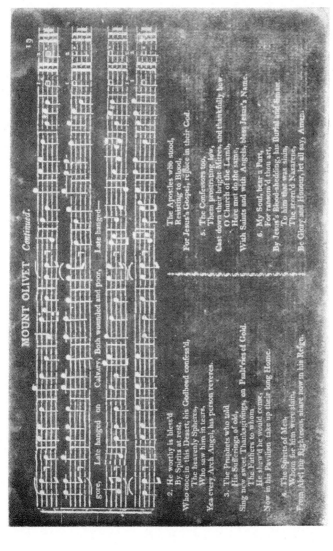

MOUNT OLIVET. STEPHEN JENKS

Jenks' Delights of Harmony, 1804. Library of Congress

five he married a daughter of the Rev. Ebenezer Gay, D.D. (Harvard, 1792), the pastor of the First Congregational Church of that place. He lived there for twenty-eight years, and wrote there most of the music which he published. His church tunes of greatest merit are "Poland," "Quincy," "London," "Spring," and "China." The last named he regarded as his best, and in this estimate the public has agreed with him, for this is the only one that now finds a place in modern hymn books. In the copy of *The New England Harmony*, in the library of the American Antiquarian Society in Worcester, there is a notation over the tune "China" to the effect that it was composed in 1790, and was first sung in public in 1794. It is written in a minor key, and is usually set to the words of Watts, "Why do we mourn for dying friends?" It has been styled "one of the most unscientific tunes ever published," but the people regarded it as the most effective. These verdicts indicate the force of that genius which could burst through the barriers by which it was surrounded and produce such results. That one could be scientific with the advantages that Swan enjoyed is not, of course, to be expected. Science did for him almost nothing—nature everything.

In 1807 Timothy Swan removed to Northfield, Massachusetts, where he continued to reside till his death, which took place July 23, 1842, the very day which completed his eighty-fourth year.

He was a fine-looking gentleman, had a well-stored mind, a retentive memory, and a genial temperament, which made him an agreeable companion. He was a great reader, sitting up till past midnight, and then lying late in the morning. This led his Northfield neighbors to say he was "Poor, proud, and indolent." He was an ardent admirer of Robert Burns, and often wrote poetry in the Scotch dialect, as the verse at the head of this sketch indicates. He is said to have been a frequent contributor of poetry to the local press, and he was for a long time in charge of the library in Northfield. He was very fond of the lilac, and planted three rows of Lombardy poplars around his house. The flocks of blackbirds that nested in their branches he guarded as his especial pets.

Books

Three if not four books may be attributed to Timothy Swan. *The Songsters' Assistant* was a collection of secular songs set to music, about half of which was the composition of Mr. Swan. The engraving was done by A. Ely, and its thirty-six pages were printed at Suffield by Swan and Ely, without date, probably about 1800. *The Songsters' Museum* was printed anonymously at Northampton in 1803. The title page of his *New England Harmony* indicates its contents, and is as follows:

THE NEW ENGLAND HARMONY
containing
A variety of Psalm Tunes in Three and Four Parts adapted
to all meters; also a number of Set Pieces of several
Verses each, together with a number of Anthems.
by Timothy Swan.
Published according to Act of Congress.
Printed at Northampton, Massachusetts,
by Andrew Wright.
And sold at his Office. Sold also at Suffield, in Connecticut,
by the author.
1801.

It was oblong in shape, and had 123 pages. His
family state that it was a pecuniary loss to him,
and never went beyond a first edition.

The other book that may have been his is *The
Federal Harmony*, first issued in 1785, in Boston
by John Norman, and attributed by Charles Evans
to Timothy Swan. Another edition was by the
same printer in 1788; the issue of 1790 had 114
pages, and one in 1792 130 pages, all four printed
by Norman.

TIMOTHY OLMSTED

1759–1848

The Musical Olio, printed in Northampton by
Andrew Wright in 1805, was compiled and composed by Timothy Olmsted. According to the prevailing arrangement of those days, it contained an
introduction to the art of singing, a variety of
psalm and hymn tunes from European authors, and
a number of original pieces never before published.
In his advertisement he says:

The pieces given out in my name [there are twenty four of
them], must speak for themselves. I have been importuned
by many of my acquaintance to insert more of them than I
intended, but to the public I now submit their trial and fate.

As the modern European authors have furnished us with
many excellent pieces of music in three parts, the air placed
for the female voice, and as that custom is prevailing, I have
adhered to it in part. Some publishers of psalmody have
exploded the alto or counter tenor and in their stead substi-
tuted second trebles; others have published in three parts
only. Objections have been made to each of those methods
singly. To obviate which I have inserted some tunes in three
parts and some in four, some with counters and some with
second trebles. Part of the airs are placed for the tenor

voice and part for the female voice, all of which I have thought best to print in characters universally made use of, having not as yet been made to perceive the utility of the simplifications and new inventions, which are so frequently presented us for our improvement by many of our modern masters. These characters are not only our old acquaintance, but that of the whole musical world, in which all nations can read and probably never will discard.

A second edition was issued in 1811 in New London, Connecticut. This contained a few more original pieces. Some of his tunes were copied into other books, even as late as Edmands' *Psalmist*, 1859; but, like most of the tunes by the writers of a century ago, they have been left out of the books of the present day.

Timothy Olmsted was descended from an old New England family, and was born in Phœnix, Oswego County, New York, November 12, 1759. When only sixteen years old he marched to Boston with the East Hartford company on the Lexington alarm in 1775; served as a musician in the Revolutionary War in the Seventh and in the Ninth Connecticut Regiments, and was present at the battle of White Plains. Just before the close of the war, on May 2, 1783, he married Alice Olmsted, a second cousin, by whom he had a large family—thirteen children. In 1785 he moved to Hartford, Connecticut, and later to Whitestown, New York. His wife died February 5, 1811, in Rome, New York. During the War of 1812 he served from August 18 to October 28, 1814, at New London, in Captain Erastus Strong's company in the First (Brainerd's) Regiment of Connecticut Militia. He died August 15, 1848.

JOHN HUBBARD
1759–1810

JOHN HUBBARD of New Hampshire was very fond of music, in fact, one writing of him has said that "perhaps one of his weak points was his excessive fondness for sacred music, on which he spent much time, it may be, at the expense of more solid and scholarly attainments." This remark also indicates the small value set upon the art of music at that time, and too much upon that which brings mere pecuniary profit. His musical publications began in 1789 with the issue of a book called *Harmonia Selecta*. In 1807 he prepared and read before the Middlesex Musical Association, at Dunstable, an "Essay on Music," which was published at the request of the society in 1808 at Boston in a pamphlet of nineteen pages. This Association was composed of musicians mostly from the northern part of Middlesex County, and in 1807 it issued *The Middlesex Collection of Church Music*, or Ancient Psalmody Revived, containing a variety of plain tunes the most suitable to be used in Divine services, to which is annexed a number of other pieces of a more delicate and artificial construction proper to be performed by a choir of good musicians occasionally, in schools and public religious assemblies." The publication of this compilation was committed by the association to the Rev. David Palmer as their agent. Mr. Palmer was the president of the society, was minister of the church in Townsend from 1800 to 1830, and during the years 1833 and 1834 represented his town in the General

Court of Massachusetts. A second edition of *The Middlesex Collection* was issued in 1808, and a third in 1811.

In 1814 there was published in Newburyport a volume of *Thirty Anthems*, which had been selected by Mr. Hubbard, one of which was original. This collection of tunes was in use for all ordinations, installations, and Thanksgivings for more than twenty-five years.

John Hubbard was born in Townsend, Massachusetts, August 8, 1759. He graduated from Dartmouth College in 1785, and after studying theology for a time he served as preceptor successively of the academies at New Ipswich and at Deerfield. From 1798 to 1802 he was judge of the Probate Court for Cheshire County, New Hampshire. In 1804 he became professor of mathematics and natural philosophy in Dartmouth College, which position he held until his death, which occurred August 14, 1810, at Hanover, New Hampshire. When the *Lock Hospital Collection* of sacred music was issued in 1809, he subscribed for sixteen copies, and this collection was doubtless used in the college. His contributions to literature were not confined to music, for an oration which he delivered July 4, 1799, was printed, also a book on *The Rudiments of Geography*, in 1803, and an *American Reader* in 1808.

AMOS BLANCHARD

THE only item found regarding Amos Blanchard, outside of his own books, is taken from Brook's *Old*

Time Music, and records that he will teach a school for instruction in sacred music on Monday and Friday evenings at the Methodist Chapel in Sewall Street, Salem, Massachusetts, beginning in November, 1823. The terms were two dollars a quarter, one half payable in advance.

The *Newburyport Collection of Sacred European Music* made its appearance in 1807 from the press of Ranlet and Norris, Exeter, New Hampshire. It had 152 pages. The following year he issued a smaller book, called *The American Musical Primer*, and its tunes were European in origin. None of the tunes in his first collection were repeated in this. His music had little usage outside of his own collections, though one tune called "Corinth" was introduced into *The Continental Harmony*, 1857, and it also appeared in the *Stoughton Collection* in 1878.

JACOB KIMBALL, JR.

1761–1826

JACOB KIMBALL, JR., was born February 22, 1761, at Topsfield, Massachusetts. He was the third of ten children of Jacob Kimball and Priscilla Smith. The father was a blacksmith, had some musical ability, and in 1765 was "chosen to set ye psalms, and to sit in ye elders' seat." Ritter, in his *History of Music in America*, attributes this honor to the son, but erroneously so, as the son was too young at that time. At the age of fourteen he was a drummer in Captain Baker's company of Little's regiment, Massachusetts Militia, from May 2 to October 2, 1775. Soon after this he entered Harvard University, from which he graduated in 1780. He then studied law and was admitted to the bar in Stratford, New Hampshire. The Rev. William Bentley, pastor of the church in Salem, called upon the elder Kimball in Topsfield, and wrote in his diary under date of December 7, 1795: "Found Mr. Kimball, the celebrated musician, at his father's. It is his purpose to establish himself in the law in Maine." But he did not like that profession, and soon gave it up for music, which suited him better. He had considerable talent as a musician, and adopted teaching as a permanent business. He taught music in the different towns in New England, endeavoring to introduce his own collection. He was not very successful as a business man, and he died in the almshouse in Topsfield, February 6, 1826, at the age of sixty-five. He was never married. The style of his music is like that of his contemporaries. He composed single psalm tunes and fuguing pieces, but was less original than Billings. He also wrote some hymns, which he set to music. His version of the sixty-fifth psalm was used in Dr. Belknap's *Sacred Poetry*, 1795. The first four lines follow:

"Thy praise, O God, in Zion waits;
   All flesh shall crowd thy sacred gates,
To offer sacrifice and prayer,
   To pay their willing homage there."

Books

He compiled two music books. The earlier one was *The Rural Harmony*, an original composition in three and four parts, for the use of singing schools and singing assemblies. It was printed in Boston in 1793 by Thomas and Andrews, and had seventy-one pieces. His other book was *The Essex Harmony*, which he also calls an original composition. This was printed by Henry Ranlet in Exeter, New Hampshire, in 1800, for T. C. Cushing and B. B. McNulty, of Salem, Massachusetts. The dedication is to the Essex Musical Association, founded in 1797, "with an ardent wish that it may contribute in some small degree toward furthering the objects of the society; the ameliorating and refining the taste for music; and that it may have a tendency to increase innocent amusement, as well as to exalt the feelings in public devotion." This book contained forty-four tunes and two anthems. An imperfect copy of it is in the Boston Public Library. This is not the same book issued by Daniel Bayley in various editions from 1770 to 1785. But it is the book to which the Rev. William Bentley refers when he writes: "Mr. McNulty has published a book of Kimball's psalmody. This young man was very amiable until he became addicted to intemperance. It is lamentable that so many publications in this country are evidently only catch-penny productions —not even suggested by genius but first asked by the promise of cash for the compilation."

The Essex Institute has a copy of *The Village Harmony* in which there is a pencil notation attributing it to Jacob Kimball, but there is some question about his connection with it. *The Village Harmony* was a very popular book in eastern Massachusetts during the twenty years following 1795, the various editions being printed in Exeter, New Hampshire; Newburyport and Boston, Massachusetts, but the compiler is not named. The tunes of Kimball had a short life. They are no longer found in the hymn books, though one or two are occasionally heard at "Old Folks' Concerts." Bentley's comment is true—"His tunes did not prove popular."

SAMUEL HOLYOKE

1762–1820[1]

THE most important contribution of Samuel Holyoke to the musical literature of America was (as shown by its title page):

THE COLUMBIAN REPOSITORY OF SACRED HARMONY, selected from European and American authors, with many new tunes not before published, including the whole of Dr. Watts' Psalms and Hymns, to each of which a tune is adapted, and some additional tunes suited to the particular meters in Tate and Brady's and Dr. Belknap's Collection of Psalms and Hymns; with an introduction of practical principles. The whole designed for the use of schools, musical societies, and worshipping assemblies.

This is the largest collection of music that had been gathered in this country up to that time. It was dedicated to the Essex (Mass.) Musical Association, of which he was a member. It was sold by subscription for three dollars, contained 472 pages, and had 734 tunes. In the advertisement he says:

It is presumed that there has no work of the kind yet appeared in the United States in which there is a greater variety of style to be found than in the present, and should

[1] From The Choir Herald.

the encouragement be equivalent to the time and labor bestowed upon it, the design will be answered.

It was published in Exeter, New Hampshire, by Henry Ranlet, but there is no date upon it. James Warrington, in his *Short Titles*, says about 1800. In the *Christian Harmonist*, published in 1804, there are two tunes credited to *The Columbian Repository*, which would indicate that the latter was in print prior to 1804. A search of the copyright records in Washington was rewarded by finding that it was entered for copyright April 7, 1802, thus fixing a date which for more than a century has been only conjectural.

Neither of the works mentioned was the first of Holyoke's collections, for in 1791 there had issued from the press of Thomas and Andrews, in Boston, a book of two hundred pages of sacred music called *Harmonia Americana*. The following quotation from the preface contains some good advice for the present time:

With respect to the design of the composition it may be observed that it is adapted as far as possible to the rules of pronunciation. Consequently, the music requires a moderate movement, for it is very difficult to follow the exact motion of the pendulum and pronounce with that propriety and elegance which the importance of the subject may demand. It may then be proper here to remark that sentiment and expression ought to be the principle guide in vocal music. Perhaps some may be disappointed that fuguing pieces are in general omitted. But the principal reason why few were inserted was the trifling effect produced by that sort of music; for the parts, falling in one after another, each conveying a different idea, confuse the sense, and render the performance a mere jargon of words. The numerous pieces of this kind extant must be a sufficient apology for omitting them here.

It is noticeable at the present time that "senti-ment and expression" are not always the "principle guide" in the rendition of vocal music.

His next effort was a third interest in the *Massa-chusetts Compiler*, a book of seventy-two pages, published in Boston in 1795 by Thomas and An-drews. The preface is dated at Charlestown (Mass.), and is signed by Hans Gram, Samuel Holyoke, and Oliver Holden. The latter is a familiar name—the composer of "Coronation"—and as he lived in Charlestown he probably did the larger part of the compiling. Hans Gram was the organist of the Brattle Street Church in Boston, and had already published anthems and hymn tunes which had been recommended by some of his contemporary composers as worthy of a favorable reception.

The next music of Mr. Holyoke which we have found was written for the funeral of Washington. The title page reads:

Hark from the Tombs, &c, and Beneath the honors, &c. Adapted from Dr. Watts and set to music by Samuel Holyoke, A.M. Performed at Newburyport, 2d January, 1800, the day on which the citizens expressed their unbounded veneration for the memory of our beloved Washington.

Opposite the title page were two odes to Washing-ton, "to be performed at the Brattle Street Church (Boston) on Wednesday, February 19, 1800."

The Christian Harmonist was printed at Salem, Massachusetts, in 1804 and contained tunes adapted to Doctor Rippon's selection, Mr. Joshua Smith's collection of hymns, and Doctor Watts' psalms and hymns. There were 195 pages of music. The tunes were partly selected and partly composed

Articles of Agreement, indented, made and concluded the 14th day of November, AD. 1806, by and between Henry Ranlet of Exeter, County of Rockingham, in the State of New Hampshire on the one Part, and Samuel Holyoke of Boxford, County of Essex in the Commonwealth of Massachusetts, on the other part. Witness that the said Holyoke has prepared for the press a Collection of Instrumental Music which he claims as Author, Compiler and Proprietor — and has committed the same to the said Ranlet to print — and has furnished the said Ranlet with paper sufficient to impress the number of Fifteen Hundred Copies of the said work, — and the said Holyoke does hereby covenant and agree with the said Ranlet — that he will attend to the printing of the said work and make such corrections for the press, as the same may require. —

— And the said Ranlet, on his part, does hereby covenant and agree to and with the said Holyoke, that he will print fifteen hundred copies of said work, and no more, that he will execute the typographical part of the work in a workmanlike manner — that, immediately after said work is out of the press, he will deliver seven hundred and fifty copies thereof to the said Holyoke, or to his order. — And the said Ranlet further agrees with the said Holyoke, for himself, his Heirs, Executors, Administrators and Assigns, that he will not, without particular license, from the said Holyoke, first had and obtained, either directly, or indirectly print, reprint, publish, or expose to sale any other copies of said work than the fifteen hundred aforesaid, — nor will he ever, without particular license, as aforesaid print, reprint, or publish any other Edition, or Editions of said work or any part thereof under the pains and penalties of the laws in that case made and provided. —

And the said Holyoke further agrees with the said Ranlet that he shall receive, as his own proper right, seven hundred and fifty copies of said work, as a compensation for printing the same. —

It is also agreed by the Parties aforesaid, that, should be a necessity for a new Edition, or Editions of said work,

CONTRACT OF SAMUEL HOLYOKE WITH HENRY RANLET, 1807
For the publication of *The Instrumental Assistant.* Original owned by the author

work, under the Title aforesaid, the said Ranlet shall
have, if he choose, the right of printing the same, on the
same terms of the first Edition, as above specified; and
should a second volume under the title aforesaid, be
thought advisable, that the said Ranlet shall, if he desire it, have the right of doing the work of said second
volume, on the terms aforesaid. —

And the Parties aforesaid further agree, each to the
other, that they will not make any alteration in
the price of the sale of said work, as published in the
title page, without their joint consent. —

And it is further agreed by the Parties aforesaid, that, in case of the decease of the said Parties, or of
either of them, before the finishing of said work and
final settlement thereof, each share of the first Edition
under the title aforesaid, shall descend to the Heirs of the
deceased, in the same manner as it would have belonged to the party himself, had he remained in
full life. —

To the true and faithful performance of the several covenants and agreements aforesaid the parties a-
foresaid do hereby respectively bind themselves and their
Heirs, Executors, Administrators and assigns, each to the
other, his Heirs, Executors, Administrators and assigns in
the penal sum of Three Thousand dollars. —

In Testimony whereof, We the Parties aforesaid,
have hereunto interchangably set our hands and seals,
the day and year above written.

Signed, Sealed, and Delivered   Samuel Holyoke
in Presence of —
    John Sawyer —
                                           Henry Ranlet

The words "intituled The Instrumental Assistant" were
interlined before signing   Samuel Holyoke.
                             Henry Ranlet

by Mr. Holyoke, and the book was especially designed for the use of Baptist congregations. Dr. John Rippon was an English Baptist whose first collection of hymns was issued in 1787, and successive editions with additional numbers were printed until his death in 1836. Joshua Smith was a member of the Baptist church in Brentwood, New Hampshire, from 1792, and his *Divine Hymns* had been first issued in 1784.

The last published work of Samuel Holyoke was printed by Henry Ranlet at Exeter, New Hampshire, in 1807, was called *The Instrumental Assistant*, and contained instructions for the violin, German flute, clarionet, bass viol and hautboy. There were two volumes under this title: Volume I, of eighty pages, bears no date; Volume II is bound with it and has one hundred and four pages of minuets, airs, rondos, marches, and is dated 1807. The original draft of the Articles of Agreement for the publication of this book is in the possession of the writer. It is signed by Samuel Holyoke and Henry Ranlet, and stipulates that "1,500 copies shall be printed, and that 750 shall be delivered to Holyoke for his compensation."

Samuel Holyoke was the second son of the Rev. Elizur Holyoke and Hannah Peabody. He was born October 15, 1762, at Boxford, Massachusetts, where his father was the minister of the Congregational church for forty-seven years. His mother was the daughter of the Rev. Oliver Peabody, one of the early ministers to the Indians of Natick, whose conversion was due to the labors of John Eliot. It is interesting also to note that his father was a nephew of Edward Holyoke, one of the early presidents of Harvard College, and a cousin of that Edward A. Holyoke who was a noted physician in eastern Massachusetts, and lived to be nearly one hundred and one years old.

Samuel was graduated from Harvard in the class of 1789. He became a noted music teacher, organizing and conducting classes in many of the towns in that section of the country. The fact that his books were printed in Boston; Salem, Massachusetts; and Exeter, New Hampshire, indicates the territory over which he traveled in his work. In 1806 we find him advertising in a Salem newspaper that he proposes to give a concert of vocal and instrumental music in the New South Meeting House on Wednesday, September 24. The tickets were a quarter of a dollar each, and the performance was announced to commence at three o'clock P. M. In the same paper he requests the aid of all those who attended the dedication of the New South Meetinghouse, and also the members of the two bands. He states that when the music is ready "notice will be given when and where to meet for preparatory rehearsals." He was a member of the Essex Musical Association, and several of the annual festivals of that society were held in the Congregational church in Boxford, where his father was minister. His most popular tune was "Arnheim," and this was among the first of his compositions. It retained a place in collections of church music for seventy-five years, but the latest books that I have been able to find it in are E. F. Hatfield's *Church Hymn Book*, printed in 1872 and 1874, and *The*

Methodist Hymnal of 1878. Of course it is to be
found in the *New Hymn and Tune Book* for the use
of the African Methodist Episcopal Zion Church,
copyrighted in 1909; but this was the Methodist
book of 1878, with a few additional hymns at the
end, which were covered by the later copyright.

In early life Mr. Holyoke had a fine voice, but in
later years it became so harsh that in the teaching
of his vocal classes he was obliged to use a clarionet.
A few days before his death he was at a social
gathering of his musical friends, February 2, 1820,
at the home of Jacob B. Moore in Concord, New
Hampshire. He asked that "Arnheim" be sung, for
he said that perhaps he would never meet with a
choir on earth so well calculated to do justice to his
first composition. They sang it over twice for him,
bringing tears to his eyes, as he seemed to realize
that he would never sing it again. He was sick
but a few days, closing his earthly career February
7, 1820, at Concord. He was unmarried. The
notice of his death that appears in the New Hampshire Patriot, printed at Concord, February 29,
1820, refers to him as "Samuel Holyoke of Boston,
aged fifty-seven, celebrated as a teacher and composer of sacred music."

The Jacob B. Moore referred to above was a
physician of Andover and Concord, New Hampshire. He was a born musician also, and composed
many pieces. I have been unable to identify any of
them, but his son tells us that some of his earliest
tunes were published in Holyoke's *Columbian Repository*. Many of the pieces in that book are
marked with * † ‡ and he explains that these were

never before published. At first I thought that the different marks were used to indicate the different composers of the tunes, but I have finally come to the conclusion that, after using all the asterisks (*) in the font of type he was obliged to use also the dagger, the double dagger (†, ‡). Besides the hymn tunes which Mr. Moore contributed to Holyoke's collection he published a number of songs in periodicals. One of his sons was John Weeks Moore, the author of a *Cyclopedia of Music*, first published in 1852, a pioneer book of the kind, and one showing much research into the history of early music in America.

The Rev. William Bently, a minister of Salem, Massachusetts, writes of Samuel Holyoke in 1791, just after his first music book had been published:

This gentleman is the first son of Harvard of whom I have heard that has published an original collection of music from his own compositions. The name given him was the American Madan, from the character of the music.

CHAUNCEY LANGDON

1763–1830

CHAUNCEY LANGDON, while an undergraduate at Yale, probably in his junior year, compiled a collection of sacred tunes, containing selections from Swan, Billings, Edson, Brownson, and other New England composers. It was called *The Beauties of Psalmody*, was an engraved pamphlet of fifty-six pages, oblong in shape, and appeared as the work of "A member of the Musical Society of Yale College." Judge Langdon, as he afterward became, was born in Farmington, Connecticut, November 8, 1763. He graduated from Yale in the class of 1787, three of whose members besides himself were members of Congress, and one of his classmates was a postmaster-general. He studied law in Hebron, Connecticut, and was married there to Lucy Nona Lathrop, a sister of one of his classmates. Soon after this he settled in Castleton, Vermont. He served as register of the Probate Court for several years between 1792 and 1813, was judge of the Probate Court in 1798-99, was a State representative in 1813-14, 1817, 1819-20, and a member of Congress from 1815 to 1817. He was given the degree of A. M. by Middlebury College in 1803, and was elected a trustee of that college in 1811, holding that office until his death July 23, 1830, at Castleton, Vermont.

JEREMIAH INGALLS

1764–1828[1]

JEREMIAH INGALLS was the eldest child of his parents and was born March 1, 1764, at Andover, Massachusetts. When he was thirteen years old his father, Abijah, died as a result of the privations of the Revolutionary War. His great-grandfather was one of the settlers of Andover, and the name was a common one in that town. To this day one of the railroad crossings preserves the name as Ingalls' Crossing. Soon after reaching his ma-

[1] From The Choir Herald, July, 1914.

jority Jeremiah settled in Newbury, Vermont, and
on April 28, 1791, was married to Mary Bigelow,
also a native of Massachusetts (Westminster). He
built for himself in 1800 a two-story house in which
he kept a tavern for ten or more years. At various
times he was engaged as farmer, cooper, or singing
master. In 1819 he removed to Rochester, Vermont, later going to Hancock in the same State,
where he died April 6, 1828, at the age of sixty-
four. He left a number of descendants who inherited a musical instinct, but not as much talent as
their father, although they were considered very
good musicians. His widow returned to Rochester,
Vermont, where she died April 18, 1848.

Mr. Ingalls had a high voice, was expert on the
bass viol, and a ready reader of music. He was a
member and a deacon of the Congregational Church,
as well as a leader of the choir, and his Newbury
singers had the honor of introducing into the sanctuary his two very best tunes, "New Jerusalem" and
"Northfield," sung from manuscript copies, though it
is believed that "Northfield" was composed at an inn
in Northfield, New Hampshire, while the author was
waiting and hungering an unusually long time for
dinner. He frequently composed both words and
music for special occasions. Of this sort we find in
his book three pieces, namely, "Election Hymn,"
"Election Ode," "An Acrostic on Judith Brock," a
funeral piece. He had a book published containing
144 pages called *The Christian Harmony*. A very
imperfect copy of this book has been examined in
the Boston Public Library. It was printed for the
compiler by Henry Ranlet at Exeter, New Hamp-

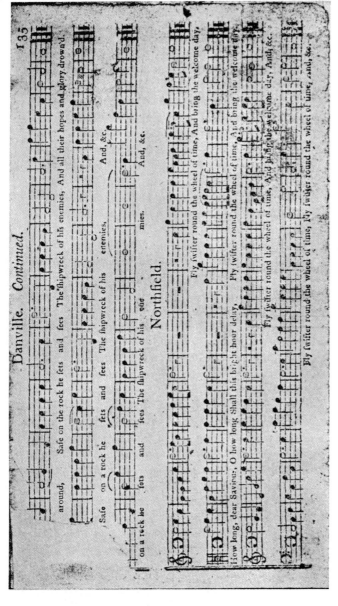

NORTHFIELD. JEREMIAH INGALLS
Christian Harmony, 1805. Boston Public Library

shire, in 1805.   The preface is dated at Newbury, Vermont, November, 1804.   The music is printed from type, and there are 134 pages of hymn tunes.

A letter before me states that "in an advertisement it is stated that nearly the whole of the tunes were the original composition of the author and there was but one in the book that was known to be composed by any one but Mr. Ingalls."   This is erroneous, for the names of the composers are given in the index, and include the well-known names of Billings, Swan, Read, Edson, and Brownson.   And, further, an advertisement in the book itself shows that "some are wholly and some in part the original composition of the author, and others selected from various authors which are credited where they are known."

An interesting story is told of him as follows:

His children were musical and his sons could play clarinet, bassoon, flute, and violin, and they would often practice for hours, the old man leading the band with his bass viol.   One Sunday they were having an excellent time performing anthems, and after a while the youngsters started a secular piece, the father with composure joining in.   From that they went on until they found themselves furiously engaged in a boisterous march, in the midst of which the old gentleman stopped short, exclaiming, "Boys, this won't do.   Put away these corrupt things and take your Bibles."

In stature he was short and corpulent.   In 1800 we find him among the list of subscribers of Samuel Holyoke's *Columbian Repository*.

Much of the old-fashioned conference meeting music is in his *Christian Harmony*, and attributed to his authorship by later compilers, making him the author of many of the tunes sung from forty to seventy years ago, to the sweet old "Pennyroyal Hymns" of those times. His "Lavonia" and "Pennsylvania" were for years very popular.

"The operatic warbler may voice her culture rare,
With Wagner, Rubenstein, and Bach, or any high-flown air,
But still her notes are lacking, they're so very straight and
  prim
By the side of that old melody, the Pennyroyal hymn."

A number of his tunes have survived in common use. "Northfield" seems to be the most popular in modern hymnals, while "Come, Ye Sinners," sometimes called "Invitation," is remembered by some of us who are not yet so very old. These two, with "Filmore" and "Kentucky," are in *The Methodist Hymnal* of 1878. The primitive *Baptist Hymn Book*, 1902, has two of his tunes not found in other recent books. The words set to the tunes in the various books are different in each one, and no hymn appears to be wedded to any one tune. This is to be expected, as when Ingalls composed his music, it was not written for any definite words.

OLIVER HOLDEN

1765–1844[1]

OLIVER HOLDEN, the carpenter-composer, is the first one of the earlier tune writers whose work is still found in the hymnals. He is known almost entirely by his tune "Coronation," and this tune is in every one of the twenty-five modern hymnals

[1] From The Choir Herald.

which I have examined, and which are used by the various denominations of evangelical churches. His other musical compositions, which were numerous, are not so well known. Born September 18, 1765, in Shirley, Massachusetts, he lived in that town with his parents till he was twenty-one years of age, and then the family moved to Charlestown. Being a carpenter, the rebuilding of that town, which had been burned by the British, promised employment. Here he prospered. He became a large operator in real estate, and when a new Baptist church was organized he gave the land on which to erect the building. Later another organization was effected, popularly called for many years the Puritan Church, of which he became the head, and was its preacher all through its existence. Their meetings were held in a one-story wooden church erected largely by the personal labors of Mr. Holden. Their services were congregational in form, and the sacrament of the Lord's Supper was observed every Sunday. He represented Charlestown in the Massachusetts House of Representatives for eight annual terms between the years 1818 and 1833. He was a prominent Mason, and the records of his lodge furnish many allusions to his musical entertainments at its meetings.

MUSIC

But circumstances turned him to music ; he opened a music store, became the leader of a choir, and conducted singing schools. Then he began to compose music and compile music books. The letter-book of Daniel Read, under date of March 12, 1793, states that he had subscribed to the periodical issues of music that were made by Oliver Holden. So many books were arranged by him that it would seem that most of his time during his later years must have been devoted to his favorite muse. Indeed, when his strength was almost gone, and he lay dying, his wife and daughter heard him whisper, "I have some beautiful airs running in my mind, if I only had strength to note them down." These were his last words and indicate his all-absorbing thoughts. He died September 4, 1844, and over his grave in Charlestown his name is inscribed as "the composer of the tune Coronation."

AMERICAN HARMONY

His first contribution to the literature of psalmody was a small volume of thirty-two pages, "the whole entirely new," and called *American Harmony*. The preface is dated at Charlestown, September 27, 1792, and Mr. Holden refers to himself as a teacher of music. His next compilation was a more pretentious effort, *The Union Harmony, or Universal Collections of Sacred Music*, in two volumes, aggregating 300 pages. It was in this collection that his "Coronation" was first printed, and set to the words of Edward Perronet, "All hail the power of Jesus' name," with which the tune has ever since been associated in this country. The name of the Rev. Mr. Medley appears as the author in Mr. Holden's book, but we know this was an error, for these familiar lines first appeared in *Occasional Verses, Moral and Sacred*, published in London in 1785, and were written by Edward Perronet. *The Union Harmony* was

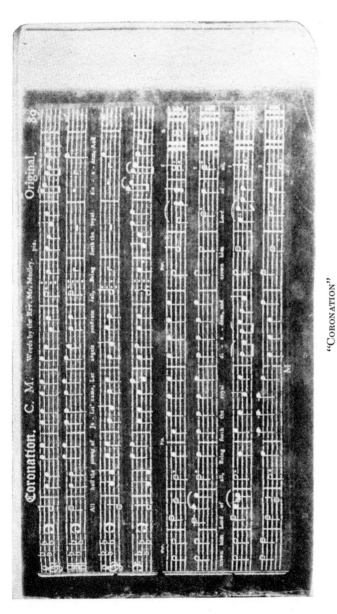

"CORONATION"

American Harmony, 1793.   Oliver Holden.   Library of Congress

issued in a second edition in 1796, and a third edition appeared in 1801.

The Massachusetts Compiler was published early in 1795 in Boston by Thomas and Andrews. It was a small book of seventy-two pages and was the joint work of Hans Gram, Samuel Holyoke, and Oliver Holden. *The Modern Collection of Sacred Music*, by an American (Oliver Holden), appeared in November, 1800. It was a book of 254 pages, and the preface is signed by the publishers, Thomas and Andrews of Boston. During this same year he prepared a collection of *Sacred Dirges*, and *A Plain Psalmody*. The latter was an original composition consisting of seventy psalm and hymn tunes. The author says he is opposed to fugue tunes and hopes that their omission will please the lovers of real devotion. The composers of five of the tunes are named; the others are, of course, by Mr. Holden. In November of this year, 1800, Mr. Bentley, minister of a church in Salem, notes in his diary that a musical composition published by Holden of Charlestown, called "West End," was performed in his church after the sermon.

The Charlestown Collection of Sacred Songs, adapted to public and private devotions, was published according to act of Congress in November, 1803, at Boston by Thomas and Andrews. It was made up principally of original compositions by Oliver Holden, never before published, but contained also seven by John Cole, of Baltimore, one by Jacob Kimball, and one by Mr. Day. In the preface Mr. Holden says,

As this work is principally designed for a supplement to a

larger collection, and as an appendix to the eighth edition of the *Worcester Collection,* it is thought unnecessary to add the rudiments. It has been the constant endeavor of the author to compose the music in a style suited to the solemnity of sacred devotion, and which he hopes will accord with the sentiments and feelings of real worshipers. As sacred poetry in general is best adapted to the pensive or solemn, he has aimed to give that air or character to the following compositions which, if he is not deceived, will produce no trifling effect on auditors or performers.

The above reference to the *Worcester Collection* requires that we notice that book which was so popular just after the Revolutionary War. It was in fact the most popular music book of the period, and was often reprinted. It first issued from the press of Isaiah Thomas at Worcester, Massachusetts, in 1786, under the title, *Laus Deo, or the Worcester Collection of Sacred Harmony,* in three parts containing

   I. An Introduction to the grounds of music or rules for learners.
  II. A larger number of celebrated psalm and hymn tunes from the most approved ancient and modern authors, together with several new ones [the index shows eight] never before published; the whole suited to all meters usually sung in churches.
 III. Select anthems, fugues and favorite pieces of music with additional number of psalm and hymn tunes, the whole compiled for the use of schools and singing societies, and recommended by many approved teachers of psalmody.

The compiler of this collection is not named. Some have assumed that the publisher, Isaiah Thomas, was also the compiler, although he says that he is unskilled in music. Still it is safe to say that even if he did have the assistance of some one else, his

was the directing mind in its preparation. This
book was also notable in being the first book printed
in New England from music type. In 1767 James
Parker had issued from his printing office in Beaver
Street in New York city the psalms of David edited
by Francis Hopkinson, with the music printed above
each line. This was the first book printed from
music type in America. The type had been imported from Amsterdam. Only the melody was
printed above each line alternating with the lines of
words. *The Worcester Collection*, however, had all
the parts printed on the double staff, as is the rule
at the present day, so that it can claim to be the
first book of complete music from type. It was
dedicated to the several musical societies in New
England, and of its contents the publisher says,

Mr. William Billings, of Boston, was the first person
we know of that attempted to compose church music in the
New England States. His music met with approbation.
Some tunes of his composing are inserted in this work, and
are extracted from The Chorister's Companion, printed in
Connecticut from copper plates. [This had been first issued
in 1782 at New Haven.] Several adepts in music followed
Mr. Billings' example, and the New England States can now
boast of many authors of church music whose compositions
do them honor. A number of their tunes are in this collection, and we hope are done in such a manner as will give
them satisfaction. A few copies of this work will by
request be published separately, in order to accommodate a
few schools which are at present destitute of books. The
Third Part is now in the press and will be published with
all possible expedition.

As a matter of fact, Part Three was not published
until the next year, 1787. With regard to his new
type the publisher says:

Having observed with pleasure the attention paid to church

music by most classes of people in the New England States, and knowing many of the books now in use, necessarily high-charged owing to their being printed from copper plates, he was induced both by inclination, and at the request of several friends, to attempt a work of this kind from types, hoping to afford it somewhat cheaper than any other book of its bigness printed after the usual manner. He accordingly engaged a set of musical types to be made in England by one of the most ingenious type founders in Great Britain, which he hopes on inspection of the tunes will be found to have answered the purpose. Many gentlemen lent their aid in furnishing tunes. Notwithstanding the expense of executing, this work has much exceeded his expectation, yet he hopes that he has so far answered the intention proposed as that the price fixed to it will not be thought unreasonable.

The Hallelujah Chorus appears in Part Three, and the publisher says:

Having been favored with a copy of the grand chorus in that celebrated work, the Messiah, by Handel, one of the greatest musicians that ever delighted the ears of mortals, I am happy to give it a place in this Collection. Although it has been thought by some too hard to be learned and too delicate to be sung even by the best performers in this country, I doubt not that there are many who have not only skill to learn, but judgment to perform it, at least equal to some of the best singers in Europe.

Two years later a second edition was printed, and the publisher says:

It gave great pleasure to the editor of the Worcester Collection of Sacred Harmony that the first edition of it was so generally approbated. Owing to the small number of which that edition consisted, it was soon out of print, and many persons who were desirous of purchasing could not obtain copies. Some persons in Boston, taking advantage of the scarcity, printed a spurious edition from copper plates, and palmed it upon the undiscerning for the real Worcester Collection. The editor, therefore, has been induced to publish a second edition. A few tunes, mostly out of use, and some others not used in public worship, are omitted, and others more modern and adapted to the present taste inserted in their room. A considerable number of psalm tunes are also added, some of which were never before published, without any addition in price.

The index indicates a number of tunes that are not in the first edition, and four that never were before published. It would be very satisfying to be able to identify the spurious edition referred to as having been made by Boston parties from copper plates, but diligent search of the music books published between 1786 and 1788 fails to reveal any one that resembles *The Worcester Collection* either in name or contents.

The third edition with large additions was issued in 1791. In the preface he notes the increasing demand for the work, and alludes to the spurious edition, saying:

Advantage has been taken of the scarcity of genuine copies to impose incorrect and spurious ones, of which those who wish to be supplied with good books will beware. . . . A complaint hath been made that good tunes soon wear out by becoming too familiar by frequent repetition. To remove this evil the editor has had a tune made by way of experiment, (Worcester, New, by Mann) long enough for the usual number of stanzas without repetition.

This tune is more like an anthem than a hymn tune.

The fourth edition was published in Boston in 1792, and besides Parts One and Two had an "Appendix containing a number of excellent psalm tunes, several of which are entirely new, and other pieces of sacred vocal musick, many of which are composed by eminent European authors, and never before published in this country." This edition was hurried through the press and "many errors escaped the observation of the corrector." These were corrected in the fifth edition in 1794. In this edition we note one composition each by Oliver Holden and Hans Gram, the latter being an anthem dedicated to the Singing Society of Newburyport. These two musicians were assisted by Samuel Holyoke in the preparation of the *Massachusetts Compiler* in 1795.

The sixth edition of *The Worcester Collection*, printed August, 1797, is by Oliver Holden, and Mr. Thomas "informs his musical friends who have so liberally encouraged the five former editions of the Worcester Collection that he has contracted with Mr. Oliver Holden, who is interested in the work, to compile and correct the present and future editions." The seventh edition, 1800, contains many new pieces, probably by the editor, though his name is not appended to any of them. The eighth edition, 1803,

has some new tunes and some European music not much known in this country. It is to be lamented that among so many American authors so little can be found well written or well adapted to sacred purposes, but it is disingenuous and impolitic to throw that little away while our country is in a state of progressive improvement. Some tunes are inserted which do not merit approbation. The motive needs no explanation. The new tunes, which are more numerous than in any former edition, are impressed by themselves in an appendix, and may be had separately.

As a separate book it was known as *The Charlestown Collection of Sacred Songs*.

ORGAN

The organ that was once the property of the Charlestown musician, and upon which he composed his tune "Coronation," is now in the rooms of the Bostonian Society in the Old State House, Boston, Massachusetts, and it was my privilege, some years ago, to be one of a company which stood around it and sang a stanza of "America" to the accompaniment of its tones. Above the keys is a case much like the old-fashioned secretary with two doors. On opening these one sees a number of short pipes, from a few inches to about twenty for the longest. The compass of the organ is four and a half octaves. It gives forth good music in summer, but it is said that in winter it is mute.

On October 21, 1789, when Washington visited the city of Boston, he was escorted along Washington Street past the State House. There a triumphal arch had been erected and an "Ode to Columbia's Favorite Son" was sung by the Independent Musical Society of that city. The words and music were said to have been composed by Oliver Holden, and it is also said that he led in the singing. This same "Ode" was sung by the Stoughton Musical Society in 1893 at the Chicago Exposition. The original print of this Ode and music appeared in the Massachusetts Magazine in 1789, and it is reproduced in facsimile in Elson's *National Music in America*.

POETRY

In 1806 *The Young Convert's Companion, a Collection of Hymns for the Use of Conference Meetings*, was published in Boston. It was edited by Oliver Holden, and there are nineteen hymns in it signed "H." One of these, beginning "All those who seek a throne of grace," is in long meter, and consisted of six stanzas. Every line has been altered to convert it into the meter of sevens, and a hymn of four stanzas has been produced which is now found in many present-day hymnals, and ascribed to Holden. The first stanza is

> "They who seek the throne of grace,
> Find that throne in every place,
> If we live a life of prayer
> God is present everywhere."

This hymn and the tune "Coronation" are all of Holden's work that has been retained in our hymn books, although up to the time that he ceased publishing music there had been no American author whose productions had been so well received and so generally sung. He was a conscientiously religious and amiable man as anyone might judge from the style of his compositions, and his "Coronation" will live for generations yet to sing and admire.

HANS GRAM

NEITHER the date of the birth or death of Hans Gram has come to our notice, but from the dates of his musical compositions we place the period of his active life in Massachusetts as about that of Mr. Graupner. Gram was a native of Denmark, liberally educated at Stockholm. He possessed a sound and discriminating mind, well stored with knowledge of men and books. For many years he was organist of the Brattle Street Church in Boston, and he taught many of the early native musicians of that vicinity, such as Jacob Kimball, Oliver Holden, and Samuel Holyoke. He wrote and published little music, though we do find a few pieces scattered here and there in the literature of the day, both secular and sacred.

In 1793 he published a small work, called *Sacred Lines for Thanksgiving Day*, November 7, 1793. "Written and set to music by Hans Gram, organist to Brattle Street Church, Boston; to which are added several tunes of different meters by the same composer." This was recommended by Jacob Kimball, Dr. Nahum Fay, and Isaac Lane.

In 1795 he was one of the compilers, with Oliver Holden and Samuel Holyoke, of *The Massachusetts Compiler*, in which appeared the first article upon harmony ever written in this country. This was written by Mr. Gram, and Doctor Bentley, of Salem, tells us in his diary that the rules were compiled mostly from the foreign writers D'Alembert, Rousseau, Selzer, and others. His other sacred pieces were an anthem for Easter, and one entitled "Bind Kings in Chains." Another anthem dedicated to the Singing Societies of Newburyport, and dated Charlestown, October, 1794, appeared in the appendix to the Fifth edition of the *Worcester Collection*. Of secular music we may note a "Hunting Song" which was printed in the Massachusetts Magazine of 1789, another "Song" in the same magazine for 1790, and an "Ode to the President" by a lady, set to music by Hans Gram. It is to be regretted that so little has been found regarding one whose influence was felt by the Massachusetts group of psalm tune writers.

GOTTLIEB GRAUPNER
1767–1836

JOHANN CHRISTIAN GOTTLIEB GRAUPNER, to use his full name, and Hans Gram were two foreign-born musicians who came to this country during the last decade of the eighteenth century, settled in the eastern part of Massachusetts, and became quite prominent in the musical affairs of that period. The former, and probably the older, was born October 6, 1767, in Verden, Germany. He was for some time an oboe player in a Hanoverian regimental band, from which he was discharged April 8, 1788. He then went to London, where he played in an orchestra under Haydn in 1791-92. From London he went to Prince Edward's Island, thence, in 1796, to Charlestown, Massachusetts, where he married Mrs. Katherine Hillier. He established himself in business in Boston as a teacher and publisher of music, and a leader of both instrumental and vocal concerts. For May 15, 1798, he advertised a concert in Salem, the tickets being priced at "half a dollar." The doors were opened at six o'clock and the performance began at precisely half-past seven. There were two parts to the program and twelve persons who took part. The numbers taken by Mr. Graupner and his wife included a clarinet quartet, in which Mr. Graupner played one of the instruments, a solo, "He Pipes So Sweet," by Mrs. Graupner, a vocal quartet in which Mrs. Graupner took the soprano, and an echo song by her, accompanied by her husband on the hautboy.

Mr. Graupner was one of those who signed the

call, March 24, 1815, for a meeting which resulted
in the formation in April of the Handel and Haydn
Society. The first concert of this society was given
at Christmas, 1815, and the program consisted
largely of selections from "The Creation." There
were one hundred in the chorus including ten ladies;
there were twelve instruments and an organ. The
tickets were one dollar apiece, 945 were sold, and the
net proceeds were $533. In 1810 the instrumental
players in Boston were organized by Graupner into
a Philharmonic Society, and soon began to give concerts. This society was continued for fourteen
years, their last concert being given on November
24, 1824. His business as a publisher of music was
located in 1801 in Sweetser's Alley. Later he established a "Musical Academy" at 6 Franklin Street,
near Franklin Place, and in 1817 we find the firm
of Graupner and Company at 15 Marlboro Street,
where they advertise they have just printed the
popular piece of music, "Strike the Cymbal," arranged for the pianoforte. One of the advertisements of this musician states that he had pianofortes for sale and to let, and that private instruments would be tuned both in town and country.

Mr. Graupner married in Charlestown, April 6,
1796, Mrs. Catherine Comeford Hillier, the daughter of a London attorney. When she appeared
in public she was known as Mrs. Heelyer, and it
was said that for many years she was the only vocalist in Boston. After her death, which occurred May
28, 1821, Mr. Graupner married again, for at the
settlement of his property his widow is given as
Mary H. Graupner.

He died of ulcerated sore throat at No. 1 Province House Court, Boston, April 16, 1836. His funeral was held April 20, in Trinity Church, and he was buried in the family vault under Saint Matthew's Church in South Boston. When this church was demolished in 1866, his body was removed to Mount Hope Cemetery, West Roxbury, Massachusetts. He left no real estate; his personal property was appraised at $975.

PETER ERBEN

1769–1861

THE Erben family were organ builders in New York. From Messiter's history of the music in Trinity Church we learn that Henry Erben built the organ that was installed in 1842, Michael Erben was an occasional organist in the church during the sixties. Peter Erben, born about 1769, was director of the society for cultivating church music connected with Trinity Church as early as 1800. Seven years later he was appointed organist of Saint George's Chapel, a mission that was supported by that church; and in 1813 he was made the first organist of Saint John's Chapel, another branch of that parish. From 1820 to 1839 he was the organist of Trinity Church, and in that year was retired on a gratuity of three hundred dollars a year. He was followed by Dr. John S. B. Hodges. Mr. Erben continued his connection with Trinity Church till his death, which occurred April 30, 1861, in Brooklyn, when he had attained the age of ninety-

one years. His funeral took place from the church
which he had served for so many years. In 1806
he published a volume of *Select Psalm and Hymn
Tunes.*

BENJAMIN CARR

1769–1831

PROBABLY the first music store in Philadelphia
was "The Music Repository," opened by Benjamin
Carr about 1793. Benjamin Carr was born in England about 1769, received a thorough musical training in that country, and had been connected with
the London Ancient Concerts before he emigrated
to America in 1793. After landing in New York
he set up as a music dealer for a short time, then
went on to Philadelphia, where he advertised himself in 1793–94 as "B. Carr & Co., Music Printers
and Importers." From 1794 to 1800 he carried on
his Musical Repository in Philadelphia. His New
York branch he sold in 1797 or 1798 to James
Hewitt. Joseph (probably a brother) Carr opened
a Musical Repository in Baltimore in 1794 in Market Street near Gay, and the next year the address
was changed to 6 Gay Street. Joseph first appears
as a music publisher in connection with Benjamin
in 1796, and the firm continued far into the nineteenth century, Joseph having the Baltimore branch,
while Benjamin remained in Philadelphia. William
Carr, probably another member of the family, was
born in Yorkshire, England, worked as an engraver
in Philadelphia, and died there January 14, 1852.
He is buried in Saint Paul's churchyard.

Benjamin Carr's distinctive work for music and musicians was the organization of the Musical Fund Society. Its history cannot be written without weaving into it many threads from Mr. Carr's brain. As early as 1816 Mr. Carr was one of a quartet of musicians who tried to form a society for regular practice. The first meetings for discussion and organization were held at his house, and before the society was finally constituted it was decided that one of its subjects should be the assistance of needy musicians. So that when it was instituted it was called the Musical Fund Society of Philadelphia. As its birth was February 29, 1820, its anniversaries must be marked in quadrenniums. A charter was granted to it February 22, 1823. Some of its earliest members included Leopold Meignen, Raynor Taylor, and John Darley, all composers of church music; Thomas Loud, sometime organist of Saint Andrew's, and Joseph C. Taws, a piano maker.

For a while Benjamin Carr was organist of Saint Joseph's Catholic Church in Philadelphia. He compiled one book of music whose title reads *Masses, Vespers, Litanies, Hymns, Psalms, Anthems and Motetts* "composed, selected and arranged for the use of the Catholic churches in the United States of America and respectfully dedicated by permission of the Right Reverend John Carroll, D. D., Bishop of Baltimore."

In 1811 he issued *Lessons and Exercises in Vocal Music,* an engraved pamphlet of sixty pages, which is marked "Opus VIII." "The Archers, or the Mountaineers of Switzerland," an opera founded upon the story of William Tell, was probably the first American opera ever composed. The words were written by William Dunlap, and the music by Benjamin Carr. It was first produced in the John Street Theater, New York, April 18, 1796.

We close this sketch with a copy of the inscription upon his monument, erected in Saint Peter's Church, which recites that

> Benjamin Carr, a distinguished professor of music, died May 24, 1831, aged 62 years. Charitable without ostentation, faithful and true in his friendships, with the intelligence of a man, he united the simplicity of a child.
>
> In testimony of the high esteem in which he was held, this monument is erected by his friends and associates of the Musical Fund Society of Philadelphia.

Of all the early musicians of Philadelphia he wrought the most vigorously to introduce the best music and especially the oratorios into the church.

JOHN WYETH

1770–1858[1]

"HALLELUJAH"—that's the title of Wyeth's "Nettleton" in Part II of his *Repository*, 1813. Thus wrote a correspondent whom I had asked to look up this tune. The hymn that is usually set to it is the well-known one by Robert Robinson, "Come, Thou Fount of Every Blessing." As originally written the tune was in the key of F, and in common time, and there was a refrain "Hallelujah, hallelujah, we are on our journey home." It was this refrain that gave it the name. I have not been able to discover when it was rearranged and given

---

[1] From The Choir Herald.

the name of "Nettleton." About half of the modern hymn books attribute it to Asahel Nettleton, while the others give it to John Wyeth, and one to the Rev. John Wyeth. In many of the older books it is anonymous. The date given for its composition by Nettleton is 1824 and 1825, while for Wyeth his collection for 1812 is noted. Its first appearance was really in the second part of Wyeth's *Repository of Sacred Music*, copyrighted in 1813, not 1812.

ASAHEL NETTLETON

The Rev. Asahel Nettleton was a noted Congregational minister, who was born April 21, 1783, at North Killingworth, Connecticut, and died May 6, 1844, at East Windsor in the same State. He graduated from Yale College in 1809. He began to preach two years later, but was not ordained till 1817. He traveled through western Massachusetts, Connecticut, and New York, preaching and holding revival services. The winter of 1827-28 he spent in Virginia and in 1831 went to Great Britain. In 1832 he was appointed professor of pastoral duty in a newly established seminary at East Windsor, and although he did not accept the appointment he settled in that town and lectured occasionally at the school. His work in hymnology was the compilation of *Village Hymns*, first issued in 1824. There were six hundred hymns, but I have never seen it printed with tunes; in fact, it is stated in the preface that a small collection of music, called *Zion's Harp* was designed to accompany the volume. To go back to the beginning of the history of his compilation:

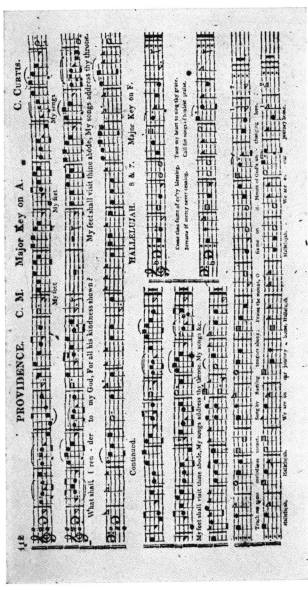

HALLELUJAH, or NETTLETON

From John Wyeth's Repository, Part II, 1813. In possession of the author

in the year 1820 the General (Congregational) Association of Connecticut appointed a committee, of which Mr. Nettleton was a member, to make a new selection of hymns, and when four years had elapsed without anything having been done, Mr. Nettleton began to compile a collection of his own. He tells us that he was guided by his experience as a preacher, and knew the demands for hymns especially suited for revivals. He spent nearly two years in gathering his materials and consulted all the collections of hymns that were available. Many of the hymns were original, while some were taken by permission from what were then recent books. Mrs. Brown's "I Love to Steal a While Away" was first used in *Village Hymns*. Robinson's "Come, Thou Fount of Every Blessing" is hymn No. 439, and the tunes suggested are "Love Divine" and "Good Shepherd." The tune "Nettleton" is not in *Zion's Harp*, and it is the only tune attributed to Asahel Nettleton; but I can find no evidence that he had anything to do with it except the name, and that is by no means convincing. One hymn, "Come, Holy Ghost, My Soul Inspire," which first appeared in *Village Hymns*, has been attributed to the compiler, though his authorship is by no means conclusive. One hymnologist has written that "he knew and could appreciate a good hymn, but it is doubtful if he ever did or ever could have written one."

John Wyeth

John Wyeth was a native of Massachusetts, having been born in Cambridge March 31, 1770. Nich-

olas, his ancestor, came from England and purchased land in Cambridge prior to 1645. John was
fifth in descent, and was the son of Ebenezer. When
a young man he was apprenticed to a printer, and
upon reaching his majority he was induced to go to
San Domingo to superintend a large printing establishment. While there the insurrection of the
Blacks occurred, and all that he had acquired was
lost. It was with difficulty that he succeeded in
escaping from the island, and this was only accomplished with the connivance of a friend, who was one
of the officers to search the vessel before it left the
port. Dressing himself as a common sailor and
working among them, he eluded the search of the
inspectors, and finally reached Philadelphia. There
he found work in various printing offices until 1792,
when he went to Harrisburg and in company with
John Allen he purchased a newspaper that had been
started the year before. Thus began his connection
with the Oracle of Dauphin, a newspaper for
Dauphin County, which he successfully carried on
until November, 1827. Mr. Wyeth's paper was a
weekly, published every Saturday morning, and supported the views of the Federal party during the
whole course of its existence. The file of this paper
in the Library of Congress, covering the last year
that it was conducted by John Wyeth, was once the
property of that great Federal Leader, Henry Clay.
Mr. Wyeth was appointed postmaster of Harrisburg in October, 1793, under Washington, of whose
administration he was a strenuous advocate and
strong admirer. He held this office for nearly five
years until July, 1798, when he was removed by Mr.

Adams, the postmaster-general, on account of "the incompatibility of the office of postmaster and editor of a newspaper." In connection with his other work he established a book store, and a publishing house, from which he issued a large number of books, the most notable of which were Judge Henry's *Narrative of the Quebec Expedition*, Graydon's *Memoirs,* and a music book.

REPOSITORY OF SACRED MUSIC

His *Repository of Sacred Music* was first issued in 1810, and continued to be printed in succeeding editions, the fifth being dated in 1820. After that two stereotyped editions were issued in 1826 and 1834. These last editions were copyrighted in 1826. This volume contained many selections from the well-known New England composers, Read, Billings, Swan, Holyoke, and Holden.

Few of the tunes introduced in this work have claim to originality. The lovers of ancient melody will here recognize a good number of old acquaintances that "dead and forgotten lie," while the friends to modern composition will find themselves by no means neglected.

The circulation of this book at that early day was wonderful, aggregating 120,000. To this he supplemented a Second Part, of which there were published about 25,000, intended especially for the Methodist Church. This book came out in 1813, and more than a third of the tunes were original, his "Hallelujah" being included among that number.

Mr. Wyeth was one of Harrisburg's most industrious and energetic citizens and became deeply interested in her prosperity and welfare. He caused the construction of several valuable improvements which remain as evidence of his enterprising spirit and good judgment. He was one of the earliest friends of Harrisburg Academy, and served as trustee, and later as president of the board of trustees. He was twice married, and had seven children. His youngest, Samuel Douglas Wyeth, was a writer, published a book entitled *The Ins and Outs of Washington*, and died in the Capital City, January 18, 1881. One of the older brothers of John Wyeth was a member of the famous Boston Tea Party in 1773; this was Joshua, at that time sixteen years of age and a journeyman blacksmith in that city.

After John Wyeth had retired from his publishing business he moved to Philadelphia, where he divided his time between reading and social pleasures. His life was marked by affability and cheerfulness. He died in the City of Brotherly Love at the age of eighty-eight, January 23, 1858.

DANIEL BELKNAP

1771–1815

DANIEL BELKNAP was a native of Framingham, Massachusetts, where he was born February 9, 1771. His father was Captain Jeremiah Belknap, captain of a company of militia during the French and Indian Wars. Captain Belknap was at one time the owner of a slave, Peter Salem, who made himself famous at the battle of Bunker Hill by firing the shot which mortally wounded Major John Pitcairn, the commander of the British forces, just as

he was about to enter the redoubt.   After a long
life Salem was reduced to poverty, and returning
to Framingham would have become a charge upon
the town had not his former owner with several
others of his fellow townsmen given bond to support him during the remaining years of his natural
life.   Daniel Belknap received only a common-school
education, and settled down on the farm in his native
town as a farmer and mechanic.   His leisure hours
were devoted to music, and he acquired such skill in
the art of singing that he began to teach at the age
of eighteen.   He taught mostly in the town of Framingham, and the neighboring towns, but once on
invitation he went to Whitesboro, New York, where,
however, he spent but a short time.   He married
Mary Parker, of Carlisle, about 1800, and had at
least five children born in Framingham between 1801
and 1809.   He continued to live in his native town
until 1812, when he removed to Pawtucket, Rhode
Island, and died there of fever October 31, 1815.

The first musical publication of Daniel Belknap
was in 1797, when a small pamphlet of thirty-one
pages was issued from the press of Thomas and
Andrews in Boston, called *The Harmonist's Companion*, containing a number of airs suitable for
divine worship, together with an anthem for Easter
and a Masonic Ode.   The latter had been performed
by the author and several brethren of the fraternity
at the installation of the Middlesex Lodge in Framingham in 1795.   In 1800 *The Evangelical Harmony*
was published by the same firm in Boston and consisted of thirty-two pages.   His third and last musical venture was *The Village Compilation of Sacred*

Music, printed in 1806, and was a more pretentious work. It had 152 pages, and contained many pieces that had never before been published, quite a number of which bore the names of Middlesex County towns. Mr. Belknap bore an unblemished reputation, and was worthy of the respect which was always accorded him. His opportunities for acquiring a knowledge of music were few, and his music, which was copied into several compilations, including *The Stoughton Collection,* 1829, *The Antiquarian,* 1849, and *The Continental Harmony,* 1857, became more or less popular for awhile, but it has not survived, and is no longer sung.

JONATHAN HUNTINGTON

1771–1838

THE musical compilations of Jonathan Huntington were issued from New England presses, and included *The Apollo Harmony,* 1807, and *Classical Sacred Music,* 1812:

> The Apollo Harmony contains Plain and Intelligible Rules for singing by note, a universal collection of Psalm and Hymn Tunes suited to all meters and keys, with a number of set pieces and anthems, proper for all occasions together with the instructions for the bass viol and German flute, selected from the most celebrated European and American compositions, with some pieces entirely new.

It was a copyrighted book, and was printed at Northampton. A dozen of the writers of that day were represented with one or more tunes. The *Classical Sacred Music* was made up from European sources, contained seventy-five pages, and was printed in Boston by the well-known printer J. T. Buckingham, in 1812.

Jonathan Huntington was a native of Connecticut, born in Windham, November 17, 1771. He married October 29, 1796, Ann Lathrop, who died in Boston, May 3, 1826, and he was married again, but the name of his second wife has not been found. He was by nature possessed of a voice of fine tone and great strength, which he had cultivated with great care while he was living in Norwich with his uncle Samuel. He had ten children, and from the places of their birth we assume that from 1797 to 1804, he was living in Windham, Connecticut; in 1806 at Troy, New York; 1808 to 1811 at Northampton, and from 1814 to 1829 in Boston. His whole life was devoted to the teaching of music in Albany, Boston, and afterward in Saint Louis, which was his home at the time of his death, July 29, 1838.

ZEDEKIAH SANGER

1771–1821

ONLY a few facts have been found about Zedekiah Sanger, but these are recorded. Zedekiah Sanger was born in Framingham, Massachusetts, July 27, 1771. He resided there till he had reached the age of manhood, was in Boston between 1813 and 1821, where he was known as a singer, a teacher, and a composer. He later removed to Albany, where he became a storekeeper, but returned to Boston, where he died in August, 1821, at the age of fifty.

In 1808 he compiled and issued from the press of Herman Mann in Dedham *The Meridian Harmony*, which he states was compiled by himself and others. Original music was contributed to it by Walter Janes, Stephen Jenks, Lewis Edson, and Abraham Wood. The fugue style, which was the prevailing type of music at that time, predominated.

BARTHOLOMEW BROWN

1772–1854

BARTHOLOMEW BROWN was born September 8, 1772, at Sterling, Massachusetts, and graduated from Harvard University in the class of 1799. He was a lawyer of standing, a friend of temperance, and "foremost in every good work." When the *Lock Hospital Collection* of music was printed in 1809, Mr. Brown was put down as a subscriber from Sterling. He left his native town in that year and took up his residence in Boston. In 1813 we find him in Abington, where he was a teacher of music, whose reputation grew continually until it extended beyond the limits of that town. He was one of the original members of the Boston Handel and Haydn Musical Society, founded in 1815, the date of his joining it being November 5, 1815. He was elected its eighth president in September, 1836, and served for one year. He was its first president to draw a salary which then amounted to $300 per annum.

When he failed of reelection in 1837, he was much displeased, and soon after joined a rival organization, "the Boston Oratorio Society," and assisted it in presenting on the same evening as the Handel and Haydn Society, Newkomm's "Hymn of the Night." It was partly for this offense that he and two others were expelled from the membership of the society of which he had been its former president.

One of the most popular of his compositions was a hymn tune called "Tilden," written in memory of a classmate and loved friend, James Tilden, who had died in 1800. He was a poet as well as a musician, and could write a song or hymn, set it to music and then sing it.

For many years he wrote the calendar pages for that famous almanac, which was founded in 1792 and later printed by Robert B. Thomas, of Sterling, and known as The Old Farmers' Almanac. Its one hundred and thirtieth yearly number was issued for 1921.

COMPILATIONS

In 1802 he was assisted by Nahum Mitchell and others in compiling *The Columbian and European Harmony*, or *Bridgewater Collection of Sacred Music*. A second edition was issued in 1804. The third edition, in 1810, was called the *Templi Carmina*, or *The Bridgewater Collection*, and the successive editions were popularly known by the second title. This collection was highly esteemed and was much used in New England for twenty-five years or more, and editions succeeded each other at short intervals until the twenty-seventh in 1839, when more than one hundred thousand copies had been printed and circulated.

He was one of the committee appointed January 14, 1810, by the parish of Brattle Street Church in Boston to prepare a collection of tunes for its use. The other members were Ebenezer Withington, Bryant P. Tilden, the Rev. Joseph S. Buckminster, and a later addition, Elias Mann. The Rev. Joseph Stevens Buckminster was the pastor of the church, was a graduate of Harvard the next year after Mr. Brown, 1800, and two years before this, that is, in 1808, he had compiled a book of hymns for the use of his society. The result of the labors of this committee was issued in 1810 as *LXXX Psalm and Hymn Tunes for Public Worship* "adapted to the metres used in churches." This book is usually known as *The Brattle Street Collection.* It is interesting to know that copies of the votes of the parish are filed in the copy of this book in the Library of Congress.

Bartholomew Brown lived to be over eighty-one years of age, and died in Boston April 14, 1854.

ELIAKIM DOOLITTLE

1772–1850

ELIAKIM DOOLITTLE was a brother of Amos Doolittle, the engraver, and was born August 29, 1772. He studied for a while at Yale College, but did not graduate, engaging in teaching both the common-school branches, and the art of singing, which in those days was taught in evening classes.

Music seemed to be his delight, and he composed with great ease.   This he published in 1806 at New Haven in *The Psalm Singers Companion,* a book of forty-nine pages, containing forty-one tunes and ône anthem.   During the War of 1812 after the Hornet had engaged and sunk the English man-of-war Peacock, in February, 1813, he wrote a popular war song, "The Hornet Stung the Peacock." His brother Amos also noted this action in a caricature engraving representing a hornet stinging John Bull, shown as a peacock.   About 1802 Mr. Doolittle had removed to Hampton, New York, and in 1811 he married Miss Hesadiah Fuller, of that town.   Six children were born to them—one son and five daughters.   He was a deeply religious man, a Congregationalist, and a devoted student of the Bible, but of a roving disposition, nervous and sensitive, impulsive and excitable; and finally he became partially insane, wandering the streets in tattered garments, with untrimmed locks and long beard, so that while living in Pawlet, Vermont, where many of his later years were spent, it is said that he was the terror of timid women and children as he roamed about in slovenly dress, and he found rest only when lodged in his grave.   He died in April, 1850, at Argyle, New York.

AMOS ALBEE

1772–

Amos Albee was the teacher in the first singing school that Lowell Mason attended.   In a copy of

Albee's *Norfolk Collection*, once the property of Mason, and now in the Library of Yale University, Mr. Mason wrote: "This is the book used in first singing school I ever attended, which was taught by Amos Albee, the compiler. I must have been thirteen years old then, and I am now seventy-three." Amos Albee was born in Medfield, Massachusetts, in 1772, where his parents, Asa Albee and Sarah Perry, had settled a year or two before. He became a musician, taught singing schools, and also taught a common school in Medfield during the years 1796-98. He was married in Medfield and three children were born there. He made that town his home until 1820, when he and his wife Judith were dismissed to the church in Watertown. I have been unable to learn how long he lived after going from Medfield. *The Norfolk Collection of Sacred Music*, compiled by him, was printed at the music press of Herman Mann in Dedham in 1805, and was an oblong book of forty-eight pages. Three years later he collaborated with Oliver Shaw and Herman Mann and produced *The Columbian Sacred Psalmonist*, which was printed at the press of Herman Mann in Dedham.

STEPHEN JENKS

1772–1856

SOME of the music of Stephen Jenks is still in use in the books of to-day. An examination of seventeen has shown his work in six. It is said that he was one of the most prolific writers of music of his time. No less than five books were published

by him. His first effort was a small book of only
sixteen pages, printed in New Haven, Connecticut,
in 1800, and called *The New England Harmony*.
Warrington says it was *The New England Harmonist*, and was printed at Danbury, Connecticut.
It was reissued in 1800 and also in an enlarged form
in forty pages, engraved by Amos Doolittle in New
Haven, Connecticut, and the name changed to *The
Musical Harmonist*. A second edition in 1803 was
printed from type. *The Delights of Harmony* was
a collection of psalm and hymn tunes and the preface is dated at New Canaan, Connecticut, October,
1805. This was also printed for the editor and
engraved by Amos Doolittle of New Haven. It had
pieces by Daniel Read, Oliver Holden, and Amos
Doolittle, and a number of others whose names as
composers have long ago gone from the indexes of
our hymnals.

His third book was called *The Delights of Harmony, or The Norfolk Compiler*, and was printed
in 1805 by the Manns in Dedham, which is in Norfolk County, Massachusetts. The Manns had been
printers in New Haven before they removed to
Dedham, and this is probably why they came to
print this book for Mr. Jenks. A large number of
his subscribers were from Connecticut. An imperfect copy of this book is in the Massachusetts Historical Society in its original binding of leather, and
appears to have had ninety-five pages with index
on page ninety-seven, and there was a supplement
of fourteen pages of "Additional Music." The Connecticut Courant in February, 1807, carries an
advertisement dated at Dedham, December 6, 1806,

as follows: "Abner Ellis publishes a supplement of 32 pages to go with Stephen Jenks *Delights of Harmony* or Norfolk Compiler." In his advertisement "The author returns his respects to the subscribers for his book; as their liberality so far exceeds his expectations he is determined to put the book to the subscribers at eighty-eight cents a book, although the conditions were one cent a page."

The next compilation upon which Mr. Jenks' name appears was called *The Hartford Collection of Sacred Harmony*, and was printed in Hartford in 1807. Jenks was assisted by Elijah Griswold and John C. Frisbie. This was a collection from the most approved American and European authors, and was designed especially for singing schools and musical societies, and contained sixty pages. The workmanship was so perfect that I thought the pages must be engraved, but the date being after the use of type had become so common I was in doubt as to whether it was a specimen of engraving or of type. After closely examining several pages, the mark of the plate was discovered on some of them, which settled the question.

His last book was called *Laus Deo, the Harmony of Zion, or The Union Compiler*, and was printed by Daniel Mann for the author, proprietor of the copyright, in Dedham in 1818. This collection was made chiefly from European authors, though there were some from the works of Americans, these last being printed verbatim from the original copies of the American composers. There were eighty pages and eighty-five tunes. His tune "Communion," also called "St. Stephen," is found in three of the seventeen books of recent date examined, and "Bartimaus" in three.   Mr. Simeon Pease Cheney, in his New American Singing Book, tells this story of Mr. Jenks: When he was about to publish his *Norfolk Compiler* he went around among his scholars and acquaintances to secure subscriptions.   Meeting a rich but miserly farmer named Sellick, he solicited his help but received such a crushing refusal that his ardor was cooled for a time.   Finding the following words, he thought them appropriate to his experience.

> "Some walk in honor's gaudy show;
>   Some dig for golden ore;
> They build for heirs they know not who
>   And straight are seen no more."

The tune which he composed to these words, while in such a frame of mind, he called "Sellick," and whenever the old farmer was present at church, or at social gatherings, he would always have this tune sung.

Stephen Jenks was born in 1772 in New Canaan, Connecticut.   He loved music and did all he could to advance its influence both by teaching and by composing.   He was married twice, first to Hannah Dauchey, who died at Ridgefield, Connecticut, August 11, 1800.   They had two sons, and it was while living at Ridgefield that his first book was published. When his second book was issued he was living in New Salem, New York.   His second wife he married in Providence, Rhode Island, and they had two sons and four daughters.   In 1829 he moved with his family to Thompson, Ohio, where he made drums and tambourines until his death, June 5, 1856.

PART III

1773–1800

ABRAHAM MAXIM

1773–1829

Two brothers, Abraham and John Maxim, contributed considerable music to the first half of the nineteenth century. Abraham was born January 3, 1773, at Carver, Massachusetts, a town which was named for the first governor of Plymouth colony. From his early youth he was noted for his love of singing and his uncommon attachment for music. His heart and mind were so absorbed in it that he was of little use on the farm. He began his composing early, and when thus engaged knew nothing else, and would be as likely to take a basket to bring water from the well as a pail.

Maxim had a bright, active mind, and at music parties would interest the company by singing, playing the bass viol, doing a sum in the rule of three, and telling what the company was talking about, all at the same time. He studied music for a time with William Billings, of Boston, and composed many of his tunes while living at Carver. After he became of age, and before 1800, he moved to Turner, Maine. This town had been incorporated in 1786, and named for the Rev. Charles Turner, of Scituate, Massachusetts, one of the proprietors. The name of one of the neighboring towns, Buckfield, he gave to one of his tunes, and his best known tune he called "Turner." This tune was retained in numerous col-

161

lections up to 1879, when it was used in Rev. Charles S. Robinson's *Songs for the Sanctuary*, and this is the latest use of it that I have noted. At Turner Mr. Maxim married and raised a family of singing children. He taught reading schools and singing school in that town and others in the vicinity, and there he compiled his books. His first book was an original composition called *The Oriental Harmony*, containing fifty-six pages and thirty-nine tunes. The preface is dated at Turner, July, 1802, and it was printed by Henry Ranlet in Exeter, N. H. His second compilation was *The Northern Harmony*, the fifth edition of which was published in Hallowell, Maine, in 1819. This was a collection of tunes from various authors, and had 128 pages. In December, 1827, he moved from Turner to Palmyra, Maine, continuing farming and teaching, and he died there suddenly of apoplexy one evening, just after leaving his singing school, aged fifty-six. He appears to have been a very cheerful, happy man with a natural taste for literature.

Just as this sketch is being prepared for print *The Gospel Hymn Book* comes to notice, copyrighted in 1818 by Abraham Maxim. It is a little book of 216 pages, without music, containing both original and selected hymns, but no authors are given.

The date of the birth of John Maxim has not been discovered. A tune called "Maxim" is found among his music which was composed for his half-century birthday, January 24, but the year is not shown. An oblong manuscript book of 140 pages is in the library of the Massachusetts Historical Society, containing 100 tunes and fifteen anthems, composed between 1842 and 1848. To a committee to whom this manuscript was submitted he wrote:

The music publishing committee are at liberty to use all or any part of the inclosed music that they see proper, free of charge, and to make any alterations either in the music or in the words or even in the names of the tunes as they deem proper. In either case no offense will be given, the tunes being original and all the author's own. Please retain what is not used until called for. Such as they are the publishers are entirely welcome to them.

No printed book of his has been discovered. He wrote many political songs about 1840, some of which were used in the *Tippicanoe Songster.*

JOEL HARMON

1773–1833

JOEL HARMON was a native of Connecticut, though his adult life was spent in Vermont. He was born in Suffield, Connecticut, in May, 1773. In 1808 he settled in Pawlet, Vermont, where he was one of the earliest merchants of that town. Music, however was his chief delight. He taught music all his life, and used his own music exclusively in his schools. He was opposed to the fugue, which had been so popular during the preceding years, and made an effort to introduce a different style; but his music did not get into general use, nor find general favor with the people. His first book was *The Columbian Sacred Minstrel,* a book of eighty pages, containing fifty-three original pieces and was sold for 75 cents a copy. It was printed in Northampton in 1809. *A Musical Primer* was printed in Harrisburg about

1814 or later, and he was preparing another when he died at York, Pennsylvania, March 17, 1833. He was a major in the War of 1812. The history of Pawlet, Vermont, says he moved to Richland, New York, in 1804.

JOHN COLE

1774–1855[1]

VERY early in the history of our country Baltimore assumed an important place in its musical development. Much of the credit for this is due to John Cole, one of the earliest printers, organists, and composers in that city. Born in Tewksbury, England, in 1774, he emigrated with his parents to the United States in 1785, being then in the eleventh year of his age. He was brought up in the Monumental city, eventually married there, and made it his permanent home. At an early age he showed a natural genius and a great love for music and attended the singing schools of that day conducted by Andrew Law, Thomas H. Atwill, Spicer, Johnson, and others. By diligent study and practice he became wiser than his teachers, and soon he himself began to instruct in psalmody. He also devoted some time to practice upon several instruments, and became the leader of a band, which gained great popularity during the War of 1812. His business as an organist and a printer brought him into the company of many distinguished musicians, from whom he received various hints and suggestions that proved very advantageous to him. At a very early

[1] From The Choir Herald.

period in his musical career Mr. Cole discovered the
necessity for a change in the then prevailing taste
of the public for music, and by extraordinary and
persistent exertions induced a few others to join
with him in this opinion, and by that means Baltimore was foremost in putting a stop to that species
of psalmody which then prevailed universally in the
schools of the continent. His voice was a baritone,
he was a most correct sight singer, and he possessed a general knowledge of the principles of composition.

Activities

For a long time he was conductor of the choir
as well as organist of the Saint Paul's Episcopal
Church in Baltimore, and during that period this
church was celebrated for the skill and taste displayed in the performances of its sacred music. The
direction of most of the public performances of
sacred music that occurred in his adopted city
usually devolved upon him as did also the presentation of the several oratorios given there. He
became a publisher as early as 1797, buying the
music stock of Mr. Carr, and continuing to publish and sell music almost up to the day of
his death. During his later career his son was
associated with him as a member of the firm,
and at the death of the latter the business was sold
to and conducted by F. D. Benteen. Mr. Cole
issued a great variety of collections and editions
of psalmody and anthems of considerable merit, as
was indicated by their extensive circulation.

As many as thirteen different compilations bear

his name as composer or compiler, and all but one of them were printed in Baltimore. In the library collected by Dr. Lowell Mason, and now owned by Yale University, there is "A Collection of Psalm Tunes and Anthems, composed by John Cole, author of the Divine Harmonist, . . . printed at Boston, Dec. 1803." Inside the cover is this note addressed to

Mr. Lowell Mason, Boston. Dear Sir: I send you this as a curiosity. Thomas and Andrews published it on their own account and sent me one hundred copies. I was then a young man, and was made very proud on hearing from them that "some of their best judges pronounced the music too good for the prevailing taste!!!" Having a few days since visited a church in which I formerly officiated I found two copies, and send you one as a memento of former times. John Cole.

This book was oblong and had fifty-five pages.

Books

Besides the book already mentioned there were the following:

Beauties of Psalmody, third edition printed in 1827.

Collection of Anthems, 56 pages, printed in Baltimore, no date.

Devotional Harmony, 1814.

Divine Harmonist, 1808.

Ecclesiastical Harmony, 1810.

Episcopalian Harmony, 1800; another edition in 1811.

Laudate Dominum, a book of chants, 1842; third edition, 1847.

The Minstrel, a book of songs, 1812.

Sacred Melodies, 1-3, 1828.

The Seraph, 1821, 1822, and 1827.

Songs of Zion, psalm tunes, 1818.

Union Harmony.

This last named book was printed in patent notes, and was "intended for the use of such teachers as are in the habit of using such notes, and to remove the prejudice of those who have never fairly examined the system."

TUNES

The most popular tune of Mr. Cole's numerous compositions is "Geneva," and whenever any of his work is selected for insertion in hymnals this is always included, and where there is only one of his, this is sure to be the one chosen. Many of the recent hymnals include John Cole among the composers whose work is used. *The Methodist Harmonist*, printed in 1833, has nine of his tunes, a larger number than in any other compilation that I have examined, with the exception of his own.

Mr. Cole died in Baltimore August 17, 1855.

BENJAMIN HOLT

1774–1861

WHEN Benjamin Holt died in 1861 at the age of eighty-seven it was said that he was the oldest American composer, and that he had been a well-known musician all his life. He was a teacher of music in Boston for many years, and had served as the second president of the Handel and Haydn Society in that city. His compositions were quite popular in his day, and appeared in many contemporary singing books. In 1853 he removed from the Hub to the country town of Lancaster, there to pass the remaining eight years of his life, and he died there March 9, 1861. Before he had reached the age of thirty he issued *The New England Sacred Harmony*, "being principally," as he says, "an original composition in three and four parts adapted to the various meters in common use." It was printed in Boston by the firm of Thomas and Andrews, the preface being dated March, 1803. This is "the first essay of the author, and rests its destiny entirely upon its own merits." "The author has taken much pains in the pieces of his own composition to have them correct." Many subscribers for his book were obtained in Boston, while of those from outside of that city the larger number were from Windham, Connecticut. This small book of fifty-six pages has twenty-two pieces by Mr. Holt never before published. There were also other pieces by both European and American authors. In 1812 Mr. Holt assisted in the preparation of the

BRIDGEWATER COLLECTION

This collection took its name from the town of Bridgewater, Massachusetts, which was the birthplace of one of the men who assisted in its compilation. Nahum Mitchell was born in East Bridgewater, February 12, 1769. His first American ancestors came to Plymouth in the third ship, which arrived there in 1623. One who knew the musician says of him, "He was one of nature's noblemen, a gentleman of the old school, courteous, compassionate, unselfish, honorable and industrious." He graduated from Harvard in 1789, taking the Bachelor's degree, which was followed in due time by the Master's degree. He studied law in Plymouth and began its practice in his native town in 1792. He was for many years in the public service of his State. He was a State representative 1803-05, and 1839-40; judge of the Court of Common Pleas for ten years from 1811 to 1821; State senator, 1813-14; a representative to the Eighth Congress at Washington, D. C.; one of the council of the governor of Massachusetts, 1814-20, and State treasurer from 1822 to 1827. He also served for a time as treasurer and librarian of the Massachusetts Historical Society. His love for music began in early life, and continued to the end. His early productions were written in the style which predominated in that day, while his later works, which were attempts at reform, were very popular. His name does not appear as the compiler of the Bridgewater Collection, but it was known by his contemporaries that his was the moving spirit in its preparation. It was the joint product of Benjamin Holt, Nahum Mitchell, and Bartholomew Brown. It was first issued in 1812, and during the next twenty-four years passed through twenty-six editions. Some of these editions were merely reprints, with the year of printing changed, while others differed in having some tunes omitted and new ones added. This collection was also called *Songs of the Temple or Templi Carmina*, and on account of its popularity exerted a great influence in promoting a reform in

the style of church music in New England; and in
some of the common tunes the compilers ventured
an improvement of the harmony.

On the first day of August, 1853, Judge Mitchell
went to Plymouth, where he was witnessing from
the steps of Pilgrim Hall the pageant of the
embarkation of the Pilgrims from Delft Haven for
America. Missing his pocketbook he stooped over
to look for it, when he fell senseless. He lived, however, to reach his home in East Bridgewater, but died
the same day at the age of eighty-four. Of him
also it was said that he was the oldest of the American composers of note. Mr. Moore, in his *Cyclopedia of Music*, published in 1856, says that Mr.
Mitchell "in conjunction with the Rev. Mr. Buckminster, of Boston, compiled a small volume of
church music called *The Brattle Street Collection*,
which was published in 1810. In that year there
was printed in Boston by Manning and Loring, a
collection of tunes which is probably the one referred
to, bearing the title, *LXXX Psalm and Hymn Tunes
for Public Worship* "adapted to the meters used in
churches." In the copy of this book which is in the
Library of Congress there is folded within the cover
the following note apparently in a contemporary
hand:

At a meeting of the standing committee of the church in
Brattle Square, January 14, 1810, voted that Mr. Bryant P.
Tilden, Mr. Bartholomew Brown, and Mr. Ebenezer Withing-
ton be a committee with the advice and assistance of the Rev.
Mr. Buckminster to have a small selection of sacred music
to be used in the publick worship of the society and to cause
the same to be published and distributed in the several pews.
At a meeting of the church in Brattle Square January 14,

1810 voted that the society approve of the above vote, and that Elias Mann be added to the said committee. Attest, Peter Thacher, clerk.

This action of the church and its standing committee was carried out and the volume prepared, but neither the book itself nor the vote of the church shows that Mr. Mitchell had any hand in it; however, as he and the others named had worked in conjunction on other selections, it is not improbable that he did some of the labor on this.

JOHN W. NEVIUS

1774–1854

JOHN W. NEVIUS was one of the three compilers of *The New Brunswick Collection of Sacred Music*, printed in New Brunswick, New Jersey, in 1817. Of the other two, Cornelius Van Deventer and John Frazee, I have been unable to find any information. John W. Nevius was born in Somerville, New Jersey, December 22, 1774. On May 12, 1796, he married Mary Rollin. He was a carpenter by trade but took a lively interest in music, taught it for several years, and was the leader of a brass band while living in New Brunswick. He was a probate judge for the decade from 1839 to 1849, and an elder in the Old School Presbyterian Church for over fifty years. The later years of his life were spent in Sunbeam, Illinois, where he died October 12, 1854.

GEORGE E. BLAKE

1775–1871

GEORGE E. BLAKE, one of the extensive publishers of music in Philadelphia, was born in Yorkshire, England, in 1775. He came to America in 1793 when the yellow fever was raging in the Pennsylvania city and the people were dying so rapidly that there were scarcely enough able-bodied left to bury the dead or care for the sick. "Every one," he said, "seemed frightened out of their wits." He did not flee from the city, as many who were able had done, but did his part in helping those in need, and when the danger had passed he began teaching the clarinet at South Third Street, in a room over John Aitken's music store. Benjamin Carr was Aitken's successor, and he was followed by Mr. Blake. The latter commenced the publishing and selling of music in 1802 at No. 13 South Fifth Street, in a small odd-fashioned building that served him both as a store and a residence for many years, and that was still standing in 1875. At the time of his death, which occurred February 14, 1871, at the age of ninety-six, he was the oldest music publisher in America.

His contribution to the literature of music included a number of books of piano music, and *The Vocal Harmony*, "a collection of psalms, hymns, anthems, and chants, compiled from the most approved authors, ancient and modern." This has over fifty pages of engraved music, is not dated, but was issued from his office when it was located at No. 1 South Third Street.

STEPHEN ADDINGTON

REFERENCE must be made to another Philadelphia book, *A Valuable Selection of Psalm and Hymn Tunes* "from the most esteemed English authors . . . and now used by the congregation at the Independent Tabernacle in Philadelphia," compiled by Stephen Addington, and published in 1808 by Matthew Carey. The congregation for which this book was especially printed was organized in 1804 under the title of "The Independent Tabernacle," and it had erected a building in Ramstead Court, west of Fourth Street and above Chestnut. In 1816 the Tabernacle was carried over to the Reformed Dutch denomination, and three years later its members renounced that jurisdiction, and were received into the Presbytery of Philadelphia as the Seventh Presbyterian Church. The old church was removed in 1842, and a new one erected in a new location. Stephen Addington was an Englishman, and his "Selection" had been first published in London in 1792.

SAMUEL WILLARD

1776–1859

SAMUEL WILLARD was the author of nearly two hundred hymns and he compiled two books of hymns, and two editions of his Deerfield Collection of music were issued. He was a native of Massachusetts, having been born in Petersham on April 16, 1776. His early years were spent on a farm, and he was nearly twenty-one before he began to prepare himself for college. He was graduated from Harvard in the class of 1803, and was a classmate of James Savage, whose *Genealogical Dictionary* did so much to preserve the records of the early families of New England. The year following his graduation from college was spent as assistant in Exeter Academy, and for the two following years he was tutor at Bowdoin College. In 1807 he received a call to the church in Deerfield, Massachusetts, but his theological views were so broad that the first council to examine him would not pass him or ordain him. Later another council was called, and he became pastor of this church. His eyes gradually failed him until he became totally blind, and in 1829 he felt it his duty to resign from his active ministry. He continued to reside in this town most of the balance of his life, preaching occasionally up to the time of his death, October 8, 1859. He was married in 1808, and had three children.

WRITINGS

He was a prolific writer, most of his work having been prepared for the press and printed after the loss of his sight. One of the first efforts of Doctor Willard in his parish was a reform of the church music, which had been degraded to the light compositions of the day. He restored the old stately tunes, training the choir, leading in church, holding singing schools sometimes Sunday evening after the two services of the day. Besides numerous religious articles he prepared a series of school readers, several books on the subject of education and several collections of music and hymns. Of these latter were his *Regular Hymns*, numbering 158 songs, composed altogether by himself, and published in 1823; a small tract, also written by himself, and printed in 1826, entitled *An Index to the Bible with Juvenile Hymns;* and a compilation, *Sacred Music and Poetry Reconciled*, which was issued in 1830, and which contained 518 hymns from various authors, nearly 180 of them being his own. In the Library of Harvard College is a manuscript in which all of his hymns appear, revised and corrected by their author, and preceded by an elaborate treatise, in which he explains and advocates the theory of "a coincidence between the musical and the poetical emphasis." The subject was one that engaged his mind and occupied his pen for many years, and all his own hymns were written or altered with a view of practically illustrating this thought. Doctor Willard claimed no high poetic merit. Yet his hymns, however modest their claim, are filled with the sanctity of his own spirit; they are musical in their rhythm and smooth in versification. To such an extent had he exercised and strengthened his memory after he was deprived of his sense of sight that he could readily repeat any one of his hymns.

His wife was born in Hingham, and thither he moved for a few years after he resigned from his church. It was while here that one collection of hymns was made, and on the title page he states that it was "adopted, while in manuscript, by the third Congregational Society in Hingham." The first edition of *The Deerfield Collection of Sacred Music* was printed in Greenfield in 1814, and a second was issued four years later containing additional pieces. Mr. Willard returned to Deerfield after a few years of absence, and there remained for the rest of his life. Harvard conferred upon him the degree of A.M. in 1810, S.T.D. in 1826, and from Bowdoin College he received the honorary degree of A.M. in 1815.

SOLOMON WARRINER

1778–1860

Solomon Warriner was a descendant of the William Warriner who settled in Springfield, Massachusetts, about 1638. He was born March 24, 1778, at Wilbraham; married in 1801 Eleanor Keep, sister of the Rev. John Keep, of Oberlin, Ohio, and a year after her death in 1810 he married Mary Bliss, the daughter of Luke Bliss, of Springfield. His family was an interesting one. The oldest son, who bore his father's name, was a singer in Saint George's Church, in New York city, at the time of the pastorate of Dr. Stephen Tyng. Another son was a minister; another a Sunday-school superintendent, and a daughter married Charles Merriam, one of the publishers of the early editions of *Webster's Unabridged Dictionary.*

The early years of Solomon's life were spent on his father's farm. When still young he gave evidence of extraordinary musical powers and used to sing the alto in the village church. At twelve he was drummer in the militia company at Wilbraham.

He became a lieutenant about 1802 and during the War of 1812 his regiment, which was an artillery regiment under Lieutenant Colonel William Edwards, of Northampton, was called out for thirty-five days duty at South Boston, from October 2 to November 5, 1814. When old enough to enter business on his own account he became a dealer in general merchandise in Springfield.

Doctor Josiah G. Holland, in an editorial published after his death, thus summarizes the musical career of Mr. Warriner:

That which has made Colonel Warriner more widely known than anything else was his devotion to sacred music and his agency in developing it in this region. He had the direction of the music in the old church of this city for a great many years with one intermission. His work led him to Pittsfield in 1815, but after remaining there for five years the people of Springfield fairly brought him back. They could not get along without him. He was here in May, 1820, when the First Church was dedicated and got up the music for the occasion. He became a somewhat noted compiler of music. *The Springfield Collection* was the name of the book of sacred music published by him in his younger days (1813). After this he was associated with the celebrated musician, Thomas Hastings, in the composition and publication of *Musica Sacra,* a first-class book of sacred music. He maintained a very pleasant correspondence with Doctor Hastings till his closing days. Colonel Warriner was the first leader of the first music society ever formed in Springfield,—the old Handel and Haydn Society. Indeed, Colonel Warriner was the great authority and standard in all musical matters throughout this region, and did more than any other man to elevate the style of sacred music in western Massachusetts. In the old church his choir numbered from seventy five to one hundred, filled all the singing seats and ran over.

His later years were spent in his garden and as prudential committee of the city schools. He led the choristers in singing Doctor Holland's hymn, "Thou didst bless the garden land," at a famous horse exhibition in Springfield in 1853. In 1886 at the celebration of the two hundred and fiftieth anniversary of the founding of Springfield the tunes were selected from Colonel Warriner's publications. He became the chorister in the First Church in 1801 and held the position for more than forty years. He could sing bass or tenor with equal ease, and he was so good a leader that when he left the city temporarily, the members of his church raised twelve hundred dollars to bring him back.

Music

Warriner's *Springfield Collection*, copyrighted and printed in 1813, was a book of 150 pages, and was oblong in shape. It is said that in this book the air was for the first time in this country given to the treble instead of the tenor voice. Thomas Hastings had about this time issued a *Utica Collection* for the use of the Handel and Burney Society of that city, and in 1816 these two were united and published as the *Musica Sacra, or the Springfield and Utica Collections United*. This became a very popular book, was reprinted in as many as ten editions, both in the oblong form, and some in octavo style.

Solomon Warriner continued to reside in Springfield until his death, June 14, 1860, at the age of seventy-two.

OLIVER SHAW[1]

1779–1848

Music has always been a favorite vocation for those who are blind, since it is their most effective means of communication with the world without them. Therefore it was most natural that Oliver Shaw, when he became blind at the age of twenty-one, should turn toward music as the most available means of earning a livelihood. He was born March 13, 1779, at Middleboro, Massachusetts. Both his parents, John Shaw and Hannah Heath, were also natives of that town. He had two brothers and five sisters, but he was the only son who reached majority. When he was a young boy he was cautioned about handling a pen knife, but in spite of the warning he stuck it into his right eye, and in a short time the sight of that eye was gone. His father was a navigator, and in order to be nearer the sea, moved his family to Taunton, in Bristol County, where Oliver had the advantages of Bristol Academy, he being one of the first pupils of that institution which had been only recently established in that city. He was then seventeen years old. As soon as he had finished his schooling he went to sea with his father and often assisted in taking the observations. On one occasion he was observing the sun when he had only partly recovered from an attack of yellow fever, and so injured his left eye that at the age of twenty-one he became totally blind. Now every avenue for advancement seemed closed before him, and for a while he knew not what he could do. Then

[1] From The Choir Herald.

his father learned that a Mr. Birkenhead had just arrived from England, and had established himself as a teacher of music in Newport, so the blind boy was placed under his instruction for two years. His next teacher was Gottlieb Graupner, of Boston. This was about 1803. Graupner had arrived in Boston in 1798, and established a music printing business, which he continued for twenty-seven years. He also kept pianofortes on sale and for rent and did tuning for those who called upon him. He was one of the founders of the Handel and Haydn Society and played the double bass in its orchestra for many years. It may be that Shaw took lessons from him on other instruments than the piano and organ; we are sure, however, that he continued to learn in Boston from another teacher named Thomas Granger, an Englishman, and by him was taught to play upon wind instruments. After two years instruction he located in Dedham, where he began his career as a teacher of music. It is probable that while he was in Dedham Lowell Mason came under his influence. Mr. Mason was a native of Medfield, a neighboring town, and on one occasion remarked that he was "indebted to him [Oliver Shaw] for his start in life—that he owed all to him." This is certainly a superb honor to have started the career of one who did so much for the cause of sacred music as Lowell Mason.

PROVIDENCE, R. I.

Dedham was not to be the scene of Mr. Shaw's life-work, for in 1807 he was induced to move to Providence, where he had a boy lead him about as he visited the homes of his pupils. For many years he was organist of the First Congregational Church, of which the Rev. Henry Edes was the pastor from 1805 to 1832. He organized several bands of music, and for many years selected the musicians that took part in the commencements of Brown University. He was a very popular teacher and often gave forty lessons in a week. Frequently he both boarded and lodged his scholars, providing for ten at a time in his own home. This home was a veritable house of music, with a piano in every room, and in a large one on the first floor there were three pianos and an organ.

THE PSALLONIAN SOCIETY

Oliver Shaw had not been in Providence long before he and seven others joined in meetings for mutual improvement in psalmody. This was in 1809, and among the members were Moses Noyes and Colonel Thomas S. Webb, of whom the latter moved to Boston in 1815, and was elected the first president of the Handel and Haydn Society there. After several years of informal meetings this group was incorporated as the Psallonian Society "for the purpose of improving themselves in the knowledge and practice of sacred music and inculcating a more correct taste in the choice and performance of it." The attendance books of this society are in the rooms of the Rhode Island Historical Society in Providence, and the first list gives the names of thirty-five men and fourteen women, while the last roll shows forty-one men and twenty women. The last annual meeting was held October 10, 1832, and so the organization came to an end. During the sixteen years of its incorporated life it gave thirty-one concerts the programs of which are still preserved in Providence. One of them, given February 15, 1820, was for the sufferers from the fire in Savannah, and the net proceeds were $82. These concerts were held at various hours, the times of opening the doors ranging from five-thirty to seven-thirty, and the concerts beginning at times from six-thirty to seven-forty-five.

FAMILY

Having settled in Providence as his home, he soon found a wife, and was married October 20, 1912, to Sarah Jencks, the only daughter of Oliver Jencks, a surveyor of that city. Their family consisted of two sons and five daughters. One of the sons, Oliver J. Shaw, inherited the musical qualities of his father, became a teacher and composer, settled in Utica, New York, and died there in 1851. Of the girls, Sarah was a singer, and often took part in the concerts given by her father. In 1834 Mr. Shaw allied himself with the church, joining the Second Baptist, now the Central Baptist Church, of Providence. He was very devout in his religious life and often used his own music for his favorite hymns, and the singing of them to his accompaniment upon the organ was an inspiring addition to his family devotions. Frequently the students from the college and other visitors stayed to family prayers. His patriotism was voiced in the stirring marches which he composed; his politics may be surmised from the names of the instrumental pieces that he wrote, and the titles he gave to his hymn tunes suggest the local geography. "Taunton" was the home of his youth, "Bristol" the county in which it was located, "Dighton" a neighboring town; and the following are streets in Providence: "Weybosset," "Meeting," "Benevolent," "Pleasant," and "Planet."

MUSIC AND BOOKS

A complete list of his vocal pieces shows at least seventy-one, written between the years 1812 and 1846; his instrumental numbers, written from 1831 to 1840, were twenty-six. This does not include the sacred music that was contained in the books he compiled. His first book was a small one of a few pages called *The Gentleman's Favorite Selection of Instrumental Music*, and is said to have been published at Dedham in 1805. *The Columbian Sacred Harmonist* was the joint work of Oliver Shaw, Amos Albee, and Herman Mann, and was printed in Dedham in 1808. Amos Albee was a native of Medfield, and in 1805 had issued from Dedham the *Norfolk Collection*. He was a teacher in Medfield during the years 1796-1798. In the book that he compiled with Oliver Shaw he had two tunes—"Tennessee" and "Medfield." Herman Mann was the printer. Born in 1771, he had established his business in Dedham in 1797, and continued there with a single year's intermission until his death in 1833. In this book Mr. Shaw had fourteen pieces.

His next book was *The Musical Olio*, consisting of songs, and it was printed in Providence in 1814. The next year he finished his *Providence Selection of*

Psalms and Hymns, a book of 110 pieces, including thirteen of his own, and had it printed at Dedham by his friend Herman Mann. This book also contained four pieces by Moses Noyes, one of the founders of the Psallonian Society. In 1819 he published in Providence *The Melodia Sacra,* to which he added a subtitle, "The Providence Selection of Sacred Music," and dedicated it to the Psallonian Society, of which he was the dominating spirit for the sixteen years of its existence. A collection of sacred songs, anthems, and other pieces, all original, was copyrighted in 1823. Another volume of *Original Melodies* followed in 1832, and then his last was *The Social Sacred Melodist,* printed for him in his home town of Providence in 1835.

Hymns

As early as 1830, when Dutton and Ives compiled *The American Psalmody,* Shaw's hymns began to be copied into other books besides his own. The book referred to has three of Mr. Shaw's. *The Melodia Sacra,* 1852, had one. Few later hymnals have contained any work of his. *The Baptist Hymnal* of 1883 has his tune "Gentleness," which is repeated in *Sursum Corda,* another Baptist book, and it is also in the book formerly used in the Methodist Episcopal Church, South. It is arranged from his most popular song, "There's Nothing True but Heaven." It is said that the proceeds from this one song amounted to $1,500. It was repeated night after night by the Boston Handel and Haydn Society, and was widely circulated. It was also one of the pieces played at his funeral.

EZEKIEL GOODALE

1780–

The Hallowell Collection of Sacred Music was the product of the Handel Society of Maine. It is not stated who was the compiler, but it was recommended by both the president and the vice-president of the society named. It was printed and published by Ezekiel Goodale at Hallowell, in 1817. For a second edition issued two years later there were added sixteen pages. Most of the tunes were by European composers, though we find Tuckey's Psalm 97, and a tune named "Canton," by Supply Belcher, a Pine Tree State musician. One tune, here called "Oporto," is the well-known "Portuguese Hymn."

Mr. Goodale was born in West Boylston, Massachusetts, in 1780. After passing his majority, in 1822 he removed to Hallowell, Maine, and having spent a few years in book-selling, he opened a printing establishment in 1813, "At the Sign of the Bible." In 1820 Frank Glazier, the son of Mr. Goodale's sister, entered the business with his uncle, and with changing partners the firm continued until 1880.

ANTHONY PHILIP HEINRICH

1781–1861

ANTHONY PHILIP HEINRICH, often called "Father Heinrich," was born in affluence in Schoenbuchel, Bohemia, March 11, 1781. When he reached manhood he became the principal in an extensive banking house in Hamburg, and during his travels in connection with his business he went to Malta, where he purchased a Cremona violin, and at once proceeded to learn to play it. His next extended travels brought him to Lisbon, thence to America in 1818, and he settled in Philadelphia for a while, where he directed the music in the Southwick Theater. It was while there that he learned of the failure of his business house, and he was reduced to poverty thus suddenly. From Philadelphia he went on to Louisville, Kentucky, supporting himself by giving violin lessons. He lived for some time at Bardstown among the Indians who then inhabited that section of the country, and many of his musical compositions refer to these aboriginal companions. He was a species of musical Catlin, painting his dusky friends upon the musical staff, instead of upon canvas. His work as an American composer is important from the fact that "though not the first to recognize the North American Indian as a fit subject for music he was the first to do so in symphonic and choral works of large dimensions calling for an orchestra of almost Richard Straussian proportions, and indeed, the first to show, as a symphonic composer, pronounced nationalistic aspirations." (See the report of the Library of Congress for 1917.)

In 1832 we find him in Boston, where he was for a while the organist in the Old South Church. It was during this year that Nathaniel D. Gould published his *National Church Harmony* and he placed therein four of the hymn tunes of Professor Heinrich. One was called "Antonia," the Latin form of his own name, and it was also the name of his daughter. In 1838 we find that this venerable and talented musician had taken up his residence in New York, and a writer in the Boston Musical Gazette for that year has the following:

Years have passed since we had the pleasure of taking him by the hand, or of seeing that hand sweep the keys with its lightning rapidity, producing its enraptured tones. We most cordially wish him success, both with his "Bonny Brunette," which no doubt is worthy of all the critical care and attention he has paid to it; also with his mighty "Condor," of which we have had a goodly account. Cannot this gigantic bird wing its way hither, or is our climate too cold and uncongenial to excite it into song? We understand that Mr. Heinrich still employs his time in composing, and that the fire of his genius is still in full glow.

In the meantime "Father Heinrich" had visited London, where he played in the Drury Lane Orchestra for thirty-six shilling a week. Then he went on to Germany, and the scenes of his youth. After his return to this country a short biography of him was printed in a Baltimore paper, which called out a correction from Mr. Heinrich, giving us some idea of his married life. He said, "Having only been wedded once and not to a lady of wealth, but one abundantly rich in beauty, accomplishments, and qualities of a noble heart, I draw a veil over my (other) private life."

His wife was an American, whom he had married, presumably, in Bohemia, for she died there in 1814, and their infant daughter, Antonia, was committed to the care of a relative at Grund near Rumburg. During his visit to his native land he tried without success to find his daughter, but on his return to America he found that she had followed her father, and they finally discovered each other.

In 1842 he took part in a Grand Musical Festival in the Broadway Tabernacle in New York, and this city was his home for most of the remaining years of his life. He died in New York, May 3, 1861, and the notice of his death states that for the last four months he was confined to his room by a serious illness which he bore with Christian resignation.

Soon after his arrival in this country he learned of the failure of the banking house with which he was connected, and so to earn a livelihood he began to compose music. He had finished seventy-five complete works, including several operas, when they were all destroyed by fire. A number of his compositions were written for such an extensive orchestra that many of them were never given, and a still larger part remain in manuscript. A fortunate purchase by the Library of Congress has placed his work where it is accessible to the music student, and there is also among his papers much material consisting of letters, memoranda, and newspaper clippings for a future biography. We will close this article with an incident from Hewitt's *Shadows on the Wall.*

The eccentric Anthony Philip Heinrich, generally known as "Father Heinrich," visited Washington, while I resided in that city, with a grand musical work of his, illustrative of the greatness and glory of this republic, the splendor of its institutions and the indomitable bravery of its army and navy. This work Heinrich wished to publish by subscription. He had many names on his list; but, as he wished to dedicate it to the President of the United States, and also to obtain the signatures of the Cabinet and other high officials, he thought it best to call personally and solicit their patronage.

He brought with him a number of letters of introduction, among them one to myself from my brother, a music publisher in New York. I received the old gentleman with all the courtesy due to his brilliant musical talents; and, as I was the first he had called upon, I tendered him the hospitalities of my house—"potluck" and a comfortable bed, promising to go the rounds with him on the following morning and introduce him to President Tyler (whose daughter, Alice, was a pupil of mine) and such other influential men as I was acquainted with.

Poor Heinrich! I shall never forget him. He imagined that he was going to set the world on fire with his "Dawning of Music in America"; but, alas! It met with the same fate as his "Castle in the Moon" and "Yankee Doodliad."

Two or three hours of patient hearing did I give to the most complicated harmony I ever heard, even in my musical dreams. Wild and unearthly passages, the pianoforte absolutely groaning under them, and "the old man eloquent," with much self-satisfaction, arose from the tired instrument, and with a look of triumph, asked me if I had ever heard music like that before? I certainly had not.

At a proper hour we visited the President's mansion, and after some ceremony and much grumbling on the part of the polite usher, were shown into the presence of Mr. Tyler, who received us with his usual urbanity. I introduced Mr. Heinrich as a professor of exalted talent and a man of extraordinary genius. The President after learning the object of our visit, which he was glad to learn was not to solicit an office, readily consented to the dedication, and commended the undertaking. Heinrich was elated to the skies, and immediately proposed to play the grand conception, in order that the Chief Magistrate of this great nation might have an idea of its merits.

"Certainly, sir," said Mr. Tyler; "I will be greatly pleased to hear it. We will go into the parlor, where there is a piano, and I will have Alice and the ladies present, so that we may have the benefit of their opinion; for, to confess the truth, gentlemen, I am but a poor judge of music."

He then rang the bell for the waiter, and we were shown into the parlor, and invited to take some refreshments at the sideboard. The ladies soon joined us, and in a short space of time we were all seated, ready to hear Father Heinrich's composition; I, for the second time, to be *gratified*. The composer labored hard to give full effect to his weird production; his bald pate bobbed from side to side, and shone like a bubble on the surface of a calm lake. At times his shoulders would be raised to the line of his ears, and his knees went up to the keyboard, while the perspiration rolled in large drops down his wrinkled cheeks.

The ladies stared at the maniac musician, as they, doubtless, thought him, and the President scratched his head, as if wondering whether wicked spirits were not rioting in the cavern of mysterious sounds and rebelling against the laws of acoustics. The composer labored on, occasionally explaining some incomprehensible passage, representing, as he said, the breaking up of the frozen river Niagara, the *thaw* of the ice, and the dash of the mass over the mighty falls. *Peace* and *plenty* were represented by soft strains of pastoral music, while the thunder of our naval war-dogs and the rattle of our army musketry told of our prowess on the sea and land.

The inspired composer had got about half-way through his wonderful production, when Mr. Tyler restlessly arose from his chair, and placing his hand gently on Heinrich's shoulder, said,

"That may all be very fine, sir, but can't you play us a good old Virginia reel?"

Had a thunderbolt fallen at the feet of the musician, he could not have been more astounded. He arose from the piano, rolled up his manuscript, and, taking his hat and cane, bolted toward the door, exclaiming:

"No sir; I never plays dance music!"

I joined him in the vestibule, having left Mr. Tyler and family enjoying a hearty laugh at the "maniac musician's" expense.

As we proceeded along Pennsylvania avenue, Heinrich grasped my arm convulsively, and exclaimed:

"Mein Got in himmel! de peoples vot made Yohn Tyler Bresident ought to be hung! He knows no more apout music than an oyshter!"

He returned to New York by the next train, and I never heard any more of the "Dawning of Music in America."

Mr. Heinrich died quite poor in New York. He was, in his earlier days, a very wealthy and influential banker in the city of Hamburg. His fondness for music, however, drew him away from the less refined but more profitable operations in the money market.

CHRISTOPHER MEINECKE

1782–1850

Much of the musical history of Baltimore during the early part of the nineteenth century centers around Saint Paul's Protestant Episcopal Church. As early as 1817 its fourth edifice was erected, and it was in this building that John Cole and Christopher Meinecke officiated. Only a very few facts have been gathered about Mr. Meinecke. First let us quote from Hewitt's *Shadows on the Wall:*

Charles Meinecke was a fine pianist as well as organist. A German by birth, he possessed the German faculty of amassing money, leading a bachelor's life and economizing to a miserly extent. He was a quiet, unobtrusive man, easy in his manners, and when he died he left a large property to his relatives in Europe. He composed many secular songs as well as sacred, and his piano music, generally variations, was quite popular. He died in 1850.

After a long search a correspondent in Baltimore found the exact date of his death to be November 6, 1850, and he quotes the following from The Sun:

Death of a musician. Mr. Christopher Meinecke, extensively known in this city as a composer and a musician, died on Wednesday evening. The deceased had attained to a considerable eminence in his profession, and was much esteemed for his integrity and virtue.

The American added that he died after a brief illness, was a native of Germany and for many years a resident of this city:

The records of the Probate Court reveal the surprising fact that at his death he possessed an estate which amounted to $190,000, a very large sum for that period. Curiosity led us to investigate the reason for the accumulation of such an amount, for surely it could not have been gathered from his receipts as a teacher of music, or a church organist. The real source of his wealth was fortunate investments. He bought real estate in the city of Baltimore, and held it until its value was greatly enhanced.

Christopher Meinecke, often called Charles, was a native of Germany. He came to this country in 1800, at the age of eighteen, landed at Baltimore, and continued to live in that city as his home until his death. His father was organist to the Duke of Oldenburgh, and consequently the son had the advantages of a complete musical education. His talents both as a composer and performer were of a very superior order. He excelled especially as a pianist; he was a brilliant concerto player, a quick reader, and accompanied the voice as only the sympathetic performer can. In 1817 he visited Europe where he was introduced to Beethoven, and submitted to him a "concerto" which won from him high approbation. Mr. Meinecke returned to Baltimore in 1819.

Music

He composed considerable music, both secular and sacred, and his productions were highly esteemed in his day. In 1821 he composed a "Te Deum" which was performed in Saint Paul's Church, and drew favorable comment from a musical journal called The Euterpiad. A "Messe, (Lateinisch)" of eighty-two pages and marked "Op. 25," is undated and was published in Leipzig; a copy of this is in the Lowell Mason Collection of Yale Library. In

1844 John Cole copyrighted a book called *Music for the Church*, "containing 62 Psalm and hymn tunes, . . . composed for the use of the choir of Saint Paul's Church," Baltimore, by C. Meinecke, organist. This was a book of 100 pages, and near the end appears his "Gloria Patri," a melody which has been the most commonly used of all the work of this composer. His music has been introduced into hymnals only to a limited extent. In 1859 the Rev. N. C. Burt, a Baltimore pastor, made *A Pastor's Selection of Hymns and Tunes* and used three of Mr. Meinecke's tunes. As Dr. Burt was a resident of the Monumental City when his book was prepared, a few words regarding him may not be out of place in this article about a fellow-citizen.

Nathaniel Clark Burt

Nathaniel Clark Burt, born in Fairton, New Jersey, April 23, 1825, graduated from Princeton in 1846, and from its theological seminary three years later. After ordination into the Presbyterian ministry he held three pastorates of five years each at Springfield, Ohio; Baltimore, Maryland; and Cincinnati, Ohio. Then on account of failing health he traveled in Europe and the Holy Land, spending the last years of his life in Southern Europe, where he undertook the care of young ladies who wished to complete their education abroad; and he died in Rome March 4, 1874. It was while pastor of the Franklin Street Presbyterian Church in Baltimore that he prepared especially for the use of his own congregation the book of music already named. He wrote considerable for the religious press, and the observations on his trip to Egypt were given to the public in a book called *The Far East*. His love for music is there manifested by numerous examples of the songs of the boatmen on the Nile, the stringed band at the hotel, and the Mohammedan worship.

THOMAS HASTINGS[1]

1784–1872

Thomas Hastings, born in Connecticut, spent the greater part of his active musical career in the Empire State, first at Utica, and later in the city of New York. To him and Lowell Mason is due a larger proportion of the psalm tunes of American origin now in common use among Protestant peoples than to any other two men. The Episcopal hymnals, however, still cling to music of English origin including many by Barnby and Dykes, though slowly introducing tunes by American composers.

Biography

Thomas Hastings was born October 15, 1784, at Washington, Connecticut, and was the son of Seth, a country physician and farmer. When the boy was twelve years old the family removed to Clinton, New York, a town which was then near the western frontier, and at eighteen he was leading the village choir. Such education as could be obtained in the country school was all the preparation he had for his lifework. In 1828 he moved to Utica, where for nine

---

[1] From The Choir Herald.

years he edited a weekly religious paper, The
Western Recorder. This gave him a channel
through which to express his musical opinions, and
these were the subject of many an editorial. In
1832 he went to New York city at the request of
twelve churches which had combined to secure his
services in the leadership of their choirs. He was
a Presbyterian, and for several years was choir-
master in the Bleecker Street Church of that denomination. His son, Thomas S., once president of the
Union Theological Seminary, said of him, "He was
a devout and earnest Christian, a hard student, and
a resolute worker, not laying aside his pen until three
days before his death." He was a diligent reader
of the Scriptures, was a concordance in himself, and
his own copies of the Word of God form quite a
little library. He is properly referred to as Doctor
Hastings, for the University of the City of New
York, recognizing his musical abilities, conferred
the degree of Mus. Doc. upon him in 1858. He
died in New York city May 15, 1872.

Musical Work

Doctor Hastings is said to have written six hundred hymns, composed about one thousand hymn
tunes, issued fifty volumes of music, and published
many articles on his favorite subject. All the recent
hymn books contain both hymns and music of his.
The first lines of some of his most frequently used
stanzas are, "Delay not, delay not, O sinner, draw
near," "To-day the Saviour calls," "He that goeth
forth with weeping," and "Hail to the brightness of
Zion's glad morning." His *Essay on Musical Taste*

was first given to the public in 1822, and it excited so much interest that he was said to be a generation ahead of his time. A new edition appeared in 1853, and a reviewer says that "it speaks well for the advance of musical knowledge and taste that this scholarly treatise should be called for anew. It treats upon precisely the topics on which correct views are most important, and it treats of them with great ability." In 1854 a book dealing with *Forty Choirs* came from his pen. These forty groups do not, he says, represent actual choirs, but all the characters had been met with in those that he had taught.

MUSICA SACRA

When Hastings was directing a County Musical Society he felt the need of a small collection of tunes for his work, and he proceeded to compose music adapted to that purpose. This was called *The Utica Collection,* and was merely a pamphlet of a few pages. A few years before this Solomon Warriner, of Springfield, Massachusetts, had issued *The Springfield Collection* (1813), a selection of 150 pages of sacred music from the works of European authors, and in 1816 these two collections were united to form the first edition of the *Musica Sacra,* which became so popular that it was reissued with slight changes almost every year up to 1836. The first four editions were printed in the quarto form, like the present-day hymn books, but the fifth was issued in two forms, the quarto and the oblong, so as to suit all tastes. The preface says:

The shape of the book which has always incommoded the

instrumental executant, is now changed for his accommodation, and though the vocalist might have preferred the former shape, yet in consequence of the present arrangement he will have the advantage of possessing a greater quantity of matter than could otherwise have been presented to him at the present reduced price.

OTHER BOOKS

A *Musical Reader* of eighty-four pages was issued from Utica, New York, in 1819: then followed *The Juvenile Psalmody*, in 1827, and many others in rapid succession. It will suffice to name only those that were the most popular. These were *The Manhattan Collection*, 1837; *The Sacred Lyre*, 1840; *The Selah*, 1856; and *The Songs of the Church*, 1862. *The Mendelssohn Collection* he edited with William B. Bradbury in 1849, and he was one of the four who issued *The Shawm* in 1853. His son, Thomas S., helped him in the preparation of the *Church Melodies* in 1858. And so we might go on with a list that would be uninteresting to the ordinary reader.

USE

During the life of Mr. Hastings his music was very popular, and some of his compositions still hold a place in the hymnals. It is but natural that some of his lesser pieces should give place to the new music that is constantly coming into use. An examination of a dozen hymnals, both denominational and unsectarian, shows at least four that are contained in eight of them. "Toplady" is in every one; "Ortonville," in ten; "Retreat," in nine; and "Zion" in eight. Each book has from one to eight of Hastings' tunes. Mr. Hastings did not always write over his true name, and for that reason did not receive credit for all the pieces that he wrote. His "Selah" is made up largely from his own compositions, and even if we take only those that bear his name, we have ninety-nine. We also find a number attributed to "Kl——ff." This is a *nom de plume* used by him, and this is his reason: "I have found that a foreigner's name went a great way, and that very ordinary tunes would be sung if 'Palestrina' or 'Pucitto' were over them, while a better tune by Hastings would go unnoticed." *The Selah* has a tune by Zol——ffer, which is probably another of his *nom de plumes*. There are also a number under the name "Carmeni," a name which I have not been able to locate in any other book, and these may be tunes by our author.

ANECDOTES

Many interesting facts are told of the Utica musician. He and two of his brothers were complete albinos. His hair was entirely destitute of color so that he looked old while he was still young. He was absent-minded at times, and it is told of him that one evening he rode to his school and walked home, oblivious that his horse was still hitched outside. He was nearsighted, and when directing his classes his head was bowed down close to the book, and moved across the page as his eyes followed the music. In spite of this defect he was able to direct with the book either side up, and when practicing with his brothers he would sometimes stand in front of them and follow from over the back of the book.

Much of his work was done in connection with

Lowell Mason and William B. Bradbury, and these three led the prevailing school of sacred music at the beginning of the last century.

ARTHUR CLIFTON

1784–1832

WHAT became of Philip Anthony Corri, the eldest son of that Dominico Corri, who came from Italy to England in 1774, and soon thereafter established himself in a music business? The members of the Corri family were all more or less musical. The second child was Sophie, a singer and a harpist, born in 1775, who married, in 1792, a Bohemian musician, J. L. Dussek. A few years later he and his father-in-law began a partnership in a music store, which soon ended in failure, and Dussek fled to the Continent, where he had varying fortunes till his death in 1812. Montague was the next son, born in Edinburgh, who became a composer and arranger of music. Dominico, the father, left London after the failure of his music venture, and went to Edinburgh, where he was a publisher and teacher for many years. He was the conductor of the Musical Society of Edinburgh, was a fine musician and an enterprising business man, and did much to improve the musical tastes of the Scottish capital. He wrote a number of operas, made a collection of the favorite songs of Scotland, and compiled a *Musical Dictionary*.

But it is the career of the oldest son which interests us just now. The *English National Biography* tells us that Philip Anthony Corri published many songs and piano pieces, and in 1813 did much to promote the foundation of the Philharmonic Society. Shortly after this date he settled in America, and there the authentic history of him seems to lose itself.

The recently published history of the London Philharmonic Society states that the first meeting for its organization was held on Sunday, January 24, 1813, and that P. A. Corri was one of those present. He was one of the original members, and also a director for the first season. The first concert was given on Monday, March 8, 1813, and Mr. Corri took one of the parts in a vocal quartet, sung in Italian, and in the second part of the program he took part in a chorus from Mozart, also sung in Italian. As no further reference to him occurs in the history of this society, it is evident that he left England shortly afterward, and that further record of him is to be sought in the United States.

The next item is an advertisement, copied from a London paper into The Euterpiad of Boston, September 14, 1822, and reads as follows:

ADVERTISEMENT. £100 REWARD

Whereas, Philip Anthony Corri, musical composer and teacher, left this country about five years ago for New York, and his personal abode is desired to be known to the advertiser, but not for any hostile purpose, this is to give notice whoever will, within six months from this date, furnish satisfaction to Mr. Harmer, solicitor, Hatton Garden, of the present residence of the said Mr. Corri, so that an interview may be obtained with him, shall be paid a reward of £100.

N. B. It has been reported that the above-named P. A. Corri, after his arrival at New York, proceeded to Philadelphia, thence to Baltimore and there married a Quaker lady.

It has also been asserted that he is returned to England. The said P. A. Corri has a sharp, Italian visage, sallow complexion, black curly hair, black eyes, and is bald on the crown of the head. He is forty years of age, five feet eight inches high, and has a soft voice and a gentlemanly manner. London, June 17, 1822.

Arthur Clifton was an early organist of Baltimore, and little seems to be known about his life before he went to the Monumental City till the appearance of a book, *Shadows on the Wall*, in 1877. This book was written by John H. Hewitt, and dealt with people of Baltimore known to the author. Many of them were musicians. Of Arthur Clifton he writes:

Clifton's real name was Arthur Corri. He was an Englishman by birth, and the son of the celebrated Corri, of London, an Italian. The reason for his changing his name when he came to this country was of a domestic nature, and I therefore avoid giving it. He was a musician of talent: composed many songs, duets and glees, also the opera of "The Enterprise," which brought out the vocal talent of Mrs. Burke (afterward Mrs. Jefferson) on the boards of the old Holliday Street Theater. Many of his songs were very popular; they were all in the English style. He was a handsome man, but a man of care, always brooding over the miseries of life, looking on the dark side, never the bright. Nevertheless, when in company, he was full of wit and anecdote, and one of the staunchest pillars of the Anacreontic Society. He was found dead in bed, some averring that he died of a broken heart, his domestic misfortunes having been given to the public.

This seems to identify Arthur Clifton as the son of Dominico Corri, and so his history acquires an added interest for us. Following the clue of the advertisement we sought the directories of New York, but were unable to find either name therein. In the Baltimore Directory for 1814 there was an Anthony Corry, who may have been the person we are seeking, and who had a dry goods and grocery store on Union street. If this was Arthur Clifton, it was before he had made the change in his name.

Arthur Clifton was the organist of the First Presbyterian Church in Baltimore as early as 1819, when he issued a book of music under the title of *An Original Collection of Psalm Tunes* "extracted from Ancient and Modern Composers, to which are added several tunes composed especially for this work."

His services were during two pastorates, those of James Inglis and William Nevins.

The First Presbyterian Church of Baltimore was at this time the only church of that denomination on the west side of the city, though the Second Church had been organized in 1804 and located in East Baltimore. Its congregation was large, wealthy, and influential, and it had a central location on the site of the present Courthouse, which it retained until 1859, when it was removed to its present corner at Madison and Park Streets. Its minister was the Rev. James Inglis, a native of Philadelphia, who had been installed its pastor in 1802. He died so suddenly of apoplexy on Sunday morning, August 15, 1820, that while his congregation was waiting for his arrival, a messenger appeared to tell them that Doctor Inglis had passed away. He was followed as pastor by Dr. William Nevins, October 19, 1820. The membership was strong in all the elements of material and social power, but was waiting for pentecostal power. In 1827 Doctor Nevins preached a sermon which resulted in awakening a revival which spread to all

the churches of the city, and added largely to their
spirituality and numbers. Doctor Nevins died September 14, 1835, thus passing beyond the lifetime
of Arthur Clifton.

A few other facts about his music have been
gleaned as follows: At the laying of the first stone
of the Baltimore and Ohio Railroad, July 4, 1828,
"The Carrollton March by Mr. Clifton was performed." He composed a March in 1824 at the
request of the committee of arrangements for the
city of Baltimore which was used during the services of welcome to General Lafayette upon the
occasion of his visit to the United States. He also
composed the music for the Annual Coronation Ode
sung at the Academy of the Visitation in Georgetown, D. C., in 1831. This was one of his last compositions.

In the Baltimore directory for 1822 his name
appears as a professor of music at number 19
Second Street. In 1824 he is at the same address.
In 1827 he was living on Holliday Street, opposite
the theater; in 1829 and 1831 he was over 69 East
Baltimore Street. We miss his name from the 1833
book (he died in 1832), but we find one, A. Clifton,
in 1836 keeping a fancy dry-goods store at 69 Baltimore Street. There is no A. Clifton in the directory for 1838, but we do have a Mrs. A. Clifton in
the dry-goods business at 69 Baltimore Street, and
in 1841 Mrs. A. Clifton is in the same business at
61 Baltimore Street.

Arthur Clifton died February 10, 1832, and the
notice of his death is thus recorded in a Baltimore
paper: "Died suddenly on Friday night, Arthur

Clifton in the 48th year of his age." His estate was administered by Catherine Ringgold, and was probated February 29, 1832. The total amount of his estate was $639.54, and included a piano, $125, music $10 and a gold watch, $25.

A few more facts from directories may be of interest: Mrs. Ringgold appears in 1824 as the proprietor of a dry-goods store at 43 Baltimore Street. In 1827 Mrs. Ringgold had a fancy-dress store at 76 Baltimore Street, and in 1829 Mrs. C. Ringgold had her fancy dry-goods store at 69 East Baltimore Street. In 1831 there is the same entry, and it will be noted also that Arthur Clifton appears in that same year as a professor of music over 69 East Baltimore Street. In 1833 Mrs. Catherine Ringgold had a fancy store at 69 Baltimore Street, and in the next directory, which is for the year 1837-38, Mrs. Ringgold's name does not appear, but Mrs. A. Clifton has a dry-goods store at the same address.

Now we seem to have partially solved the mystery of his marriage and family life, though the record is not entirely complete. He was baptized December 31, 1817, according to the register of Saint Paul's Protestant Episcopal Church, perhaps by Bishop James Kent, who was then its rector, and the next day, January 1, 1818, he was married to Miss Alphonsa Elizabeth Ringgold, the city records state, by Minister Kent, while the newspaper reports of the event give the name of the officiating clergyman as the "Right Reverend Archbishop Marechal," who was then at the Roman Catholic Cathedral. The burial records of the Cathedral have this record: "October 9, 1829 was buried the child of Mrs. Clifton, whose age and sickness are not known." These records would seem to indicate that Mrs. Clifton was a Catholic, yet Mr. Clifton may have been an Episcopalian, though he was organist in a Presbyterian church. Catherine Ringgold, who administered his estate, was probably a sister of Mrs. Clifton, lived with them, and conducted the dry-goods store at the same address. Several further facts are necessary for a complete record, but we must be satisfied for awhile with the results of the long search, which has been so well rewarded.

SAMUEL DYER

1785–1835[1]

SAMUEL DYER, who introduced the tune "Mendon" into this country, was a native of England. His father was James Dyer (1744–1797) and his mother was Sarah Barton (1744–1833). His parents lived first at White Chapel in Hampshire, but in 1782 they removed to Wellshire, where Mr. Dyer, Sr., was ordained as preacher and ministered in the Baptist church of that place. There were eight children born to this couple, Samuel being the seventh, born November 4, 1785, after their removal to Wellshire. This date is verified by the statement of Mr. Dyer himself in one of his books when he says that in 1811 he was in his twenty-sixth year. In the summer of 1806 the family moved to Coventry. Samuel spent his childhood in his native land of England. He received some instruction in

[1] From The Choir Herald.

music from Mr. Thomas Walker, of London, beginning in 1808. Mr. Walker was an eminent singer and leader, and the most distinguished chorister in London, one hundred years ago. His voice, Mr. Dyer tells us, "was a fine counter-tenor, and of extraordinary compass and power, and his style animated and expressive."

In 1811 Mr. Dyer came to New York, where he began his musical career in the United States as a choir leader and a teacher of sacred music, being then in his twenty-sixth year. His first residence in the metropolis continued only for about one year, for in 1812 he went to Philadelphia, where a society was soon afterward formed for the practice of oratorio music, and a series of sacred concerts was given under his leadership. In July of 1815 he visited his father's home in England, and while in London had the great pleasure of meeting his former instructor, Mr. Thomas Walker, and of singing with him at the regular rehearsal of the Cecilian Society. Mr. Walker was the compiler of a collection of tunes to accompany Doctor Rippon's hymn book, first brought out about 1797. Just before Mr. Dyer's visit, that is, in 1814, he had published a selection of his own, intended as a supplement, and entitled *Walker's Companion to Rippon's Tune-book*.

SACRED MUSIC

When Mr. Dyer returned to America he brought with him a large amount of new music, to be used in his work. In November he was induced to settle in Baltimore, and he was so much encouraged by the patronage offered him that he undertook the publication of a book of tunes and anthems. This was *Dyer's New Selection of Sacred Music*, and was printed in Baltimore in 1817. This collection comprised not only a great variety of psalm and hymn tunes, but anthems, odes, and choruses from many ancient and modern composers, most of them being such as had never before been published in this country. He aimed to correct the faults he had found in previous books, and mentions among others, the following: insufficient attention to the insertion of the useful and pleasing description of church music, the alteration and mutilation of tunes, inaccuracy in engraving, indifferent paper, and the use of shaped notes. He calls attention to the clear type and letters in his book and notes that this class of music is mostly used "by candle light." For the purpose of introducing the work to more general notice he visited, in 1818, many places south of Baltimore, traveling even as far as Savannah, Georgia, and then back along the Atlantic coast as far north as Salem, Massachusetts. In numerous places he taught singing schools and conducted public performances, and was generally "successful in effecting some improvements in church music." He also had a good opportunity of forming an opinion of the class of pieces that were most likely to prove generally successful.

OTHER EDITIONS

The first edition of his hymn tunes having been sold, he left out the anthems and issued a second edition in Baltimore in 1820, a third in 1824, a fourth in 1828, and the *Philadelphia Collection of Sacred Music*, known as the sixth edition, enlarged, was printed in New York the same year, 1828. The second edition of his anthems was issued separately in Baltimore in 1822, the third in 1834, and the sixth, though copyrighted in 1835, was printed in 1851. Years afterward a reprint was issued by the Oliver Ditson Company in Boston. The second and third editions of his *Anthems* are especially valuable to the historian, as they contain biographical sketches of the composers and much data about himself. He is authority for the statement that the words to the music of Pucitta's "Strike the cymbal" were written by William Staughton. This piece is contained in *Father Kemp's Old Folks Concert Tunes*, and is a favorite for such concerts. The author of the words is not shown in any copies I have seen. But Mr. Dyer writes in the third edition of his *Anthems*:

Familiar as this piece is and extensive as its circulation has been, it is yet probable that great numbers of those who perform it are unacquainted with its origin and introduction into this country. It was originally set to Italian words, "Viva Enrico," and was received by Mr. Benjamin Carr, organist and professor of music in Philadelphia, with a variety of other music from England about 1812. On inspection Mr. Carr was confident this piece was of a character that would please; he accordingly applied to the Rev. William Staughton of that city to adapt English words to it, and brought it forward first as a grand oratorio held under his immediate direction in Saint Augustine's Church, April 13, 1814, at which I had the pleasure to be present. It was published by Mr. Carr immediately afterward and became, as was predicted, a universal favorite. The author is an eminent composer. We have no means of ascertaining the date of its composition, but think it probable that it was first brought out in Italy about 1800.

William Staughton was an Englishman by birth, and removed from Philadelphia to Washington, D. C., in 1820, to become the first president of Columbia College, now known as George Washington University.

In the preface of his secod edition of *Anthems*, Mr. Dyer says that he "proposes to publish a supplement of from twenty-five to fifty pages, to appear upon the first of October of each year, consisting of gleanings from the latest European works and the productions of living authors in the United States." One other publication, copyrighted in 1830, comprising "Choruses, solos, etc.," is often found bound in with the 1834 edition of his *Anthem* book.

Biographical

Samuel Dyer was married in 1807 at Bedford, England, to Sarah Owen, and had four children. Their second child was Samuel Owen Dyer, who was born at Norfolk, Virginia, August 4, 1819, and died in Brooklyn, New York, April 2, 1894. During the years from 1829 to 1834 he was in England studying music. After returning to the United States he lived for a while in New Orleans. In 1839 he went to New York, where he was married the next year to Emma Price, and where he entered into employment with Firth, Pond and Company. Here he learned the trade of piano-tuner, and it was this company that issued the edition of his father's *Anthems* that he edited. After this he devoted all of his time to music—teaching, tuning instruments, and playing church organs. For many years he served churches in Brooklyn in that capacity. Samuel Dyer was a member of the Musical Fund Society of Philadelphia, and in 1829 was the conductor of the New York Sacred Music Society. The name "Samuel Dyer" appears in the New York directories from 1824 to 1828 as residing at 44 Lumber Street, and his New York *Selection of Sacred Music*, the fourth edition of 1821, shows upon its title page that it will be sold by him at that address. The next directory, 1829-30, shows him as a music teacher in Brooklyn. As his name then disappears from the New York directories, it may be that he moved across the river into New Jersey, for he died at Hoboken, New Jersey, July 20, 1835.

"MENDON"

The tune "Mendon" usually attributed to Lowell Mason, first appeared in the "Supplement of Samuel Dyer's Third Edition of Sacred Music"; but there it had an extra note in each line. In his fourth edition he omitted this additional note, saying, "It is believed that the present arrangement is the original form." He called it a "German Air." Later when it was introduced into other hymn books, the melody of the last line was altered, and it became the tune as it is now known in most of the present-day collections. It is supposed that this change was made by Lowell Mason, and that he gave it the name of "Mendon." Most of the recent hymnals give the credit for its introduction into this country where it properly belongs, to Samuel Dyer.

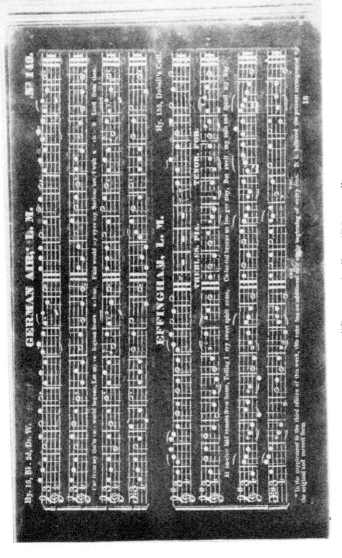

"GERMAN AIR" or "MENDON"

Sacred Music, fourth edition, 1828. By Samuel Dyer. Library of Congress

LOWELL MASON

1792–1872[1]

LOWELL MASON was eight years younger than Thomas Hastings, and both died within a few months of each other in 1872. The first named was born in Medfield, Massachusetts, January 8, 1792, and was the son of Johnson Mason and Catherine Hartshorn. His aptitude for music showed itself at an early age and he became the leader of the choir in his native town. The weaving of straw and its manufacture into hats had been introduced about 1800, and young Mason started in on this work with his father; but when he had reached his majority he set out with two other young men for Savannah, Georgia, traveling by post chaise, and the expense of this trip has been recorded as ninety-seven dollars. For the next fourteen years Savannah was his home, his business that of a clerk in a bank, while incidentally he was leading church choirs and making a collection of music. For seven years he was organist in the Independent Presbyterian Church, and just before he left the city he was one of the four who asked dismission for the purpose of forming the First Presbyterian Church of Savannah.

HANDEL AND HAYDN COLLECTION OF SACRED MUSIC

It is interesting to note the extreme modesty with which his first collection of music was placed before the public. While in Savannah he had compiled from various sources a large manuscript, and return-

---

[1] From The Choir Herald.

ing North had offered it in Philadelphia and Boston, but without finding a publisher. He was about to start back to Georgia when he was introduced to the Handel and Haydn Society, and his music was submitted to Dr. George K. Jackson, the organist of the society, and having been approved by him an agreement was entered into by which the book was to be issued as the work of that body. The name of Lowell Mason was omitted at his request, for, he says, "I was then a bank officer in Savannah and did not wish to be known as a musical man, and I had not the least thought of making music my profession."

It is rather amusing to see the studied effort to make it appear that the book was the product of the Society, and in later editions we read, "In the selection of the music and the arrangement of the harmony the Society are happy to acknowledge their obligations to Mr. Lowell Mason, one of their members," etc. This book became very popular, running through seventeen editions beginning with 1822; and during the thirty-five years following over 50,000 copies of the various editions were sold. This was a profitable investment for the Handel and Haydn Society, as well as for the compiler, for first and last it brought to each over $30,000. Doctor Mason was a prolific writer of books, and an enumeration of those that were issued from his pen would more than fill the space allotted to this article. *The Choir*, 1833, sold more than 50,000; *The Modern Psalmist*, 1839, as many; *Carmina Sacra*, 1841, and the *New Carmina Sacra*, 1852, more than 500,000, while in its revised form as *The American Tune*

Book, the circulation of the three books reached more than a million.

When the Handel and Haydn Collection was issued in 1822 Mason was thirty years old, and returning to Savannah he remained there for five years longer, when he received an offer from Boston to go there and lead the music in three churches, six months in each in succession, for which he was guaranteed an income of $2,000 a year. This contract he did not carry out, and on being released returned to banking for a short time, serving also as organist in the Bowdoin Street Church. But music was to be his life work, and he needed all his time to devote to his plans. One of his objects was to secure the teaching of music in the public schools as a regular study. This he accomplished only after a long period of labor culminating in 1838.

Boston Academy of Music

When Mason went to Boston he became a member of the Handel and Haydn Society, was elected its president in 1827 and served in that capacity for five years. In 1829 W. C. Woodbridge, well known by his series of school Geographies, returned from Europe, where he had been to study the methods of instruction used by Pestalozzi, and Mr. Mason, slow in being impressed with the advantages of this method, but seeing the results attained, adopted it in his musical work. For the purpose of promoting his plans for the introduction of music into the public schools he withdrew from active work in the society that had fathered his first book and that was wedded to oratorio and organized the Boston Academy of

Music in 1832. He associated with himself in this work George J. Webb, and together they began to instruct children in music. Their first classes were held in one of the rooms of the Bowdoin Street Church, where he was organist, and the children were taught free, the only condition being that they would promise to attend for the entire year. By persevering with the school officials he was at length allowed to teach one class as an experiment, and at no expense to the city. Thus he carried his point, and in 1838 music was adopted as one of the regular school studies. The chief objection had been that this study would no doubt divert the minds of the pupils, so they would not make the desired progress in their other work. The result was that music really added to the zest with which their other work was done.

CONVENTIONS

One of the most important means for teaching music to the people was the Musical Convention, introduced by Lowell Mason in 1834. These conventions were meetings, which usually held for ten or twelve days, and were attended by those who wanted to learn to sing by note; and on returning home many of them became teachers. At first these conventions were held in or near Boston, but when their good effects were realized, demands were made for them at other places, both west and south, and good music was brought to the attention of the mass of the people.

Mason continued to reside in Boston until 1851, when he removed to New York, making his home with his sons, Daniel and Lowell, Jr., who had established a music business in that city. The degree of Doctor of Music was conferred upon him in 1855 by the University of New York, the first instance of the granting of such a degree in this country. His later years were spent in Orange, New Jersey, where he died August 11, 1872, at the age of eighty years.

LIBRARY

Doctor Mason's library was one of the largest and most valuable of the kind in America. A considerable addition was made to it in 1852 when he purchased that of C. H. Rinck, who had died six years before. This library included 830 manuscripts and 700 volumes on hymnology, and among its rarities were volumes printed in Venice in 1589, Heidelberg in 1596, and a French book of songs in Paris, 1755. When he learned that the books of Professor Dehn, a famous teacher in Berlin, and a former librarian of the Musical Library of that city, were to be sold, he sent an agent to secure them for his collection. It is said that he was unable to read one of the books that were thus acquired, but he wanted them to add value to his growing collection. After his death his family presented this library to Yale College, where it is kept as a special collection.

OPPOSITION

It is not surprising that a man with such pronounced as well as advanced ideas in music as Lowell Mason should have met opposing minds. In fact, it is only the man who moves along with the current that finds his progress easy.

The following is taken from a reply by L. O. Emerson in 1916 to an attack which had been made years before by John S. Dwight in his Journal of Music upon the methods of teaching that subject by Lowell Mason, I. B. Woodbury, and Mr. Emerson himself, to which his attention had then been called. He says:

So it was Dwight's Journal of Music that said Lowell Mason and other psalm-tune writers were degrading and cheapening music? Well, we could not have expected anything better than that from that source, for Mr. Dwight was not in sympathy with the good work we were doing.

In reality we were doing more to help his cause than he himself was doing.

His Journal was a good one, the best published at that time. It stood for the highest and best music of all kinds. It did not have a large circulation. It did not go abroad among the masses of the people.

He could talk about the musical giants of the past and of his own time, if there were any, criticize the performances of their music, the soloists, etc., which was all very well.

While he was doing this we were carrying the best choral music of the various kinds, from church music to the oratorio and opera, and also the best soloists obtainable, to thousands and thousands of musically hungry singers and people all over the country, teaching them how to render it and giving them opportunities to hear the best solo singers of the country.

If this kind of work was degrading and cheapening music, then revive the convention and musical festival and let the good work go on, for it is still needed.

If the thousands of singers who attended the festivals, and the greater number of thousands who attended the concerts, could speak with one voice, they would send up a shout in their favor that would be heard across the continent.

When Lowell Mason organized the musical convention in Boston and carried it from thence into the country, he set in motion an influence that for forty years or more did more to make this nation a musical one than any one thing else has done.

First printing of Lowell Mason's OLIVET from *Sacred Songs*,
1832.　In the author's collection

In 1846 W. H. Day, editor of the American Journal of Music in Boston, and the promoter of a numerical notation, which he had used in a recent book, denounced Doctor Mason for his methods of teaching, and his use of the round-note notation, and spoke sneeringly of his Academy of Music. Even Theodore Seward, who wrote a pamphlet on *The Educational Work of Dr. Mason*, records the fact that he did not always agree with the plans and methods of the doctor. It is therefore pleasing to note in this connection that Mrs. Mason wrote upon her visiting card, and inclosed it in the copy of Mr. Seward's essay now in the Library of Congress, "The accompanying pamphlet gives the best representation of my husband's work, and the only one of any value to the world."

Tunes

Doctor Mason's compositions are still very much used in the hymnals. Ten of the different books now used by as many different denominations and not more than twenty years old have from eleven to sixty; six tunes are in each of the ten books. Of these six "Missionary Hymn" is said to have been the first of his published tunes, having been issued in sheet form in Boston, before it was included in the ninth edition of the Handel and Haydn Collection in 1829. It is there used with Heber's hymn, "From Greenland's Icy Mountains," and because hymn and tune are usually found together, the tune is called in some books "Heber." "Hamburg" was in the Handel and Haydn Collection of 1824. "Olivet," with Ray Palmer's hymn, first appeared in print in Hastings and Mason's *Spiritual Songs*, 1832. "Boylston" was printed the same year in the Choir. "Bethany" appeared in 1858 in *The Sabbath Hymn and Tune Book*. "Hebron" dates from 1830. "Olmutz," found in nine of the ten books examined, was arranged in 1834 from the eighth Gregorian Tone. Three were found in eight of the books—"Laban," "Uxbridge," and "Ward." Had books bearing dates nearer the lifetime of Mason been examined, the proportion of his tunes would have been much larger. But it will be a long time before all of his work has passed out of common use.

THE REV. JONATHAN MAYHEW
WAINWRIGHT

1792–1854

JONATHAN M. WAINWRIGHT was born in Liverpool, England, September 21, 1792. His parents were American citizens and were on a business sojourn there at the time of his birth, and two of their other children were of English birth. The family returned to this country when Jonathan was eleven years old, and he entered Harvard college, from which he was graduated in the class of 1812. He was a tutor at his Alma Mater from 1815 to 1817, and part of the time while at college he served as organist in Christ Church, Boston. Having fitted himself for the ministry in the Protestant Episcopal Church, he was made a deacon in 1816, and two years later became rector of Christ Church in Hartford, Con-

necticut. While in that city he was also a member
of a literary club, associated with Peter Parley and
William L. Stone. His service to his church may
be briefly stated as follows: From 1819 to 1821
he was an assistant at Trinity Church in New York;
from 1821 to 1834, rector of Grace Episcopal
Church, New York. In 1834 he was at Trinity
Church in Boston; from 1837 to 1854, rector of
Saint John's Chapel in New York; and from 1852
to 1854 was provisional bishop of New York. He
died September 21, 1854, and his funeral was conducted from Trinity Church in New York.

His musical talent was displayed from early boyhood. In college he served as organist; he presided
over the meeting at which the Harvard Musical
Association was organized. In 1819 there appeared
as his compilation "A set of chants adapted to the
Hymns in the Morning and Evening Prayer, and to
the communion service of the Protestant Episcopal
Church."

Music of the Church was copyrighted in 1828, and
was an oblong book having two sets of double brace
music at the top, and several hymns at the bottom
of each page below the music. In 1852 a new edition under the same title appeared, the page made
narrower by the omission of the hymns at the bottom, and printed from entirely new plates. Many
tunes occurring in the former edition were omitted,
either from the inferior character of the music or
because they were to be found in the majority of
books of psalmody; and many new tunes were added.
In the first edition there were two compositions with
his initials attached, and the plates used in this

book were used also for the second part of *Psalm-odia Evangelica*, "a collection of Psalm and Hymn Tunes by the author of the Music of the Church, printed in New York by Elam Bliss in 1830."

CHARLES ZEUNER[1]

1795–1857

THE town of Eisleben, near Gotha, in Saxony, where Martin Luther was born in 1483, claims also to have been the birthplace three hundred years later of Charles Zeuner, the distinguished organist and composer, September 20, 1795. He was baptized Heinrich Christopher Zeuner. We are quoting from the Musical Cyclopedia of John W. Moore when we write that we have no means of knowing why, on coming to this country, he took the name of Charles. But such was the fact. He came about 1824, and settled in Boston, Massachusetts. After a residence of thirty years in that city, during which he composed most of his music and assisted in editing several music books, he removed to Philadelphia, where he served as organist first of Saint Anne's Episcopal Church, and afterward of the Arch Street Presbyterian Church. For several years before his death his friends had noticed a peculiarity in his demeanor, indicating at times a certain aberration of mind. On Saturday, November 7, 1857, he left his boarding house and was seen to cross the Delaware by steamboat ; and walk into the woods. Not long after this

---

[1] From The Choir Herald.

the body of a man was found with the head entirely
shattered with a gun, and the body was proven to
be that of Mr. Zeuner.   An examination showed
plainly that he had taken his own life.

Before leaving his native land he had been a court
musician, and after he had become established in
Boston he was considered one of the best educated
musicians and organists in the country.   For several
years he led an active life in the musical circle of
the Hub, and when he was to remove to Philadelphia
in 1840 one of the magazines wrote of him:

He has contributed materially toward elevating our style
of church music by his publications, and yet at the present
time his loss is comparatively little felt.   He has lately kept
much retired: he has hidden his talent and wasted it on trifles.
We hope that his new career will excite him to new exertions
and will again place him in that station in regard to the art
which he is qualified and ought to fill.

But it did not.   Few if any new compositions were
written and no new books edited.

In Boston he had been president of the Handel
and Haydn Society, 1838–39, during a period when
it was expected that the president would also be the
director of the society's chorus.   But his temper was
such that he could not keep harmony among the
singers, and he resigned when requested to do so.
It is said that when he did not know there was any
critic in his audience he would often play very indif-
ferently, although he was well able to perform in a
masterly manner.   One morning while he was organist in Philadelphia his fancy led him to improvise
an exquisite fugue which astonished the few appre-
ciative members of his audience, but others were

shocked at the wonderful performance that they could not comprehend. One of the latter, meeting him in the vestibule after the service, said to him: "Mr. Zeuner, pray is our organ out of order? There was such an unaccountable jolting and rumbling in the pedals this morning that altogether it sounded very strange indeed." This lamentable display of musical ignorance entirely overcame the testy and sensitive harmonist, and with a contemptuous hiss between his teeth he strode from his interrogator and never went near that stately church again either professionally or otherwise.

THE AMERICAN HARP

The year 1832 seems to have marked the climax of Mr. Zeuner's musical work. In that year his *American Harp* appeared, and so successful was it that a second edition was issued before the close of the same year. The second edition was merely a second printing, the contents being the same save the arrangement of some of the pages, and the addition of a preface, explaining why this collection was so different from those usually put forth. Up to this time the usual collection was made up largely of tunes from the older composers, and a few only that were new or original. *The American Harp* was an entirely new composition of Mr. Zeuner, with the exception of five tunes, one of which was "Old Hundred." He deprecates the adaptation of music from secular or operatic sources. "Church music," he says, "ought to be the most perfect in character and style, and ought always to be free from unhallowed associations; and its dignity and solemnity ought to be constantly guarded and as far as possible religiously preserved from all derogatory influences and corrupt and debasing tendencies." His two tunes that are now most commonly used, "Hummel" and "Missionary Chant," are in this book. During this same year of 1832 he composed three pieces for Lowell Mason's *Lyra Sacra,* and also some piees for N. D. Gould's *National Church Harmony.* Many of his compositions were used in *The Psaltery,* 1845, by Mason and Webb. These two musicians were members of the Boston Academy of Music, and the choir of that organization had presented Zeuner's oratorio, "The Feast of Tabernacles."

A writer in 1873 says that this oratorio was probably destroyed—a belief which arose from the following incident: The manuscript was first offered to the Handel and Haydn Society; the price set on it was three thousand dollars, but the Society declined to purchase. It was presented, however, at the Odeon by the Boston Academy for eight evenings, but the result was a financial failure. Incensed at this, Zeuner stole into the Academy, tore up and burned all the manuscript and printed score that he could find. One copy at least escaped destruction, and is in the Library of Congress. Its date is 1837.

The Ancient Lyre

His second book, *The Ancient Lyre,* was issued under the approbation of the Professional Music Society of Boston, and was different from *The American Harp,* in that it contained both old and new music. It was copyrighted in 1836, became very popular, and passed through at least twenty editions. A copy of the 16th, printed in 1848, is in the library of the American Antiquarian Society in Worcester, Massachusetts. A book of anthems was issued in 1831 and considerable secular music came from his fertile mind at short intervals—marches, songs, a quickstep, etc.

PSALM TUNES

Out of the large number of psalm tunes that were composed by Charles Zeuner only two are still in common use. "Missionary Chant" is by far the most popular, and is to be found in nearly all of the larger books in use at present in the churches. Lowell Mason once asked him why it was so popular. He said, "I was sitting on one of these seats on Boston Common on a most beautiful moonlight evening, all alone, with all the world moving about me, and suddenly 'Missionary Chant' was given me. I ran home as fast as ever I could and put it on paper before I should forget. That is what makes it please." His tune "Hummel" is almost as frequently used. In this name he records his esteem for the teacher of his early years.

Zeuner was never married, and was without relatives in this country. He is described as a plump, good-looking man with a florid, bright face, and of a quick nervous temperament. His compositions are well written and based on real original merit. In religion he was a Lutheran, and his chief object in all his compositions was to establish a chaste and pure style in church music.

SIMEON BUTLER MARSH[1]

1798–1875

ONE of the first pieces of sacred music that the amateur tries to learn is "Martyn." The reason for this is its simplicity and its slow movement; and it is also probably that the words, which are usually those of Wesley, beginning, "Jesus, Lover of my soul," attract by their noble sentiment and their appeal to rest from the troubles that assail us all at one time or another. The tune was written by Simeon Butler Marsh, and one is surprised to learn that there is no other music of his in common use, though he wrote many other pieces. He loved music from the time when, as a boy of seven, he joined a children's choir; and he wrote other music which was sung more or less in his day. But "Martyn" alone has survived in the hymnals of the present time. This tune and the words of Wesley are now so firmly wedded that the one suggests the other, and in recent hymnals it is seldom that the tune appears without these words. The tune was written in 1834, but where it first appeared in print I have been unable to determine. In the Plymouth Collection, compiled by Henry Ward Beecher in 1855, we find Martyn with words of John Newton, "Mary to the Saviour's Tomb"; the hymn by Robert Grant, beginning, "Saviour, when in dust to thee," is set to this tune in a book printed in 1859. But during the last fifty years the joint product of Marsh and Wesley has appeared together in every hymnal.

[1] From The Choir Herald.

The parents of our author had five children, four of whom were born in Weathersfield, Connecticut. In 1797 the family removed to Sherburne, New York, and here Simeon was born on the first of June, 1798. His father was Eli, and his mother Azubah Butler. He was reared upon a farm, and before he was eight years old he began to sing in a children's choir in Sherburne. When he was sixteen years of age he secured a music teacher, and in 1817 began to teach the singing school, which at that period was so popular throughout the entire country. The following year he met Dr. Thomas Hastings in his school in Geneva, and from him received much help and encouragement. For the next thirty years he labored with congregations within the Albany Presbytery, teaching choirs, and leading singing schools with great success. In 1837 he undertook another line of work, starting a newspaper at Amsterdam, New York, which he called The Intelligencer, and which later became The Recorder. This paper he conducted for seven years, and later established the Sherburne News in his home town.

Not all of his work was for remuneration. For thirteen years he gave free instruction to the children of Schenectady in his own hired room. He made use of his knowledge of the printer's art by setting the type with his own hand and preparing for the press the forms of three juvenile books. In 1859 he returned to Sherburne, where he taught voice, piano, and violin to large classes of men, women, and children. He was the superintendent of the Sunday school in Sherburne for six years and for half that time the leader of the choir. Among his compositions were two cantatas, "The Saviour," for mixed voices, and "The King of the Forest," arranged mostly for boys' voices.

On his twenty-second birthday, June 1, 1820, he married Eliza Carrier, of Hamilton, New York. Two children were born to them, one of whom, John Butler Marsh, was for a number of years professor of vocal culture and organ instruction in the Elmira Female College, New York. Mr. Marsh celebrated his golden wedding in 1870. His wife died in 1873, after which he removed to Albany to live with his son, and died there July 14, 1875.

SAMUEL LYTLER METCALF

1798–1856

THE payment of one's college expenses from the proceeds of the publication of a music book is of such rare occurrence that it is worthy of note. This happened in the case of Samuel Lytler Metcalf, a native of Virginia, who was born near Winchester, September 21, 1798. While he was yet young his parents moved to Shelby County, Kentucky, and he began his education in Shelbyville. His aptitude for music led him to take up the teaching of music. He gave lessons once a week, and when only nineteen years old he wrote a volume of sacred music, which was published in Cincinnati at his own risk, and which gave him sufficient funds with which to enter college.

This book was *The Kentucky Harmonist*, and was a "choice selection of sacred music from the most eminent and approved authors of that science, for the use of Christian Churches of every denomination, Singing Schools and Private Societies, together with an explanation of the rules and principles of composition and rules for learners." It was copyrighted in 1817, and printed in Cincinnati for the author. A second edition was called for and was dated at Lexington in 1819, while a fourth edition, to which he adds the letters of his degree M. D., was printed in 1826.

Just as he was entering upon manhood, in 1819, he began his studies in Transylvania University, a school in Lexington, Kentucky, which had been founded during the year of his birth, 1798, and which was absorbed in 1865 by the Kentucky State University. Here he continued for the regular course of four years, and from this university he received his degree of Doctor of Medicine. He began the practice of a physician in New Albany, Indiana, later removed to Mississippi, where he met a lady who became his wife, but who died four years later. For many years he was a professor of chemistry in Transylvania University, his Alma Mater. He was a close student of a number of subjects, and possessed a well-chosen library, which was at one time unfortunately destroyed by fire. The results of his studies he put into permanent form in a history of the *Indian Wars in the West*, a volume of *Terrestrial Magnetism*, and two volumes on the subject of *Calorie*, the latter of which was first issued in 1845, and this was followed by a second edition in 1853. This book was well received abroad, and Doctor Metcalf was solicited to become a candidate for the Gregorian chair in the University of Edinburgh, but this honor he declined. He had studied his favorite science in London, and in 1846 was married a second time to an English lady in that city. Doctor Metcalf died at Cape May in July, 1856, leaving, besides his widow, a daughter eight years old.

THOMAS LOUD

THOMAS LOUD was one of the musical group in Philadelphia, and was probably a native American. He is found in that city as early as 1812, where he finished musical training under George Pfeffer. He became so efficient that the rivalry between him and his teacher was settled by a public performance in favor of the pupil. His ability made him popular as an organist and a conductor of choruses. He was one of the directors of the Musical Fund Society of his home city. In 1824, when he was organist of Saint Andrew's Church, he published *The Psalmist*, "a Collection of Psalm and Hymn Tunes arranged for the organ or pianoforte." This was a book of sixty-four pages, contained some of his own music, and was written and engraved by Joseph Perkins. Another book of his was printed in New York in 1853 and was called *The Organ Study*, "being an introduction to the practice of the organ together with a collection of voluntaries, preludes, original and selected, and a model of a church service." This was also a small book, having only seventy-five pages. The date of Mr. Loud's death has not been discovered.

HENRY KEMBLE OLIVER

1800–1885

"FEDERAL STREET," the best known of the tunes of Henry K. Oliver, was one of his first compositions. In a collection of his original hymn tunes, made in 1875, which gives the dates of the various compositions, 1832 is assigned to "Federal Street." One other tune is credited to this same year, but none earlier. Its name comes from the street on which he lived in Salem, Massachusetts. It is said that he first thought of naming it for his wife, whose name was Sally Cook, but finally decided upon the street which ran past his door. The origin of the tune is thus described by S. J. Barrows: "One afternoon he was sitting in his library reading Theodore Hook's novel, *Passion and Principle*, an affecting story, terminating with the saddest results. Laying down the volume, and walking around the room, thinking of what he had read, Miss Steele's hymn came into his mind, beginning "So fades the lovely blooming flower," and the last verse,

> "Then gentle Patience smiles on Pain.
> And dying Hope revives again;
> Hope wipes the tear from Sorrow's eye.
> And Faith points upward to the sky."

An unbidden melody floated into his mind. He was not attempting composition, but without effort the words somehow melted into music. He sat down to the piano and played the tune, adding the harmonies; he then put it upon paper and threw it into a drawer, where it remained two years. When

Lowell Mason was teaching in Salem, he asked if anyone had attempted musical composition. Oliver produced this piece, and Mason was so well pleased with it that he asked permission to publish it in *The Boston Academy Collection* of church music which he was then preparing. This book issued in 1836 and "Federal Street" appears in it set to the words of the last stanza, but changed in the first word to "See gentle Patience smiles on Pain."

No other words than the first stanza quoted are given in the composer's collection of original tunes, nor in his *Collection of Church Music* issued in 1860. This setting does not appear in any recent books. In fact, this tune is not wedded to any particular hymn. In nine of the thirty books examined it is set to the hymn of Joseph Grigg, beginning, "Jesus, and shall it ever be."

During almost all of the long life of Henry K. Oliver's eighty-five years, music held him captive. "He was familiar," he tells us, "with music from his mother's knee, and sang with her the old melodies of Billings, Holden, and other early American writers. The divine art had become to him as the years increased more alluring, more loved, and more venerated." He was born November 24, 1800, in Beverly, Massachusetts, the son of Samuel Oliver and Elizabeth Kemble. His education was thorough and his public life active. From the Boston Latin School he went to Phillips Andover, then two years to Harvard College, entering Dartmouth College in the middle of his course, and at the age of sixteen graduating in 1818. Harvard honored him in 1862 by granting him his degree of A. B. and also A. M.

and placed his name among the graduates in the class of 1818. In 1883 Dartmouth granted him the degree of Mus.D. He entered the choir of the Park Street Church in Boston at the age of ten years. He was a church organist for thirty-six years and a school teacher for twenty-four. He married, August 30, 1825, Sarah Cook, of Salem. A rapid survey of his labors from 1844 shows him Adjutant-General of the State of Massachusetts for four years, superintendent of the Atlantic Cotton Mills in Lawrence for ten years, mayor of that city for one year, treasurer of his native State during the period of the war, and the first chief of its Bureau of Labor for ten years. After four years as mayor of his home town of Salem he retired to his home on Federal Street, where he died August 12, 1885. This old house has been famous in Salem history. On the parlor walls there is so-called landscape paper representing scenes in Paris. There was an old-fashioned tall clock on the stairway, and when I visited his daughter some years ago I found upon the wall in the hallway a picture of the old gentleman as he was winding the clock. The door is in the colonial style, and has been made the subject of a souvenir postal.

He was the boy soprano in Boston when the only instrument was a bass viol. Later the bassoon and the flute were introduced, and before many years, but not until after much discussion and opposition, the organ had become the accepted accompaniment to the hymn tunes and anthems. As early as 1826 he organized and managed the Old Mozart Association in Salem; for the twenty years from 1832 he was connected with the Salem Glee Club. His *Collection of Original Hymn Tunes* is dedicated to the Salem Oratorical Society, which he refers to as an association of amateurs which has successfully rendered the most difficult and the best work of the great authors within the brief period of a half dozen years, and has attained a conspicuous rank among the most eminent of kindred associations. In this work he had no small part. The ease with which he composed tunes is illustrated by "Merton," which was done in church during the time of the sermon. Not finding any tune that suited him for the hymn to be used at the close of the service, he wrote out the four parts of this tune, gave them to the members of his choir, and they rendered it so acceptably that the pastor inquired where the organist had obtained the new tune. When he confessed that he had made the tune during the service, the minister rebuked him, but forgave him when reminded that he was known to make notes on the margins of his sermons of thoughts that came to him, which could be developed later. For many years "Merton" was one of his most popular hymn tunes.

PART IV

1801–1863

JOHN HENRY NEWMAN

1801–1890[1]

One of the most difficult to sing of the hymns to be found in many of the recent collections of church music is Newman's "Lead, Kindly Light." First, the irregularity of the verse. By this I do not mean that the rhythm is irregular, for if the sense of the words be disregarded, it will be found that the words flow along smoothly, but I mean that the sentences are irregular, running over from line to line, with stops in the middle of some lines, whereas, in most hymns each line is a sentence or a clause by itself. A second reason is that the music too is irregular. The short notes come in unusual places, and the time must often be changed to suit the words in the various stanzas. The chief reason, however, I think, is the fact that few singers know what the writer meant to express, and as they do not understand what the idea really is, they cannot reproduce it in song. One of the early compilers of tune books says, "Sentiment and expression ought to be the principal guide in vocal music." But the expression cannot be correct unless the singer feels the sentiment of the words that are sung.

In order, therefore, to understand this hymn, we must stop awhile and recall the facts of Cardinal Newman's life, and try to realize to some extent his feelings when the words of this hymn came from

[1] From The Choir Herald.

his heart. John Henry Newman was born in London, February 21, 1801. Both his parents were religious. His mother was Huguenot. His father, a banker, died when John was quite young. Of himself he says: "I was brought up from a child to take great delight in reading the Bible, but I had no formal religious convictions till I was fifteen." We may hastily follow his education by noting a few dates. He was graduated from Trinity College, Oxford, in 1820, became a Fellow in Oriel College in 1822, and a tutor in 1826. He had been ordained a deacon in the Church of England in 1824, and the following year was ordained a priest. In 1828 he became vicar of Saint Mary's, the university church, a position which he retained until 1843, just a short time before he joined the Church of Rome. His theological studies and discussion had inclined him toward the Roman Catholic Church, and he was received into that communion in 1845. From 1848 to 1884 he was the Father Superior of the Oratory of Saint Philip Neri at Birmingham, and for the next four years he was the rector of the Catholic University in Dublin. In 1879 he was made a cardinal, and he died August 11, 1890, at Birmingham, England.

The Tractarian Movement

Beginning about 1830 there was a strong movement which arose within the Church of England, tending to clear up some of the obscure points of difference between that church and the Church of Rome. In 1828 Newman had met John Keble, that quiet and zealous advocate of the doctrines of the

Established Church, who refused an influential and remunerative position in the West Indies, preferring rather "a better and holier satisfaction in pastoral work in the country." They became firm friends, though the future cardinal always held the quieter man in awe, and when their ways diverged in 1845, it was a source of deep regret to Keble. On July 14, 1833, Keble had preached a sermon in the university pulpit under the title of "National Apostasy," and this date has often been referred to as the beginning of the so-called Tractarian Movement, for this sermon brought about a series of ninety tracts in which the disputed doctrines were discussed.

THE HYMN

Keeping in mind the fact that his religious convictions were not firmly established until his entrance into the Catholic Church in 1845, we may now go back to the year 1832, when he was vicar of Saint Mary's, and when on account of failing health he was obliged to seek rest and change of scene in a trip to Italy. Regaining health and strength, he was anxious to return to England, where he felt that he had a mission. He says: "I was aching to get home, yet for want of a vessel, I was kept at Palermo for three weeks. At last I got off on an orange boat, bound for Marseilles. Then it was that I wrote the lines, 'Lead, Kindly Light,' which have since become well known. We were becalmed a whole week in the Straits of Bonifacio. I was writing verses the whole time of my passage." In another place he gives the date of its composition as June

16, 1833. In the above quotation, taken from New-man's "Apologia pro Vita Sua," it is noted that the word "light" is not spelled with a capital letter. This hymn was first published in the British Magazine, and then in his *Lyra Apostolica* in 1836. With these facts in mind, let us read over the words with no reference to the lines of poetry, but with a desire to get the meaning from "between the lines."

> "Lead, kindly light,
> Amid the encircling gloom, lead thou me on;
> The night is dark, and I am far from home,
> Lead thou me on.
> Keep thou my feet.
> I do not ask to see the distant scene:
> One step enough for me.

> "I was not ever thus,
> Nor prayed that thou should'st lead me on;
> I loved to choose and see my path;
> But now, lead thou me on.
> I loved the garish day; [bright or splendid day]
> And spite of fears, pride ruled my will:
> Remember not past years.

> "So long thy power has blessed me,
> Sure it still will lead me on o'er moor and fen,
> O'er crag and torrent, till the night is gone,
> And with the morn, those angel faces smile
> Which I have loved long since and lost awhile."

His writings are in faultless English style and show a devout and saintly spirit. The hymn just quoted is written in the simplest Anglo Saxon words. Some one has called attention to the fact that at least thirty consecutive words of one syllable may be found in the first stanza, and it is most interesting to note that of the one hundred and thirty words in the three stanzas, only sixteen are pro-

nounced as of more than a single syllable.   Mr.
Newman himself, with becoming modesty, attributed
much of the popularity of his hymn to the music
which was written for it by Joseph B. Dykes, but as
the tune to which a hymn has become wedded always
suggests the words which are usually sung to its
notes, it is certain that it is the hymn itself that
attracts the soul of the listener.

Several years ago the following appeared in a
weekly paper:

Andrew Carnegie has engaged one of the most prominent
organists in the city [New York] to awaken him on the organ
with the strains of "Lead, Kindly Light." If it is true that
our first thoughts in the morning have much to do with our
conduct during the day, surely Mr. Carnegie has chosen a
most heavenly way of beginning the day.

GEORGE JAMES WEBB[1]

1803–1887

A CAREFUL study of the names of the tunes given
by George J. Webb to his compositions in the *Massachusetts Collection of Psalmody*, 1840, would
make one familiar with many of the people and
places mentioned in the Bible, for fifty-four of the
ninety-nine are from that source.   Some of those
commonly   known   are   "Abednego,"   "Drusilla,"
"Jubal," and "Naomi."   Another series might be
made of the mental and moral qualities, such as
"peace, joy, adoration and sincerity."   Still another
group suggests geography, as "Genoa," "Piedmont,"
"Thebes," "Corea" and "Amazon."   He was a pro-

[1] From The Choir Herald.

lific composer, contributing nearly one hundred
pieces to this one book alone, which he edited.

His long life embraced the period covered by
George Kingsley, George N. Allen, W. B. Bradbury, and John Zundel, and included the active
musical careers of Lowell Mason, George F. Root,
Benjamin F. Baker, and Thomas Hastings. He was
born June 24, 1803, at Rushmore Lodge, Wiltshire,
near Salisbury, England. His father was a large
landowner, and though possessing little technical
musical knowledge, he was a good singer, and
wanted his children to have instruction in that
branch. His mother was a cultured musician, and
began the training of her son before he was seven
years old. His first experience at a boarding school
was at Salisbury, where he came under the instruction of Alexander Lucas, father of the Charles
Lucas who was at one time principal of the Royal
Academy of Music in London. Here he learned to
play the piano and violin, without any idea of making more out of his music than his own pleasure.
At sixteen he had gone back to his father's house,
but it was evident that farming was not to be his
life-work. He had felt a drawing toward the ministry, but realized that more education was necessary for that calling than he felt that he could
afford the time to secure. When his father asked
him what he would choose for his vocation he replied
that he would be a professor of music. To fit himself for that work he went to Falmouth, and placed
himself under the instruction of a teacher named
Sharp, who was also an organist there, and in a
short time he was able to take the place of his

teacher at the organ. About this time some visitors
at his home told of the opportunities that were
offered in America, and he decided to try his fortunes in the New World. He had engaged passage
to New York when he fell in with the captain of a
boat running to Boston, and was prevailed upon to
change his plans and sail to the latter city. It was
only a few weeks after his arrival in America that
he was engaged as organist in the Old South Church,
and for the next forty years Boston was his home,
and many of the churches of that city enjoyed his
services as a performer. The change of destination
proved fortunate for him, as he soon met Lowell
Mason, and for the rest of their lives they were
associated in musical work. The bonds that bound
them were later strengthened by the marriage of
Mr. Webb's daughter, Mary, and Dr. Mason's son,
William.

Lowell Mason had begun his plans for the instruction of children in music, and he found Mr. Webb
a valuable helper in this work. The Boston Academy
of Music was organized with this end in view, and
its classes were first held in rooms of the Bowdoin
Street Church, where Mr. Mason was the leader of
the church music. Later an unused theater was
leased and called "The Odeon." A series of Normal
Musical Conventions for teachers was begun in 1836.
The attendance at the first one was only fourteen,
but in 1849 there were one thousand present. In
1871 he moved to Orange, New Jersey, whither
Lowell Mason had preceded him, and gave vocal
lessons in New York city, while during the summers he held a "Normal" at Binghamton, New York.

Mr. Mason died in Orange in 1872, and the younger musician died there October 7, 1887.

Mr. Root, who was associated with him in normal work, says of him, "He was the best vocal teacher in Boston, and the most refined and delightful teacher of the English glee and madrigal that I have ever known, an elegant organist, an accomplished musician and a model Christian gentleman."

BOOKS

His compilations of music include *Scripture Worship*, 1834; *The Massachusetts Collection of Psalmody*, 1840; and *The American Glee Book*, 1841. His work with Lowell Mason comprised both secular and sacred music, the more important books in the latter class being *The Psaltery*, 1845; *The National Psalmist*, 1848; and *Cantica Laudis*, 1850. During this period the two men were professors in the Boston Academy of Music. Mr. Webb edited two different journals—The Musical Cabinet with T. B. Hayward in 1841, and The Melodist with William Mason. When he issued *The Massachusetts Collection* in 1840 he was president of the Handel and Haydn Society in Boston.

TUNES

Out of the large number of tunes that George J. Webb composed, only one has survived the period of his lifetime, and is found in recent hymnals. This is known by his name "Webb." It was originally written to the secular words, " 'Tis dawn, the lark is singing." As a church tune it was set to the words, "The morning light is breaking," and given the name "Goodwin." I have not traced it to its earliest appearance, but it is found in *Cantica Laudis*, compiled by Mason and Webb in 1850, where it is called "Goodwin." This name is used as late as Hatfield's *Hymn and Tune Book*, 1872, which gives both names, but after that date the title "Webb" is adopted. In twenty-six hymnals examined there are as many as thirteen different hymns set to this tune, but there are two that are most favored by compilers. Duffield's hymn, "Stand Up for Jesus," is found thirteen times, while Samuel F. Smith's missionary stanza, "The morning light is breaking," the one first used with it, still leads, and is in nineteen of the books.

GEORGE HOOD

1807–1882

THE earliest historians of sacred music in America were George Hood and Nathaniel Duren Gould. Both were composers of music and compilers of books, but the facts they put into print regarding the early history of psalmody and those who had a part in its making are of greater value to-day than the music which they wrote. George Hood was the younger of the two and was the first to turn his attention to the subject. It was in 1846 that his *History of Music in New England* appeared, when he was not quite forty years old, for he was born February 10, 1807, in Topsfield, Massachusetts. He was, therefore, only a few days older than the poet Longfellow and a few months the senior of Agassiz, the naturalist. Mr. Hood's interest in music led him to take up the teaching of that subject, first in the public schools and then in a female seminary. He afterward became a Presbyterian minister, and served several churches until his death September 24, 1882.

MUSICAL PRODUCTIONS

He did not compose much music, but in the same year that his history appeared he published *The Southern Melodist*, intended for use in the South. This book had shaped notes and a figured bass, and contained two tunes under his name, and two composed by his brother Jacob. In 1864 George published a *Musical Manual* to be used as an instruction book. His *History* is a small book of 259 pages, and in its preparation he spent ten years of research, the amount of matter that he was able to collect being remarkable, considering that his was a pioneer work. At the end of his book he has described all the music books that were available to him. The list, he tells us, was made from his own library, supplemented by Mr. Lowell's large collection of American music books. It was his intention to include all those printed before 1800, and in this he was quite successful. In spite of its deficiencies the results of his labors still have considerable value for the historian. In 1882 Mr. Hood furnished for the Musical Herald, published in Boston, a series of sketches of the early writers of church music, from which much information has been taken for the sketches in this book.

DEODATUS DUTTON

1808–1832

THE career of Deodatus Dutton was a short one, yet it gave great promise during the few years of his public life. He was born in Monson, Massachusetts, in 1808, and as his name carried a Junior, his father's name must have been Deodatus also. He was a precocious musician, and at the age of sixteen was chosen to play the first organ in the Center Church in Hartford. He completed his college course in that city, graduating from Washington (now Trinity) College in 1828. His poetical abilities had already been discovered, and at the commencement he was selected as the class poet, and delivered a poem, whose subject was "Hartford." He was licensed to preach by the Third Presbytery of New York, but was never ordained, as he died in New York December 16, 1832, while he was continuing his theological studies in that city. He was buried from one of the Dutch Reformed churches there.

AMERICAN PSALMODY

This joint compilation of Elam Ives, Jr., and Deodatus Dutton, Jr., was first issued in 1830 in a small edition, and reissued in the same year in a second edition greatly enlarged with alterations and improvements with 368 pages. The improvement considered of most importance by the compilers was the system of teaching music, which had been tested in practice for some time. A third edition was copyrighted and issued in 1834 with the name of Elam

Ives only upon the title page, for Dutton had died two years before.

Mr. Ives tells us that Mr. Dutton versified many of the hymns in this book, and also that he did the same for the book called "The Juvenile Lyre" issued in 1831 in Boston, by Lowell Mason and Elam Ives, though he had no credit for his work.

WOODSTOCK

"Woodstock" is his best-known tune, written for the words of Mrs. Brown's hymn, "I Love to Steal Awhile Away," which had been printed in the *Village Hymns* of Asahel Nettleton in 1824. It is in *The American Psalmody*, was copied into *The Boston Academy's Collection* in 1836, and appears in many of the present-day hymnals. It was probably named for the town of Woodstock in Connecticut, as a number of his tunes are named for towns in that State.

Mr. Gould, in his *History of Church Music in America*, has this to say: "Dutton, who was preparing for the ministry, in connection with Mr. Ives, published a book of church music in Hartford, called *The Hartford Collection*, in which were many tunes of his own composition. His skill and taste were of the most promising order, and the tune 'Woodstock,' with the words 'I love to steal awhile away,' will be associated with his name and handed down to future ages, and sung by many on earth, while he is singing the song of Moses and the Lamb in heaven."

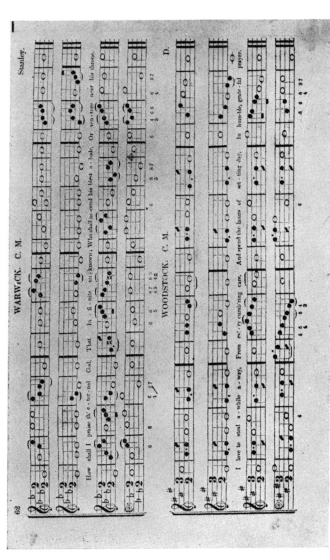

WOODSTOCK

By Deodatus Dutton, in his American Psalmody, second edition, 1830.   In the author's collection

DAVID CREAMER

1812–1887

THE first book of hymnology written about an American hymn book was prepared by a native of Baltimore, Maryland, who published in 1848 a *Methodist Hymnology*, which was made up of annotations upon the hymns in the 1836 edition of *The Methodist Hymn Book*. For many years David Creamer had been investigating the history of the Methodist hymns; he had employed agents in Europe to purchase for him all the editions of Wesley's poems and hymns that could be found until he had all but a single small tract, and had also sought other books of hymns from which selections might have been made for Methodist use.

David Creamer was the fourth in descent from one Henry Creamer, who had come from Germany, and had settled in Westminster County, Maryland. David was born in Baltimore, November 20, 1812, the son of Joshua Creamer and Margaret Smith. Both his parents were Methodists, and his mother's father, John Merryman Smith, was also of that faith. He was one of twelve children, eight of whom arrived at maturity, married, and had families. He was educated in private schools in Baltimore until he was seventeen, when he entered his father's counting room, and in 1832 he became a partner in the business under the name of "Joshua Creamer & Son, Dealers in Lumber." The firm lasted for eleven years, when his father withdrew to engage in a commission branch of the business. In the financial crisis of 1857 his profits were swept away, and the next year he retired from active commercial life.

He was married November 27, 1834, by the Rev. G. G. Cookman, to Eliza Ann Taylor, a daughter of Judge Isaac Taylor, of the Orphans' Court, who was also a local preacher of the Methodist Episcopal Church. Of this union there were four children—two boys and two girls. Mr. Creamer was loyal to the government before and during the Civil War, and when the inquest was held over the persons killed in the attack on the Sixth Massachusetts Infantry, April 19, 1861, as it passed through the streets of Baltimore, he was foreman of the jury. There is in the Library of Congress a memorandum book, once the property of Mr. Creamer, in which among other notes he has put down a number of items about the trial, which appear to be summaries of the testimony of the witnesses. It was through his efforts that the citizens of Massachusetts learned of the care given to the wounded and the dead by the authorities of Baltimore. In August, 1862, he was appointed a recruiting officer for the State of Maryland, and in September of that year was selected by Governor Bradford to visit the regiments in and around Washington to find out their needs. In July, 1863, he was made an assessor of the internal revenue, and from 1882 he was a clerk in the post office department in Washington. A copy of his *Methodist Hymnology* in the possession of the present writer contains his photograph, the date of his birth, and a presentation to Ephraim Wheeler, a fellow clerk in the same office.

Mr. Creamer was a life-long member of the Methodist Church, having joined it when he was seventeen years old. At that time he was a member of Philip Shepherd's "Sunrise Class" which met in the Old Town Meeting House on Green Street in Baltimore, and in 1878 he was the leader of the North Baltimore "Sunrise Class." He was for twenty-one years a trustee of Dickinson College, resigning only when the infirmities of age made it difficult for him to attend the meetings of the Board. In 1855 he was one of the School committee of the city of Baltimore, and he was also one of the Board of Managers of the "Baltimore Association for the Education and Improvement of the Colored Race," traveling, speaking and writing in its interests.

In 1836 David Creamer and John Nelson McJilton started a weekly journal, The Baltimore Monument, devoted to literature, science, and music. This contains some poems of Mr. Creamer, several of which are set to music. The Rev. G. G. Cookman was among its list of contributors. Mr. Creamer seems to have withdrawn from its editorship after Volume II, for Volume III shows T. S. Arthur as coeditor with McJilton.

The one outstanding result of the labors of David Creamer was the *Methodist Hymnology*, published in 1848. At the General Conference of the church, held in Pittsburgh in May, 1848, the matter of a new hymn book was brought up, and on the second day of the Conference James Floy, of the New York Conference, moved that a committee of seven be appointed to consider whether a revisal of the hymn book were necessary. This committee reported that a revision seemed desirable, and that it was expected by the people, whereupon a committee of five bishops and two laymen was appointed to make the necessary revision. David Creamer of Baltimore and Robert A. West of New York were the two laymen. Later it was moved that William Hunter be added to the committee, but this motion was lost. The result of the work of this committee was issued in 1849 as the *Methodist Hymn Book* of that date. Much of the work of selecting the hymns for the new book was done in New York, Mr. Floy assisting Mr. West in this direction, though Mr. Floy was not of the official committee.

The edition of 1836, which was used as the basis of the new book, was carefully annotated by these laymen, who placed opposite each hymn its original source, and a number of books of various denominations in which it was then used. This book was in the possession of Mr. West, and is now owned by his son, and a copy of many of the notations has been made in an edition of the 1836 book now in the hands of the present writer. Mr. Creamer doubtless was the leading authority of sources. When past seventy he writes of this book:

I was a young man in 1848 when as a native American I received from the General Conference of that year the first office it ever conferred upon a layman, in connection with another member of the church, Mr. R. A. West, an Englishman, by being placed upon the Hymn Book Committee together with five ministers of the gospel. To-day, though in my three score and tenth year, I am not in feeling an old man, and with almost pristine vigor of soul and body it falls to my lot in this unexpected and informal way not only to bid farewell to the old "Collection of 1849," but to welcome with hearty approval and high appreciation of its superior merits, the New Hymnal of 1878.

The fraternal delegate sent from England to this Conference in Pittsburgh was James Dixon, who had been a minister from the year 1812, and continued to preach till 1871. Mr. Creamer met the delegate on his arrival in New York, and accompanied him through Philadelphia to Baltimore, thence by way of Washington, D. C., to the seat of the Conference. After his return to England Mr. Dixon put into book form his impressions of this visit, and he has this to say regarding David Creamer, to whom he refers as a merchant living in Baltimore: "This gentleman left an employment dear to his heart at New York for the purpose of accompanying me to his native city. He had been employed for several years in studying the hymns and poetry of the Wesleys, and was at the time employed in bringing out a work partly historical and partly critical, through the press, on this interesting subject. He had spared neither trouble nor expense in the pursuit of his object, employing all sorts of agents in Europe to collect every edition in existence of Charles Wesley's poetic effusions. I am not able to give an opinion of this work, as it was not published at the time I left: but from a portion of 'copy' shown me on our route I judged it would prove an acceptable addition to the literature of the American Methodist Church. It had been submitted to the inspection of a committee of the Baltimore Conference, who reported favorably, and the Conference recommended the work to the public. This gentleman, like all fine enthusiasts, seemed to live in Wesleyan poetry. It was his ideal of everything beautiful and glorious; his mind was fascinated and absorbed in his theme; he discoursed not of politics, or merchandise or material things, but of Charles Wesley, of sacred songs, of meters, sublimities, and devotional praise to God. It was really refreshing to see a young man (thirty-six years old), a merchant in active life, enabled to turn his thoughts so completely from buying and selling and getting gain as to devote his time and energies to a subject so delicate and sacred."

From the report of the committee of the Baltimore Annual Conference in March, 1848, the following extract is of interest:

The book contains the results of six years of absorbing study of this engaging branch of sacred poetry, with unequaled aids and facilities, embodying a brief memoir of each lyrist to whose sanctifying genius the church is indebted for these "Songs of Zion"; verifying the authors of the hymns in our book, as far as they have been discovered, giving in many instances the time and occasion of their composition, and, besides, a mass of critical observations, which we are convinced will give new information to a majority of readers. The entire production is so fully Wesleyan and Methodistic that your committee are of opinion that this conference may safely advise its immediate publication by our Book Concern; and as the hymnology of the church is in various quarters attracting increased attention, we may, as a Conference, recommend the book to the favorable consideration of the coming General Conference of our church.

The authority of Mr. Creamer as a hymnologist was recognized by no less a person than Daniel Sedgwick, a bookseller of London who devoted his energies largely to the location of hymn books. There is in the library of the Episcopal Diocese in Baltimore a little book of *Hymns and Spiritual Songs,* by James Maxwell, printed in 1768 and sold by Samuel Brown in Smith Street near the foot of

Potbaker's Hill in New York. In it is the following
letter from Daniel Sedgwick to Bishop W. R. Whit-
tingham, of whose collection it now forms a part:
He writes under date of January 31, 1871:

My anxiety to see "Maxwell" was that I supposed it to be an
English book (Mr. Creamer not informing me that it was
American) and not knowing in all my researches of such a
volume. It now appears to be a reprint of his little volume,
"Hymns and Spiritual Songs, in three books, with a prefatory
essay on Psalmody, 18mo. Birmingham, 1759." This is the
only copy of his work I ever saw, and the person I sold it to
had been looking for it twenty years and though this is some
twelve years ago, I have never been able to procure another
copy. The little volume is valuable as containing several
hymns now in use in various collections. There is never a
copy of this book in the British Museum, or in any other
person's possession than the one I possessed. I wonder if
Mr. Bird has a copy of the American edition.

The library of Mr. Creamer was sold at a public
auction sale in December, 1884. About seven hundred volumes of sacred poetry went to Drew Theological Library and furnished the nucleus of the fine
hymnological collection of that institution. The
wealth of material relating to the history of Methodism is indicated by the statement that the library
consisted of several thousand volumes, embracing
102 volumes of the Arminian and Wesleyan Magazines, fifty years of The Christian Advocate, sixty
volumes of the Evangelical Magazine, besides other
magazines and pamphlets of denominational value.
There were also in the sale many relics and memen-
tos of the Civil War.

Mr. Creamer died on Good Friday, April 8, 1887,
in the seventy-fifth year of his age.

HENRY WELLINGTON GREATOREX[1]

1813–1858

THE family of Henry W. Greatorex were famous both as musicians and as artists. His father, Thomas, was one of the foremost organists and conductors of his time in England. For the last twelve years of his life, covering the reign of George IV, he was organist in Westminster Abbey, and was honored at his death with a burial within the walls of that famous shrine. There is a tradition in his family that while talking one day with the king he claimed higher power than his sovereign. When his Majesty pressed him for his reason, he replied, "You are only a king, I am a Greater-Rex." It was during the period just preceding the birth of Henry that the Duke of Wellington was winning favor by his military genius, and it may be that this will account for the middle name of our musician.

The date of the birth of Mr. Greatorex is variously given, and in the absence of official documents to determine which is correct, we will state what we find. Appleton's *Cyclopedia* says that he was born at Burton-on-Trent in 1816, and this date has been followed by others who have written about him. But in the notice of his death, printed in the Charleston (S. C.) Daily Courier of September 18, 1858, the very definite date of December 24, 1813,[2] is given.

---

[1] From The Choir Herald.
[2] "DIED, Henry Wellington GREATOREX on the morning of September 10, 1858, of yellow fever (in Charleston, S. C.). He was born December 24, 1813, in London, came to America in 1836, and removed to Charleston in 1853.

HENRY WELLINGTON GREATOREX

It is possible that the person who had the notice written had access to his papers and that this is the correct date. As to his birthplace it may be said that his grandfather lived at Burton-on-Trent in Derbyshire, and that his oldest aunt, Martha, also had an estate there; later when his father had settled in London, several years before the birth of Henry, he retained a country residence at Burton. It is therefore more than likely that though his parents had their home in London, they were at Burton at the time of Henry's birth, and this surmise is verified by the records of the family. Of his early life we have found no record, but as his father was a thorough musician there is no doubt that the boy received a complete training in that branch. In 1839, so one record shows, he was engaged to go to the United States to play the organ in Center Church in Hartford, Connecticut. He remained there for two years, and then after an absence for a short period returned to play the organ in Saint John's Church for a while. He was considered a remarkable player for the times, and enjoyed an unusual popularity.

His next location was in New York, and in November, 1846, a local item referred to him as of Saint Paul's Church. Later he was organist and director

---

To his absent relatives it will be a consolation to know that he was surrounded by the kindest friends.

> "What is this absorbs me quite,
> Steals my senses, shuts my sight,
> Drowns my spirit, draws my breath,
> Tell me, my soul, can this be death?
> Heaven opens on my eyes, my ears
> With sounds seraphic ring,
> Lend, lend your wings, I mount, I fly,
> O grave, where is thy victory,
> O death, where is thy sting?"

of the music in Calvary Protestant Episcopal Church in the metropolis. In 1853 he went to Charleston, South Carolina, as organist of an Episcopal church, and fell a victim to the yellow fever in 1858. He was buried in this Southern city.

FAMILY

So little regarding the family of Mr. Greatorex has appeared in print, and the members of it have been so difficult to locate, that an unusual interest has been aroused to persevere until all the scattered threads should be found and woven into a complete whole. The following may be taken as a correct record: Across the river from Hartford is the town of Windsor, and here on March 11, 1822, was born Samantha Filley, daughter of Horace Filley and Thirzah Thorp. (This statement is from the history of Windsor, by Henry R. Stiles.) The family records give her name as Frances. She became the first wife of Mr. Greatorex, and while they were living in New York there was born to them a son, July 11, 1846. This son, called Frank Henry, for his mother and father, inherited the musical instincts of his father and became a splendid singer. While yet a young boy he enlisted during the Civil War as a drummer in the eighty-fourth New York State Militia, and later in the one hundred and forty-sixth New York Infantry. During this service he was detailed to instruct the band in one of the colored regiments of volunteers in Texas. After his discharge from the Volunteers he enlisted again in the regulars July 7, 1866, in the seventh United States Infantry;

and on December 19, 1867, he was discharged in
Saint Augustine, Florida, where he settled, married,
and raised his family, and one of his granddaughters
is now singing in the oldest church in the United
States in that city. Thus the musical tastes of the
father have persisted in the line of the oldest son.
The mother died soon after the birth of her son and
was buried in her native town.

While located in New York, Henry W. Greatorex
met Miss Eliza Pratt, the daughter of a retired
Methodist minister from Ireland, the Rev. James
Calcott Pratt, and they were married in 1849.
She became as famous as her husband, though in a
different line of work, for she studied art, and won
considerable reputation with her pen-and-ink
sketches. Her pen drawing of "Durer's House in
Nuremberg" is in the Vatican. Mrs. Greatorex
was born December 25, 1810, at Manor Hamilton,
Ireland, and died February 9, 1897, in Paris,
France. Her family consisted of one son and two
daughters. The son grew to maturity, moved to
Colorado, and died there several years ago. The
daughters followed their mother's bent and became
artists, and some of the paintings of these three
ladies, mother and daughters, adorn the home of
relatives in the city of Washington, D. C. Let no
one be misled by the statement of Mr. Stiles, who
says in his *History of Ancient Windsor, Connecticut*, that the first Mrs. Greatorex died "leaving two
daughters, now well-known artists in New York
city," for these daughters were members of the
second family, as stated before.

The Greatorex Collection

In 1851 Mr. Greatorex published a *Collection of Sacred Music*, which was in popular use for many years thereafter, and was considered one of the best collections made in this country up to that time. It was copyrighted by A. C. Goodman, of Hartford, and many copies bore his imprint. I own two copies of this book, one printed in New York by the Church Publishing Company, and the other printed in Boston by Oliver Ditson Company, who were then owners of the copyright. When the transfer of copyright took place the Ditson Company are unable to state. Both the books referred to are identical as to contents though one is thicker than the other, owing to the quality of the paper used. The music in this book is printed on four staves, as most of the music of that period was, but, unlike other books, the alto and tenor were also written on the two lower lines in smaller notes, so that the organist could follow the melody more easily by having only two staves to read.

The Library of Congress has a piece of sheet music called "Love Me," the music by Henry W. Greatorex, and the words by Eliza. This was doubtless his wife. The piece was printed in Richmond, Virginia, and is contained in a book of "Confederate Music," most of which was printed on separate sheets by the same firm, but collected and bound together for preserving. Both Mr. and Mrs. Greatorex were fine singers, and their visits to the parents of the latter were significant events in the life of the little town. Saint Mark's Church in LeRoy,

New York, was assured of a good audience when it was known that the musicians from the metropolis would be present. Mr. Greatorex was a good tenor, his wife was none the less proficient as a contralto, and when members of the local choir joined them an excellent quartet was formed. On some of these occasions a concert was given, and the visitors appeared in solo parts, winning deserved applause from those who were so fortunate as to hear them. Mr. Greatorex had a commanding presence, being rather portly in physique.

INDEX

Much may be learned, or at least verified, from the index of Mr. Greatorex's *Collection*, if we read with discerning eyes. There we find "Burton" attributed to "A. G." This was Anthony Greatorex, Henry's grandfather, who was organist in the town of Burton, England, and after his death a tablet was placed in the parish church:

> Sacred to the memory of Anthony Greatorex, forty-three years organist of this church, born July 15, 1730; died November 19, 1814.

"Tottenham" is marked "T. G." Mr. Love in his *Scottish Church Music* says that this tune appears in some of the Scotch Hymnals, and is usually credited to Thomas Greatorex, but though there seems no proof that he wrote it, it is likely that he did. It is taken from his *Parochial Psalmody* of 1823, and the fact that his son marks this tune with his father's initials, goes far to determine the authorship. "St. Anselm" is also marked "T. G."

TUNES

His *Collection* of 1851 has thirty-seven pieces marked "H. W. G.," besides seventeen chants and other pieces. This was a very popular book and was in common use for many years, the copyright being issued in the name of Mrs. H. W. Greatorex at its expiration in 1879. Some of these tunes have never been used in any other books, but a few have been introduced into a number of recent hymnals. The most popular tunes are "Leighton," "Geer," "Bemerton," and "Grostette"; "Manoah" and "Seymour" are used as arranged by him, and his "Gloria Patri" is found frequently. Had it not been that the scourge of 1858 claimed him in early life, there is no doubt that much more excellent music would have come from the pen of Henry W. Greatorex.

JONATHAN CALL WOODMAN[1]

1813–1894

JONATHAN CALL WOODMAN is known to hymn-book compilers by the one tune "State Street." He was born in Newburyport, Massachusetts, July 12, 1813, and died in Brooklyn, New York, February 5, 1894. He was the first assistant of Lowell Mason in introducing the teaching of music into the public schools of Boston. He was one of the first soloists of the Boston Academy of Music, and on one occasion took a solo part in the "Messiah." Several members of the Woodman family were in Professor

[1] From The Choir Herald.

202

Holbrook and State Street, Jonathan Call Woodman.
From *Musical Casket*, 1858. In collection of the author

Mason's choir, and when George F. Root went to Boston as Mr. Mason's assistant in the schools, he became acquainted with them, and in 1845 married Mr. Woodman's sister, Mary Olive. Mr. Root once said of his wife, "She was an accomplished singer, and if my children inherit musical qualities they get quite as much from her side of the family as from mine." Mr. Woodman married Sarah Ann Copeland in 1839, and their only son, Raymond Huntington Woodman, is one of the prominent music teachers and organists in Brooklyn. The father was a fairly good organist for those early days, and his excellent taste and ability as a choir director made up for any lack of technical facility. He played in the First Presbyterian Church in Brooklyn, and at the Packer Collegiate Institute, both of which places have in later years been filled by the son. He was one of the assistant teachers in the first Normal Musical Institute held in New York by Lowell Mason and George F. Root in 1853. He composed a number of pieces, seventeen of which appeared in *The Musical Casket*, compiled by him in 1858. The copyright of this book was reissued in 1886. A large part of its contents was from foreign writers; of his own compositions more than half were secular. One of his hymn tunes he named "Call"—his own middle name, and the maiden name of his mother. "State Street" is the last tune in the book, and is set to the hymn of Isaac Watts beginning, "Blessed are the sons of peace." No single hymn is wedded to this tune, each compiler having used a different one with the melody. The tune, however, is a very popular one, and scarcely a book is issued without it.

ABNER AND DARIUS ELIOT JONES[1]

ABNER and DARIUS E. JONES, father and son, have at least seven books to their credit. Abner Jones was a music teacher in New York for a number of years. In 1835 he conducted the New York Institute of Sacred Music, and in May of that year a concert was given under his direction by the children of the Seventh Presbyterian Church, corner of Broome and Ring Streets, the proceeds of which were to be used for continuing the instruction of the youth of that congregation in singing. He had a tenor voice, and took a tenor part at the dedication of Trinity Church, May 21, 1846. Very few biographical details have been found regarding him, but without doubt much of his time was occupied in teaching music and arranging the collections of sacred music that he issued.

BOOKS

In 1830 he prepared the introduction for *Psalmodia Evangelica*, a collection of psalm and hymn tunes, published by Elam Bliss in New York.

The preface states that he brings "to the work not only skill and science, but a practical knowledge of the art of teaching sacred and vocal music." His *Melodies of the Church*, 1832, was a collection of psalms and hymns adapted to public and social worship, seasons of revival, and various similar occasions, accompanied with appropriate music. There were twelve pages devoted to an explanation of the

---

[1] From The Choir Herald.

rudiments of music, so that the book could be used in schools or in families where the study of the subject was desired. Five of Mr. Jones' compositions were inserted. He was assisted in this compilation by William Blondell, organist of the Saint Paul's Church, who examined and corrected the music, and by Cyrus P. Smith, organist of the First Presbyterian Church of Brooklyn, who set the marks of expression. In this same year he published *Church Melodies*, a collection of hymns without music. In 1834 he issued in New York another book, which a review states was his fourth. This was *Evening Melodies*, a collection of sacred music, both original and selected, together with a new and improved system of elementary instruction in the art of singing. His next compilation, on which he had been at work for a long time, was not issued till 1854. This was *The Psalms of David*, rendered into English verse of various measures by Abner Jones, "professor of music in New York." The completion of this book had been delayed, he states in his preface, for two reasons, partly by financial embarrassments, and partly by the affliction which had come upon his family in the loss of his two surviving daughters during the years 1837–38. This is the only reference I have found to his family except his son Darius, who will be noticed later. In 1860 he issued *The Psalter*, defined and explained.

In June, 1835, there was an Abner D. Jones second vice-president of the Handel and Haydn Society of Newark, N. J., and as we know that his son was employed in Newark during his early manhood, it seems likely that the family were living there, and that the father may have been a member and officer of the musical society in that city. Some of his tunes were copied into the singing books for the next twenty or more years, but none of them are found in recent hymnals.

DARIUS ELIOT JONES

1815–1881

Darius was the son of Abner, and was born at Carroll, New York, October 18, 1815. For twenty years his interests were with the business world in New York and Newark, New Jersey. He was employed by the Mason Brothers in the former city for a considerable time, and when in June of 1850 they began the publication of a musical monthly called The Choral Advocate, Lowell Mason became its editor, and Mr. George J. Webb and Mr. Jones assistant editors. At the same time Mr. Jones was conducting the music in Plymouth Church, and when his pastor, the Rev. Henry Ward Beecher, wanted a new hymn book for the use of his church, he suggested that Mr. Jones prepare it. The result was *Temple Melodies*, issued in 1851. In Chicago he edited the Congregational Herald; then, feeling the call to the Christian ministry, he entered Iowa College at Davenport as a student, and on February 13, 1858, was ordained as a Congregational minister. He served churches at Columbus City and Newton Center until 1863, when he became treasurer of the Iowa General Association. For a year he was agent for the American Bible Society, and during the four years from 1866 to 1870 he was agent for Iowa College with residence at Grinnell. This school is now located at Grinnell and is called Grinnell College. It was while here that he issued his second hymn book, *Songs for the New Life*, in 1869. From that time on he supplied various churches in the Hawkeye State until his death August 10, 1881, at Davenport, Iowa.

BOOKS

He compiled two collections of hymns, both of which have been already mentioned. *Temple Melodies* was the first hymn and tune book that secured any extensive use among the Congregationalists. In it he placed six tunes composed by his father, two of which had been previously used in the *Melodies of the Church*, 1832. There were also two of his own compositions, including the tune "Stockwell." *Songs for the New Life* was copyrighted in 1869, and the preface is dated at Grinnell, Iowa. In it there are eighteen tunes by the compiler, including his "Stockwell," which appears twice, and also one of his tunes which he named "Magoun" in honor of the Rev. George F. Magoun, the president of Iowa College.

STOCKWELL

The one tune of his which has been used in most of the recent hymnals is "Stockwell," and it usually appears with the date 1851. It was written at least a year earlier, for it is found in Lowell Mason's *New Carmina Sacra*, copyrighted in 1850, set to the words that are generally sung to it, "Silently the shades of evening." The *Carmina Sacra*, by Lowell

Mason, was first issued in 1841, and proved such a popular compilation that 400,000 copies of it were sold. In 1850 a new edition of it was prepared, called the *New Carmina Sacra*, and Mr. Jones contributed this tune. During the same year it was copied from this book into the first volume of the Choral Advocate, a musical monthly magazine of which he was one of the assistant editors. A word may be said about the hymn that has been so long wedded to the tune. "Silently the shades of evening" was written by Christopher C. Cox (1816–1881), a physician of Baltimore, and was first published in Woodworth's Cabinet in 1847, set to music; but after Mr. Jones had set it to his tune "Stockwell" the hymn and tune have seldom parted company.

MARCUS M. WELLS[1]

1815–1895

MARCUS MORRIS WELLS was born in Otsego, New York, October 2, 1815. In early manhood he went to Buffalo, in the same State, where he was converted in a Baptist mission church. Later we find him at Cooperstown, and then at Hardwick, where he had a farm which he cultivated, and where he also made farm implements. He died July 17, 1895, and a memorial window was placed in the Baptist church of that town in January, 1903. The one hymn by which he will be known begins "Holy Spirit, faithful Guide," and the tune which he wrote for it usually is found with it. Concerning the origin of the hymn he

[1] From The Choir Herald.

says: "On a Saturday afternoon in October, 1858, while at work in my cornfield, the sentiment of the hymn came to me. The next day, Sunday, being a very stormy day, I finished the hymn and wrote a tune for it and sent it to Professor I. B. Woodbury." Mr. Woodbury was the editor of the New York Musical Pioneer, but when this piece came into the office he was in the South on account of ill health. The hymn and tune therefore came to the attention of Hubert P. Main, who was selecting the music for the paper in the absence of the editor, and it was first published in the November number of the Pioneer for 1858. It was afterward printed in *The Psalm King*, 1866, and gradually crept into use in the church hymnals. It is a classic as a devotional hymn. It appears under different names; often under the first line of the words, once as "Taylor," twice as "Eucharist," sometimes as "Faithful Guide," but more frequently under the single word "Guide." In sixteen books which were examined it appears six times with the words written for it, beginning "Holy Spirit." Nine times it is set to as many different hymns. In most of the later books, however, both hymn and tune as written are used together.

JOHN ZUNDEL[1]

1815–1882

JOHN ZUNDEL was German-born, but the greater part of his life was spent in this country. He lived here during thirty of his maturer years, and then

[1] From The Choir Herald.

returned to his native land. He was born December 10, 1815, at Hochdorf, and died July, 1882, at Cannstadt, Germany, in his sixty-sixth year. He was an accomplished musician before he came to America. He had been organist at Saint Anne's Lutheran Church in Saint Petersburg, and had served as bandmaster of the Imperial Horse Guards in that same city; he was also the instructor of the children of Madame Sontag, who by her marriage in 1829 became the Countess Rossi. In October, 1847, Mr. Zundel arrived in New York, and began his work which was to have such an influence on the development of sacred music. For a short time he was organist of the First Unitarian Church in Brooklyn, and then of Saint George's (Doctor Tyng's) in New York. On the first of January, 1850, he became organist of Plymouth Church in Brooklyn, and during the twenty-eight years that followed he retired from and returned to the church three times. Beginning with a salary of seven hundred dollars, it was gradually raised until at the end of his services he was receiving fifteen hundred dollars a year. During the last few months of his American career he was organist of the Central Methodist Church in Detroit, Michigan. When he left that appointment he sailed for Europe with no intention of returning.

PUBLICATIONS

Three books were issued by him for use in the services of the church. *The Choral Friend*, 1852, was a small book of ninety-five pages, and was printed in a limited edition, but it was warmly welcomed by his musical friends and contained a number of his earlier compositions that were used in his later books. Some of the tunes had been composed to German words, and had been sung from manuscript at Saint Anne's Lutheran Church in Saint Petersburg. Zundel's *Psalmody* appeared in 1855. It contained many original tunes and was recommended to the musical public because it was a smaller book than those then in use, and was therefore less expensive. *Christian Heart Songs* was copyrighted in 1870. "It has required," he says, "almost a lifetime to compose its contents." He also prepared a number of works for instruction on the melodeon and the organ, a work on harmony, and a number of collections of voluntaries and anthems. Twice he was an editor of periodicals; in 1863 he started the Monthly Choir and Organ Journal, which ran for a year, and a decade later he edited Zundel and Brandt's Quarterly, a magazine each number of which was made up of twelve pages of music, both vocal and instrumental.

Tunes

Only two of his tunes are in common use at the present time. The most popular one appeared in his *Christian Heart Songs*, 1870, under the name of "Beecher," with the words of Wesley, "Love divine, all love excelling." In some books it is known as "Love Divine" or "Zundel." "Lebanon" is the other tune that is found in several collections. At least a half dozen others appear in one or more recent books. He divides his compositions into two classes, and says that the tunes composed during the early years that he was in New York were mainly for quartet singing, and some for the Episcopal service, but by far the greater portion of them were composed during his connection with Mr. Beecher's church, with a view to their use by large choirs, or for congregational singing. He says in the preface of *Heart Songs:*

As a German-born citizen, I may take the liberty of saying that, superior as musical education in Germany may be, or even is, church singing has little profited by it. The Germans sing their chorals mostly after hearing them, they learn them partly at school, and the parents sing them to the children from generation to generation. To introduce a new choral into a congregation is no less trouble than to make a new tune go in any American church, provided the tune be singable and enjoyable at all.

THE PLYMOUTH COLLECTION

The most important work that Mr. Zundel did was in connection with Henry Ward Beecher in the successful introduction of congregational singing into Plymouth Church. Mr. Beecher became pastor of this church in 1847. He was not a musician himself, but was very desirous that all the people should sing, and as there was no book that satisfied him he suggested to Mr. Darius E. Jones, who was then leading the music in his church, that a suitable book should be prepared. The result was *Temple Melodies*, issued in 1851. Mr. Zundel assisted in arranging the music for this book. There were nearly five hundred hymns, with appropriate tunes upon each page. This, however, was not Mr. Beecher's ideal of a church hymn book, though it was a good beginning. There were not enough hymns in this compilation for him, so during the next few years he devoted what time he could snatch from his busy days to the collection and arrangement of materials for a larger book, and in 1855 the *Plymouth Collection* appeared. No publisher could be found who had faith enough in the success of such a large collection for congregational use as to undertake its printing, so two members of Plymouth Church agreed to furnish the money. Never before had such boldness been shown in the selection of materials. The poetry of all denominations and the standard verse writers of his day were drawn upon. Many exquisite hymns were taken from the Moravian collections. Hymns from the Wesleys, Watts, Cowper, and Newton were included. "Some of the most touching and truly evangelical hymns have been gathered from Roman Catholic sources. It has been a joy to us to learn, during our research, how much food for true piety is afforded through Catholic books."

The storm of protest that greeted this book because of the introduction of Catholic hymns for use in the churches of Protestantism may better be imagined than described. The words of the hymns were chosen by Mr. Beecher; but the selection of the tunes was placed in the hands of his brother, Charles Beecher, who was an excellent musician, and being also a Congregational minister, was well acquainted with the kind of music that was best fitted for the use of congregations. An assistant musical editor was found in Mr. Zundel, who was the organist of Mr. Beecher's church. His ideas were conformable with those of his pastor, and he introduced into the new hymn book twenty-eight of his own compositions. The success of the book was all that could have been desired, and two years later a committee from the Baptist churches of New York asked permission to have an edition issued that would have some additional hymns especially suited to Baptist usage. This was granted, and a Baptist edition came from the press. The part that Mr. Zundel had in the music of his church is indicated in the statement of Mr. Beecher, written in 1871: "Mr. Zundel has cooperated with me for nearly twenty years in building up congregational singing in Plymouth Church."

WILLIAM B. BRADBURY[1]

1816–1868

LOWELL MASON was twenty-four years old, and had just begun his musical career, when William B. Bradbury was born, October 6, 1816, at York, Maine, and he outlived the younger man four years, both dying in New Jersey towns, where their homes were only a few miles apart. William Batchelder Bradbury was the middle child of the five in his father's family. Both of his parents were excellent singers, and from them he inherited his musical taste. Before he was fourteen he had learned to play on all the instruments that came in his way, but the organ was not known in his Maine home. When a young man he went to Boston, entering the family of Sumner Hill, a musician and teacher, from whom he

[1] From The Choir Herald.

received his first lessons in harmony. He was further encouraged in his musical efforts by Calvin
Allen, a foreman in the employ of the Chickering
Piano Company. It was not long before he met
Lowell Mason and George J. Webb, entered their
school, the Boston Academy of Music, and joined
Professor Mason's choir at the Bowdoin Street
Church. Here he served as organist for three
months, performing the double duty of pressing the
keys to make the music, and pulling them up again
to stop the sound. For this he received twenty-five
dollars a month. At the end of the quarter he
obtained another place where he was paid one hundred dollars, and did not have to pull the keys up.

TEACHING

He was recommended by Mason to Machias,
Maine, and he lived there a year and a half, teaching singing schools in the evenings, and giving piano
lessons during the day. There he doubtless found
much musical talent; for America's first psalm-tune
composer, James Lyon, the compiler of *Urania,*
1761, was located as minister of that settlement in
1771, continuing twenty-three years until his death
in 1794. We can imagine that some of the older
people of the village could remember the musical
pastor of forty years before, and that his teachings
had been handed down to the later generation. For
the next few years Bradbury alternated between
Boston and Maine, and then went to New York,
becoming organist in a church where a new organ
had been introduced. There was considerable objection to this innovation, but he overcame the oppo-

sition by playing softly, and producing a subdued effect. Here in the metropolis he began his juvenile classes, giving his instructions freely, and closing the sessions with a concert. At one of his Musical Festivals he had a chorus of one thousand children, and so far as the performance was concerned it was a grand success, but financially it was a failure, the deficit amounting to two hundred dollars. The concert given by his Sunday-school classes of the Baptist Tabernacle in 1847, was in the nature of a testimonial and a benefit, as at its close Mr. Bradbury was presented with a watch. A few months later, taking his wife and daughter, he sailed for England. Later he went to Germany, where he remained for two years. He studied at Leipzig, making the most out of his time, practicing six hours a day, the result being that he overworked his right arm so that it was lame for several months after his return home. On November 4, 1847, Mendelssohn died in Leipzig, and the student attended the funeral. On his return to America he called his next compilation *The Mendelssohn Collection*, 1849.

CONVENTIONS AND INSTITUTES

Mr. Bradbury held his first musical convention in 1851 at Somerville, New Jersey. Later he joined forces with Lowell Mason, Thomas Hastings, and George F. Root, and these four formed the faculty of the various Normal Institutes that were held in the East during the next few years. In 1854 he formed a partnership with his brother, and engaged in the piano business, manufacturing and selling the instruments, and dealing in other musical supplies.

His excessive labors induced disease of the lungs, and during the last years of his life he was in feeble health. He died January 7, 1868, at his home in Montclair, New Jersey.

BOOKS

He was a prolific composer and compiler, and during the twenty-six years of his active work, between 1841 and 1867, fifty-nine separate books had his name upon the title page, an average of more than two a year. *The Young Choir*, 1841, was his first book. For Sunday schools he prepared *The Oriola, Fresh Laurels*, and the *Sunday School Choir*. In the oblong shape there were *The Choralist, The Psalmodist, The Mendelssohn Collection,* the very popular *Shawm,* and *The Jubilee,* which sold over two hundred and twenty-five thousand copies. There were also Glee books—*Alpine, Metropolitan,* and *New York Glee Books.* In the small hymnal size there was *The Devotional Hymn and Tune Book,* intended for Baptist Societies. Many of these books sold in large numbers, and it has been estimated that over two million of his works have been sold. This success was not won without opposition. When his book *The Golden Chain* came out in 1861 it became exceedingly popular, and attained a large sale, but it was mercilessly criticized by his rivals on account of a few trifling errors that it contained. These were corrected by Doctor Hastings, who also assisted Bradbury in much of his other work.

USAGE

Taking the same ten books that we used in our

search for the tunes of Lowell Mason, we find that Bradbury's tunes are found in them in an aggregate of eighty-eight times, one book having twenty-one different ones, and the lowest having but three. Only one tune, "Woodworth," is found in all of the ten books. The next most popular tune is the one usually set to the hymn "He Leadeth Me," and it is found in nine of our list of hymnals. In one book it is called "Aughton," and another has it under the name of "Smither." *The Pilgrim Hymnal* is the only one that omits it. It has the hymn, but uses another tune. This too is the book that has the least number of Bradbury's works. Seven books have the tunes "Rest" and "Zephyr"; six have "Aletta," "Brown," and "Even Me." "Sweet Hour of Prayer," which is so much used in books prepared for the use of Sunday schools and social meetings, is in only four of the church hymnals referred to. In one of them it is called "Walford," for the blind writer of the hymn. This is a very good showing for a composer whose tunes have been in use for more than fifty years. As much of this composition was for children, and appeared in books intended especially for Sunday schools, an examination of similar books compiled in recent years will show the retention of a large proportion of Bradbury's tunes.

VIRGIL CORYDON TAYLOR

1817–1891

VIRGIL CORYDON TAYLOR was born in Barkhamstead, Connecticut, April 2, 1817. His father bore

VIRGIL CORYDON TAYLOR
Copy of a photograph furnished
by his daughter, Mrs. Peter A.
Porter, Buffalo, New York

the same name, and he traces his ancestry back,
partially through the female lines, to Elder William
Brewster, the pilgrim who drew up the compact on
the Mayflower in 1620. In his old home in the Nutmeg State his father had placed for his benefit what
was called in those early days a church organ, and
on this instrument many of his musical compositions
were first played. His entire life was devoted to the
development and advancement of music, teaching
singing schools, holding institutes, and as an organist and private teacher. He located for a while in
Hartford, then removed to Poughkeepsie, New York,
in 1851, to take the leadership of the Poughkeepsie
Union Musical Association, which had been founded
the previous year. Upon his departure from the
city the Union disbanded. While there he was also
organist and chorister of the Central Baptist
Church. His wife was a fine soprano, and sang in
his choir. Later they went to the First Dutch
Church, where they performed similar parts. In
1861 he was organist and conductor of the music
in the Strong Place Baptist Church in Brooklyn.
He was organist in Niagara Falls, and finally settled
in Des Moines, Iowa, where he served Saint Paul's
Church, and where he was residing at the time of his
death, January 30, 1891.

Books

Mr. Taylor compiled a number of books of music,
both sacred and secular. His first effort was *The
Sacred Minstrel*, published in Hartford in 1846;
The Concordia was a book of glees, issued in 1852
at New York; *The Golden Lyre*, 1850; *The Chime*,

1856, New York; *The Celestina*, 1856, was a revision of *The Sacred Minstrel* of 1846; *The Enchanter*, songs and glees, 1861, New York, and a book of chants called *The Venite*, in 1865. *The Praise Offering* was copyrighted in 1867, and contained a new idea, by which the location of the key note was shown either by a heavy line or a wide space. Only a part of the tunes in this book were printed in the new notation, for to have delayed it for a complete font of type would, he said, have deferred the work for another year. It was prepared especially for his choir at Saint Paul's Church in Des Moines, Iowa. A compilation of *Greenback Campaign Songs* was issued in 1878 at Des Moines.

Louvan

His single contribution to the stock of American tunes was the tune "Louvan." It appeared in his first book, *The Sacred Minstrel*, in 1846, and in most if not all of his succeeding books. He considered it one of his best, and hymn-book editors have confirmed his judgment by continuing its use in their hymnals up to the present time. It was first set to words of Thomas Moore, "There's nothing bright above, below." Several of his tunes were used in other hymn books published during his lifetime, but "Louvan" is the only one now in common use.

Mr. Taylor introduced many fugue tunes into his first book, *The Sacred Minstrel*, realizing the popularity with which they had been held for the fifty years previous, but "with such modifications as to render their arrangement conformable to the rules of harmony without destroying their character."

The music was written in only four varieties of time. In *The Celestina* there were a number of tunes marked "H. H. H." of which he makes especial mention, and for which he claims the copyright.   In 1859 B. F. Edmands introduced three of them into his edition of *The Psalmist* with tunes, and attributed them to H. H. Hawley. A fourth tune by this same composer was presented for Edmands' work. As a few of the tunes in Taylor's book are under the name of H. H. Hawley, it is safe to assume that those under the initials are by the same writer, and not by the editor, Virgil Corydon Taylor.

ISAAC BAKER WOODBURY[1]

1819–1858

BEVERLY, Massachusetts, the birthplace of Isaac B. Woodbury, lies to the north of Salem, and further on, toward Asbury Grove, the placid waters of Wenham Lake are seen on the left, while on the right, and high up above the street, is the house that was built and occupied by the musician as his country home.   October 23, 1819, was the date of his birth.   When thirteen years old he moved to Boston, and began the study of music, and learned also to play the violin.   At nineteen he went to Europe to spend a year in further study in London and Paris.   Returning to Boston, he taught music there for six years; later he joined the Bay State Glee Club, and traveled throughout New England giving concerts.   When he reached Bellows Falls,

---
[1] From The Choir Herald.

Vermont, he met the postmaster and proprietor of the country store, John Weeks Moore, who prevailed upon him to remain there for a while. The result was that he organized the New Hampshire and Vermont Musical Association, and continued as its conductor for a number of years.

He next went to New York, and for a number of years prior to 1851 he directed the music in the Rudgers Street Church. On account of ill health he was obliged to resign this work, and again he went to Europe. Before he left he had become the editor of the New York Musical Review and he made good use of the time that he was away in search of health in seeking also new music for use in his paper. On his return he brought a large supply to use in the preparation of the books that he then had in mind. In the fall of 1858 he left New York, intending to spend the winter in the South. An accident to the vessel on which he was a passenger compelled him to return, but again he started south by land. Going by easy stages of about one hundred miles a day, he passed through Philadelphia and Baltimore, and on his thirty-ninth birthday he had reached Columbia, South Carolina. Too weak to proceed farther, he remained there for three days until his death on October 26, 1858. He left a wife and six little ones.

Gentleness was the characteristic of the man and his music. His compositions were for the church, the fireside and the social circle. He wrote with remarkable fluency, and it was surprising how much he could accomplish in a short space of time. Just before his death it was said that his music was sung by more worshipers in the sanctuary than the

music of any other man.   He had a beautiful voice
and sang various styles, but excelled in the ballad
and descriptive music.   For sport he was fond of
hunting and duck-shooting.   And in a letter to his
paper he wrote that even in winter it was his daily
custom to ride on horseback, or, when Old Boreas
blew cold, in his carriage, among the leafless trees
or the evergreen pines.

Books

Music cheered and solaced him almost to his last
hour.   It was but a few weeks previous to his death
that he turned from his desk, almost sinking from
exhaustion, with the remark to his broken-hearted
wife, "No more music for me until I am in heaven,"
and from that moment his thoughts were wholly
given to preparation for the expected change. *The
Dayspring*, which was published soon after his
death, was a sort of memorial to him, for it was
largely made up of his music, some of which had
been used before, but much of it was taken from
manuscript found in his portfolio after his decease.
This book was compiled by Sylvester Main.   His
first book had been arranged with the assistance of
Benjamin F. Baker in 1842, and was called *The
Boston Musical Education Society's Collection*.
With this same coworker he issued *The Choral* in
1845.   Some of his other works were *The Dulcimer*,
1850; *The Cythera*, 1854; *The Lute of Zion*, 1856.
For use in the South we find *The Harp of the South*,
1853; and *The Casket*, 1855, the latter being published by the Southern Baptist Society in Charleston, South Carolina.   Besides those just named,

which were collections of sacred music, he prepared several instruction books, one for the voice, one in composition, and another for the organ. He also compiled three glee books, books for children's singing schools, and books for the Sunday school. He assisted in compiling *The Methodist Hymn Book* in 1857, and also the book prepared by Philip Phillips in 1867.

Usage

Woodbury's hymn tunes are fast going out of use. Leaving out the Episcopal book, because there is none of his work therein, we have examined nine books, and in these there are nineteen different tunes occurring thirty-eight times. Only two of these appear in more than two different books. "Siloam" is in eight of them, and so is the tune set to the words "Forever with the Lord." This tune is found under three names: in two books it is called "Woodbury," and in three is entitled "Nearer Home," while in the other three it takes the first line of the hymn. It is interesting to note that when *The Methodist Hymnal* was revised in 1849 one of the members of the committee wrote on the margin of his book, opposite the words of Montgomery, beginning "Forever with the Lord," "These verses were objected to by a majority of the editors and bishops"; but Doctor Nutter, in his annotations of the hymnal, expresses quite another opinion when he says, "This is no doubt the most valuable and widely used hymn the author wrote."

One of the most popular of his secular pieces is "Speed Away," and this melody has been used lately with sacred words. Another song was "The Indian's Lament," written to his friend and neighbor in Salem, Luther O. Emerson; the first line is familiar: "Let me go to my home in the far distant West." For the first song that he wrote he received the sum of ten dollars. Its words seemed to express his every endeavor in life, and the first line was placed upon his tombstone in Norwalk, Connecticut: "He doeth all things well."

SAMUEL PARKMAN TUCKERMAN

1819–1890

Samuel Parkman Tuckerman was a native of Boston, where he was born February 11, 1819. His musical education was obtained largely abroad. He had been an organist in his native city from 1840 to 1849, and in the latter year he went to Europe, where he spent four years of study. He secured his degree of Doctor of Music from Doctor Sumner, Archbishop of Canterbury, by special decree after an exercise of eight real parts was approved by three of the most prominent English musicians. The next year, 1852, he received the degree of Master of Sacred Music in the Academy of Saint Cecelia, Rome. On his return to Boston in 1853 he spent three more years as an organist there, and then removed to New York, where he became organist of Trinity Church.

Besides *The National Lyre* he compiled a book of *Cathedral Chants*, in 1858, and *The Episcopal Harp*, in 1844. He lectured on music, and gave many organ recitals. He died in Newport, Rhode Island, June 30, 1890.

ROBERT C. KEMP

1820–1897

ROBERT C. KEMP, also known as "Father Kemp," compiled a selection of "Old Folks' Concert" music, and conducted many concerts of the old music during the fifties and sixties. He was born at Wellfleet, on Cape Cod, Massachusetts, June 6, 1820. At the age of nine he went with his uncle upon a fishing boat and for three years was engaged in fishing either on the Grand Banks or along the New England coast. At the age of twenty we find him in Boston engaged in the boot and shoe business on Hanover Street, the junior member of the firm of Mansfield and Kemp. While in Boston he was married, and soon afterward moved to Reading, where he purchased a farm, intending to enjoy the pleasures of rural life in connection with his city business. In those days there were not the many calls for social evenings that there are at the present time. Music and the singing schools took up much of the time of the young people. Reading was a model New England town, and the idea came to Mr. Kemp that it would be a good plan to learn the old music of the generation past, and so he invited some of the young people to gather at his home to pass the time in singing the familiar songs of the day. "It then occurred to me," says Mr. Kemp, "to revive old mem-

ories by singing some of the tunes which strengthened the religious faith of our grandfathers and
grandmothers, and had often been the medium
through which our sturdy and pious ancestors had
lifted their hearts in thankfulness to their Maker,
for planting their home in the land of liberty."
Then he put his idea into effect.

The rehearsals were kept up, and soon "The Reading Old Folks Musical Society" was organized. Its
first public concert was given in Reading on December 5, 1854, and was a grand success. The hall was
filled and many stood outside and listened as the
"Old Folks" sang. News of this concert spread,
and an invitation was received to visit Lynn. This
trip was made in sleighs. Boston was the next place,
and Tremont Temple was engaged, with the under-
standing that if this attempt met with success others
would follow. On this occasion a special train was
chartered to take the singers from their homes in
Reading. There were eleven members in the troupe
at this time, and eleven concerts in Boston followed.
The company was then increased to forty-seven and
a trip to Washington planned. In New York they
sang before an audience of seven thousand and in
Washington they appeared before President Bu-
chanan, while on their return they gave concerts in
Baltimore and Philadelphia, and the proceeds of the
trip were given to charity. "The laughable song,
called 'Johnny Schmocker,'" says Mr. Kemp,
"which has obtained such a wide popularity, was
first sung in public by the 'Old Folks.' It was given
to me by a student in Middletown, Connecticut, with
the agreement that it should not be published. It

was published, however, and somebody must have made considerable out of its sale."

MORE CONCERTS

At the close of the year 1860 the troupe decided upon a trip to England. There were thirty, including the singers and managing agents, and they set sail on January 9, 1861. After a trip of twelve days they landed at Liverpool and proceeded directly to London, where a series of forty concerts was given. These were not such a success as Mr. Kemp had anticipated; but as he was the only one that was ready to return, he left the party and went back to Boston alone. The others spent some time in seeing the sights of England before they returned. The troupe was again reorganized and another series of concerts was given on Monday evenings in Tremont Temple in Boston, and a trip was made through the Western States.

About 1870 the concert business was given up and Mr. Kemp again went into the business of selling shoes in Boston. His wife died about 1882 and the later years of his life were spent in the Old Men's Home in Charlestown, where he died May 14, 1897. In 1857 he assisted in the preparation of *The Continental Harmony*, and in 1889 he compiled *Father Kemp's Old Folks Concert Music*, which will be the book to furnish for years to come the songs of the olden time. Mrs. Kemp compiled in 1876 the *Faneuil Hall Temperance Song Book*, a paper-covered book of words containing only forty-eight pages.

GEORGE FREDERICK ROOT[1]

1820–1895

DOCTOR ROOT was one of the group of music teachers, which included Mason, Bradbury, Baker, and Woodbury, whose activities covered the middle third of the last century. George Frederick Root, to call him by his full name, was born at Sheffield, in the western part of Massachusetts, August 30, 1820. When he was six years old the family moved to North Reading, not far from Boston, and there his youth was spent. He does not claim that his bent toward music was due to the local surroundings, yet it is of interest to note that much musical history is connected with the town of Reading. As early as 1795 Reuben Emerson, a young man preparing for college, held a singing school here, and gave to Nathaniel D. Gould his first and only instruction in the art of singing. After graduating from Dartmouth College the singing master came back to Reading, and was pastor of its church for fifty-five years. The pupil became a music teacher, and wrote the first *History of Church Music in America.* Here too lived "Father Kemp," who organized the Reading Old Folks' Musical Society, and gave so many popular concerts of old-time music during the "sixties" both in the United States and in England.

But as to Mr. Root, his one ambition was to become a musician. Opportunity soon led him to Boston, and it was not long before his teacher, B. F. Baker, asked him to learn some hymn tunes to play

---

[1] From The Choir Herald.

at prayer meetings. Soon he was given a pupil to instruct, and then he began to teach singing schools. Thus he was launched upon his musical career. He helped Lowell Mason teaching in the public schools of Boston, and there met the composer of "State Street," J. C. Woodman, whose sister, Mary Olive Woodman, he married in August, 1845.

He had already been settled in New York for a year, having gone there to teach in a Young Ladies' School, which was being conducted by Jacob Abbott, and later he added to his work instruction in Rutgers Female Institute, and the New York Institution for the Blind. It was in this latter school that he had as a pupil the blind Fanny Crosby, who in after years wrote so many of the verses that he set to music. In 1852 he conceived the idea of conducting a three-months' session of a Normal Musical Institute for the instruction of teachers, but owing to the absence of Lowell Mason, whom he wanted as one of its instructors, the first session was not held until the following year. From this time on much of Mr. Root's labor was devoted to the Institutes. In 1859 he went to Chicago, where his brother had opened a music store with Mr. Cady. He was interested to a small degree in the business of the firm, and much of his publishing was now done by Root and Cady. In 1871 the big fire in Chicago swept away in a few minutes the work of years, but it did not stop his work. As soon as the losses could be adjusted, and new stocks provided, the business went on. He made two trips across the Atlantic, the first in 1850, when he gave many hours to study in Paris, and in 1886 he visited England. The

degree of Doctor of Music was conferred upon him
in 1872 by the University of Chicago. The last
sentence of Mr. Root's *Story of a Musical Life*
expresses the hope that he may live to see his golden
wedding day. He was married in August, 1845; he
died August 6, 1895, at his summer home on Bailey's
Island on the coast of Maine, being only a few weeks
less than seventy-five years old.

BOOKS

A list of the musical productions of Mr. Root
would be long and uninteresting. In his *Story* he
gives the names of seventy-four (one for each year
of his life). His first compilation was *The Young
Ladies' Choir*, issued to supply the needs of the
school where he was teaching, and only a few copies
were made. Among his other works were collections
of church music, *The Shawm* and *The Diapason;* for
Sunday schools, *The Prize, The Glory* and *The
Triumph;* instruction books for the organ and the
piano, cantatas, and books of selections for day
schools. He also gives us the titles of one hundred
and seventy-eight pieces of sheet music that bear his
name.

TUNES

No one of his hymn tunes has been so popular as
to have been retained in many books of recent date.
Most hymnals have at least one of his compositions,
several have three, and one has five, but this latter
book has twice the number of pieces as in the average
church hymnal. "Varina" appears in seven of the
twelve examined that contain his work. This is an

arrangement made by Mr. Root from a piece by Charles H. Rinck, and the words usually set to it are by Watts, "There is a land of pure delight." "Rialto" is in five books, and "Shining Shore" in four. "One day," he tells us, "his mother, passing through the room where he was working, laid a slip of paper from one of her religious weeklies before him, saying, 'George, I think that would be good for music.' I looked and the poem began, 'My days are gliding swiftly by.' A simple melody sang itself along in my mind as I read and I jotted it down and went on with my work. That was the origin of 'The Shining Shore.' " Other tunes of his that many will recall are "Knocking, Knocking, Who Is There?" "When He Cometh," "Where Are the Reapers?" and "Ring the Bells of Heaven."

Songs

When Foster's music was becoming so popular Root thought that he would also write something that would catch the prevailing taste, and so, getting his words from his former pupil, Fanny Crosby, he set to music "The Hazel Dell," "There's Music in the Air," and "Rosalie, the Prairie Flower." Hesitating to put his own name to them until they should be proved successes, he signed them "Wurzel," the German for "Root." Just about this time he went to Boston, and a friend who had begun to issue music importuned him for some songs. Looking over his stock Mr. Root found six that he offered. Most of his music had been published on the royalty basis, but for this lot of six he asked six hundred dollars. His friend thought this a large amount, and made a contract on the royalty basis. "Rosalie" brought the composer nearly $3,000, to say nothing of the other five, so that the lump sum would have been a better bargain for the printer.

WAR SONGS

The best-known compositions of Mr. Root are doubtless his war songs. In 1861 he wrote "The Battle Cry of Freedom" to the words "Yes, we'll rally round the Flag." This was first sung in Chicago, was later taken up by the Hutchinson family, and by them carried over the country. "Just Before the Battle, Mother," was written the next year, and "Tramp, Tramp, Tramp"—produced in 1864—made such a hit that over ten thousand copies were sold the first year, and for a while fourteen presses were running off this one piece. At the battle of Balls Bluff, October 21, 1861, Willie Grout, a second lieutenant in the Fifteenth Massachusetts Infantry, was killed. A friend of the family, Henry S. Washburn, wrote "The Vacant Chair," and when the latter was brought to the attention of Mr. Root he made a tune for it which became very popular both in the army and at home. The first line runs, "We shall meet, but we shall miss him." About thirty war songs were written by Mr. Root during 1861–65.

SILAS A. BANCROFT

1823–1886

SILAS ATKINS BANCROFT was not a large composer, nor did he compile many books, but he was a musician and organist all his life, and the few facts that have been gathered from his niece and from printed notes found in various places are here recorded for preservation. He was one of the trio whose *National Lyre* appeared in 1848. Three tunes of his are found in this book. By far the greater number composed by any of the three were by Samuel P. Tuckerman.

Silas A. Bancroft was born in Boston, April 14, 1823, and was the son of Jacob Bancroft, a merchant of that city, and Martha Howland Gray, the daughter of Captain Robert Gray, who discovered the Columbia River in 1792, and a lineal descendant of John Howland, who came over in the Mayflower. Silas was one of ten children and was musical from his early years. It is a family tradition that while still a small child he listened to a neighbor playing a Mozart "sonata" across the street and when it was finished he went to the piano and played it through without a mistake. He could always play by ear, was bright in his studies, and very original in his conversation, thus making many warm friends, especially among the musical people of his day. He befriended many poor students, taking them into his own pleasant home and introducing them to his brothers and sisters, who were also musical, so giving them a friendly start, and a lift until they had made a place for themselves. Among them was the late Benjamin J. Lang.

He took lessons from A. N. Johnson and George F. Root, who were for a number of years the leading teachers of music in Boston. As his father was comfortably well off, Silas did not have the incentive to work very hard, and therefore left few works behind him; still he was for over thirty years one of the prominent organists of the New England metropolis.   From 1848 to 1860 Mr. Bancroft was organist of the Mount Vernon Congregational Church, Boston, of which Edward N. Kirk was then pastor, and during this period he made a trip to Europe. From this church he went to Emmanuel Church, a position which he held for over twenty years.   At one time he conducted a class of two hundred choir singers who met for impromptu sight-reading and singing.

Besides *The National Lyre*, he assisted William Mason in 1848 in the compilation of *The Social Glee Book*, and some of his pieces are to be found in this book. He died November 18, 1886. He was never married.

STEPHEN COLLINS FOSTER[1]

1826–1864

It will be a surprise to many to learn that Stephen Collins Foster made a considerable contribution to Sunday-school music. In a book printed in 1863 by Horace Waters in New York—*The Atheneum Collection of Hymns and Tunes for Church and Sunday Schools*—there are twenty-nine pieces from his pen. This was among the last of his work, for he died the following year, 1864. Some of these tunes were older melodies newly harmonized, and some of them were new compositions.

[1] From The Choir Herald.

WATERS' BOOKS

Henry Waters (1812–1893) was a New York publisher who added much to musical literature. Seventeen different books have his imprint, covering the thirteen years from 1858 to 1871. The most popular one was *The Sabbath School Bell*, 1859. This, he says, was the first popular Sunday-school book issued in this country, and 300,000 copies were sold before any other Sunday-school book of note was published. During the next ten years nearly one million copies were sold. We are especially interested in those books that have contributions from the pen of Mr. Foster. In a recently published bibliography of the writings of Foster, prepared by the Library of Congress, it is stated that the *Atheneum Collection*, copyrighted in 1863, has twenty-nine pieces by him, written expressly for that work. Another book printed by Mr. Waters, *Heavenly Echoes*, 1867, has fifteen pieces, four of which are not in the collection of 1863, while a number of the pieces appear on correspondingly numbered pages in both books, indicating that the same plates were used. *The Sabbath Bell*, No. 2, 1860, has another piece by Foster that is not found in any other book that I have examined. Another and a smaller book, *The Golden Harp*, also called *The Choral Harp*, and issued in the same year that the *Atheneum Collection* appeared, contains fourteen pieces, all of which are to be found in the larger work, and on the same numbered pages—evidently printed from the same plates.

In more recent hymnals, we find in *The Revivalist*,

1872, a piece with words, "Sorrow shall come again no more," the tune being Foster's "Hard Times, Come Again No More." A Sunday-school Hymn Book of 1903 has the following first line, "Hear the gentle voice of Jesus," set to Foster's "Massa's in the cold, cold ground," and another hymn, called "Our Shepherd True," set to "The Suwanee River." Another recent book has the tune "Old Black Joe," with the words, "Gone from my heart, the world and all its charms." Editors are often criticized for using the words of sacred hymns with tunes that are more familiar in their secular setting, but when the tunes do not have to be learned the words are more quickly adopted. These are some of Foster's tunes that are found in recent church hymn books. But Foster is much better known and will be longer remembered by his secular compositions.

BIOGRAPHY

Stephen C. Foster was born on the Fourth of July, 1826. Morrison Foster, his brother, thus writes:

The day was a memorable one for several reasons. Independence had reached its half century. A grand celebration was held in my father's woods back of the house. The volunteer soldiers from Pittsburgh, and the Regulars from the United States arsenal were there. At noon a national salute pealed from the cannon at the arsenal, and the bands played the national hymn. At that hour my brother Stephen was born. The same day John Adams and Thomas Jefferson died.

Mr. Foster's father was of Irish descent, and had gone from Virginia to western Pennsylvania, where he had founded the town of Lawrenceburg, now a part of the city of Pittsburgh, and was living there at the time of Stephen's birth. The mother was of English ancestry from Maryland, a lady of education and culture, and it was from her that the son inherited his taste for poetry and music. Without a teacher he learned to play the guitar and flute, and at the age of thirteen, when he was attending the public schools in Athens, Pennsylvania, he composed a waltz for four flutes which was performed at the commencement there in 1839. It was called "The Tioga Waltz" and first appeared in print in the collection of his songs prepared by his brother Morrison, in 1894, and written out from memory by him. At fifteen Stephen entered Jefferson Academy at Canonsburg. Most of his later education was obtained from private tutors.

He was married in 1850 to Miss Jane Denny Mc-Dowell, soon removed to New York, and spent part of the remaining ten years of his life in that city. He died there January 13, 1864, from the effects of a fall. His body was carried to Pittsburgh at the expense of the Pennsylvania Railroad and was buried beside his father and mother, and not far from the place of his birth. Thirty-nine years after this, in the month of January, 1903, his widow, then Mrs. Wylie, was fatally burned, her clothes catching fire as she sat in front of an open grate. He left one daughter, Marion, now Mrs. Welch, of Pittsburgh.

Secular Songs

Mr. Foster's songs fall into two classes—those in the Negro dialect, and those in the king's English. In order to acquaint himself with the Negro, his language, sentiments, and expressions, he attended their camp meetings as frequently as possible. His success in this line is seen in the familiar songs, "Old Black Joe," "Old Uncle Ned," and "Massa's in de Col', Col' Groun'." In his latter compositions he abandoned dialect and wrote "Old Dog Tray," which became so popular that one hundred and twenty-five thousand copies were sold in the first eighteen months. Two other songs of his are "Under the Willow She's Sleeping" and "Hard Times, Come Again No More." The copyrights of "Oh Susanna" and "Uncle Ned" were given to W. C. Peters, who made ten thousand dollars out of them, and was enabled thereby to establish himself in business. Most of his songs, however, were published under an agreement by which he received three cents royalty for each copy sold. The first edition of "The Old Folks at Home," 1851, bore upon its title page the statement that it was an "Ethiopian melody sung by Christy's Minstrels, written and composed by E. P. Christy." For this privilege of claiming its authorship Christy paid $500, but the publishers continued to send the royalty to Foster, and later to his heirs. This was his best-paying piece, for it brought him over $15,000 in royalties. The popularity of this song will continue as long as the home is loved. There are times in the lives of men and women when their thoughts turn tenderly to the scenes of their childhood, and then it is that "The Old Folks At Home" charms them. No matter where that home may have been, the State makes no difference, for the strains of "My Old Kentucky Home" carry them back. These are the songs that reach the heart, for they recall the commonplace affairs of life, and appeal to the tender sense of sympathy, love and *home*.

WILLIAM D'ARCY HALEY

1828–1890

THE life history of William D'Arcy Haley, who was for a short period pastor of the First Unitarian Church in Washington, D. C., now the All Souls Unitarian Church, has been hard to follow, but from several sources the principal events of his career have been compiled. He was born in London, England, May 2, 1828. His mother, who was Harriet D'Arcy, having died when he was a mere boy, he came to America with his father. He attended Harvard College for a year or more, then went to Meadville Theological School in Pennsylvania, from which he graduated after two years' attendance in the class of 1853. He entered the ministry, and was pastor of the First Congregational Church in Alton, Illinois, from 1853 to 1856. Thence he came to Washington, D. C., and became pastor of the First Unitarian Church in that city. He was chosen January 10, 1858, and remained in charge until February 1, 1861. In a statement which he wrote he says that before the beginning of the Civil War he assisted in building the barracks around the capital. When the war broke out he went to Massachusetts and offered his services to Governor Andrews, and became chaplain of the Seventeenth Massachusetts Volunteer Infantry. This regiment was organized at Lynnfield, and mustered into service at Rochester, Massachusetts. He served with the colors till May 30, 1862, when he resigned. After a short visit to England he returned, and from August, 1863, to the spring of 1864, he was a first lieutenant in Company A, Second North Carolina Infantry. On September 13, 1864, only a month after the Twenty-fifth New York Cavalry had defended the capital at Fort Stevens from the attack of General Early, Mr. Haley entered the army a third time as a captain in Company I, from which he was discharged June 10, 1863.

For the twelve years following the war Mr. Haley led a wandering life as a printer and newspaper correspondent, wherever a job could be found, never staying more than one year in a place. During this period we find him in Boston, in several places in the State of New York, in New Jersey, Pittsburgh, Pennsylvania; Columbus, Ohio; and Chicago, Illinois. In 1877 he went to California, where he made his home for the remainder of his life.

He married first Archidamia Maria Gammons, daughter of Grace Alton Gammons, who was afterward Mrs. Grace Gammons Barnum of New Haven, Connecticut. After her death he married, December 10, 1873, Eizabeth Holmes, of New York, by whom he had two children, Herbert Holmes Haley, and Ione D'Arcy Haley. For two years he was a clerk in the custom house in San Francisco. Then followed a long service as editor of the San Jose Mercury, and he died in that city, March 2, 1890.

He was a thirty-third-degree Mason, and from an obituary published in the "Transactions of the

Supreme Council" in 1892 we extract the following: "He received all the degrees of Freemasonry in the city of Washington, including the thirty-third, which was conferred upon him at the session of 1860. He served his country faithfully in the late war, and his death was the result of wounds received in battle."

While in Washington, Mr. Haley compiled and arranged *A Manual of the Broad Church*, "containing an order of public service, catechism, forms of administration of Broad Church rites, private devotions and hymns for the use of the families and children of the Broad Church," which was published in New York in 1859. There are one hundred and ten hymns, and the collection includes the following, which have stood the test of time, and are still used in the hymnals of the various denominations: "I Love Thy Church, O God," "How Precious Is the Book Divine," "By Cool Siloam's Shady Rill," "When Marshaled on the Nightly Plain," "In the Cross of Christ I Glory," "Jesus Shall Reign Where'er the Sun," "Lord, Dismiss Us With Thy Blessing."

Following the hymns there is bound in another section of twenty-five pages containing "The Order for Evening Prayer, compiled for the use of the First Unitarian Church of Washington," which was printed in Washington in 1858, and "Dedicated to the church by its affectionate pastor, W. D. Haley." This seems to be an uncommon book. I have not found any copy in the Library of Congress, in the Boston Public Library, nor in the library of the Unitarian Historical Society in Boston. In fact, the only copy I have been able to locate is my own.

HORATIO G. SPAFFORD[1]

1829–1881

"It Is Well With My Soul"

This beautiful hymn appeared in several books as early as 1883, set to music by P. P. Bliss. It is in itself expressive of calm resignation and submission to the will of God; but when one knows the sorrow and grief through which the author had come triumphant, its meaning is increased many fold. Mr. Horatio G. Spafford had been a successful lawyer in Chicago, but in the financial crisis of 1873 most of his property had slipped away. His wife and four daughters had, on the advice of friends, been started on a trip to France, in order that they might be far from the scene of worry. A conference of the Evangelical Alliance had just closed its sessions and a number of the delegates from France had embarked upon the same boat with Mrs. Spafford and her daughters. The company of the Ville-Du-Havre numbered over three hundred, and as there were many Christians among them, religious services were held every morning and on the Sabbath a Sunday school was organized especially for the children, of whom there were fifteen or twenty. The four sisters, whose ages ranged from eighteen months to twelve years, seem to have attracted much attention and to have made many friends.

The Ville-Du-Havre left New York on November 15, 1873, and everything went well until the twenty-second. It was a clear, caim night, when shortly after midnight the Loch Earn, bound for New York, came into collision with her, and in a few minutes the French packet sank, carrying down with her two hundred and twenty-six souls. Those who were res- cued were taken aboard the Loch Earn, which did not seem to be much injured by the impact, and as soon as a count could be made it was found that there were eighty-seven present, but this number included only twenty-eight of the passengers. The four girls were lost, but Mrs. Spafford was among the survivors. She was nearly distracted by the loss of all her children, but in a few days became more quiet and could say: "God gave me my four little daughters, and it is he who has taken them from me. He will make me understand and accept his will." As soon as she reached land she tele- graphed from France (as reported in one of the Chicago papers, which gave an account of the wreck): "Saved alone. Children lost. What shall I do?" Mr. Spafford immediately left his home to join his wife, and when passing the place where the shipwreck occurred, he said: "I was deeply agi- tated, it is true, but I could not represent to myself my four little girls as buried there at the bottom of the ocean. Involuntarily I lifted my eyes to heaven. Yes, I am sure they are there—on high—and hap- pier far than if they were still with me. So con- vinced am I of this that I would not, for the whole world, that one of my children should be given back to me."

He and his wife returned to Chicago for a short time, and it was during this period that this hymn was written. As we read it over, knowing what

called it from the soul of the father, does it mean
much more to us?

"When peace, like a river, attendeth my way,
   When sorrows like sea-billows roll;
Whatever my lot, Thou hast taught me to say,
   'It is well, it is well with my soul.'

"Though Satan should buffet, though trials should come,
   Let this blest assurance control,
That Christ hath regarded my helpless estate,
   And hath shed his own blood for my soul.

"My sin—oh, the bliss of this glorious thought—
   My sin—not in part, but the whole,
Is nailed to his cross and I bear it no more,
   Praise the Lord, praise the Lord, O my soul.

"And, Lord, haste the day when the faith shall be sight,
   The clouds be rolled back as a scroll,
The trump shall resound, and the Lord shall descend,
   'Even so'—it is well with my soul."

Mr. Spafford was born in Lawrenceburg, near
Troy, New York, October 20, 1829. He was an
elder in the Fullerton Avenue Presbyterian Church
in Chicago, and having become impressed with the
fact that the spirituality awakened by most forms
of Christian activities in the church, the Sunday
school, and the Young Men's Christian Associations was painfully limited, in the noon prayer
meeting he cried to God for the baptism of the Holy
Spirit and fire on his workers, that his work might
be carried out. Mrs. Spafford writes: "It is not to
be wondered at, then, that passing through that
baptism of God, by the shipwreck, which was the
experience that wrung from his inmost soul the hymn
referred to, his former yearning after God should
have become intensified and that with his whole heart

he should have turned to the Bible to find there what the kernel of the matter might be, which seemed to be 'to love God with the whole heart, and one's neighbor as oneself.' To this, then, we yielded ourselves, and Mr. Spafford's conviction and example drew others with like aspirations, who were seeking fellowship for the expression and development of these spiritual yearnings." This was the nucleus of the colony which, in 1881, left Chicago and settled in Jerusalem, there to carry out his ideas of overcoming sin. They reached Jerusalem on September 26, 1881, and it was just seven years from that date that Mr. Spafford was buried.

"Mrs. Spafford is still living, and strong and bright as any other. She is a very kind lady, very intelligent indeed, and has a good heart. All call her mother." One writing of her on her sixty-fourth birthday says: "Her hair was white, but her form proud and erect, her face kindly, but firm."

The followers of Mr. Spafford now number about one hundred and twenty, and are known as the American Colony, though they say it is not a name of their own choosing. It is a sort of religious and cooperative community, each one having his work to do for the benefit of all. They have a store in which they sell the products of their workers. There is a botanist who collects and prepares for sale the flowers of the Holy Land; a photographer who has gathered a large stock of pictures; a carpenter makes articles of wood for sale to tourists; and other trades are represented. Their home is outside the walls, about a mile from the Damascus Gate.

While Mr. Spafford was living in Chicago he

issued a small collection of hymns, and after removing to the Holy Land he wrote others, which have not been printed but which are used in the services of his followers.

SAMUEL A. WARD[1]

1848–1903

Samuel Augustus Ward was born December 28, 1848, in Newark, New Jersey. For more than twenty-five years he conducted a music store in his native city, selling pianos and music, and his business had grown to such large proportions that at the time of his death he was having his store enlarged. He was the leader of the Orpheus Club of Newark for fourteen years, and was a familiar figure among the musical people of that city. He had resigned as conductor at the close of the season 1902–03. His death occurred at Newark September 28, 1903.

A single tune of his composition is found in many of the recent hymnals. It has appeared under several names. In one book its title is "Caldwell," in another it is found as "Resurrection," but more frequently it bears the name of "Materna," and the words placed to it are usually those of the old hymn, "O Mother, Dear Jerusalem." Four other hymns were used in the twelve books examined. During the Great War, however, it became associated with Miss Bates' patriotic hymn, "America, the Beautiful," and the more recent books use this tune and

---

[1] From The Choir Herald.

hymn together. The hymn "America, the Beautiful" was written by Katharine Lee Bates, professor of English Literature in Wellesley College, in 1893, soon after she had visited the Columbian Exposition in Chicago. It was not printed till 1895, when it was given to the public in the pages of the Congregationalist in Boston. Several tunes were written for it, one by Charles S. Brown, which was adopted by the Christian Endeavor Society and was printed in some of their song books. But the tune of Mr. Ward is now sung to these words in the schools, and the two seem destined to become wedded in popular use.

PART V

REVIVALIST GROUP—CAMP MEETING
MUSIC—WASHINGTON HYMNODY

THE REVIVALIST GROUP[1]

1868–1872

The Revivalist was the most popular collection of evangelistic hymns and tunes issued during the latter half of the last century. During the seventies it was a best seller. The first issue seems to have appeared in the early part of 1868. There is a statement in print (in the biography of George A. Hall, to be referred to later) that this book came out in 1866, and a recent letter from the musical editor says that he is "quite sure that the first edition was in the fall of 1867." But the records of the copyright office show that it was entered for copyright February 10, 1868. The writer has a copy of that year, and as it contains two recommendations dated in January of the same year, it is certain that the first number appeared early in 1868. It was a book of 240 pages and contained 265 numbers (hymns). It was compiled by Joseph Hillman (1833–90), a well-to-do merchant of Troy, New York, a man very zealous for his church, and devoted to the extension of Christ's kingdom by means of the revival, the praying band, and the camp meeting. Furthermore, he wrote a history of Methodism in his home town of Troy, in 1880. Mr. Hillman gathered about him a number of consecrated workers, whom he organized into a praying band, and they traveled extensively in New York State

---

[1] From The Choir Herald.

311

and in New England, stopping wherever they could find openings. He conducted meetings in the South Street Methodist Church in Utica when the pastor was the Rev. Lewis Hartsough, and later this minister became the musical editor of *The Revivalist*. The hymns were gathered from many sources, and were at first printed on sheets which were distributed throughout the congregations. The popularity of the book increased so rapidly that it was reissued time after time, and changes were made at nearly every printing. In 1869 another copyright was taken out, and the contents enlarged to 264 pages; the arrangement was also considerably altered. A second edition to this copyright of 1869 was printed with the addition of twenty-four pages. Again, in 1871, twenty-six pages were attached at the end under a copyright of that year. In 1872 another copyright was entered, and the book at its seventh printing had grown to 336 pages, while to its eleventh edition under the same copyright twenty-four pages had been added. Whether there were later editions I have been unable to discover. The combined circulation of this collection was over 150,000 copies.

Lewis Hartsough

Lewis Hartsough, the musical editor, writes of himself as follows:

I was born in Ithaca, New York, August 31, 1828. Afterwards as I became known by the use of some hymns of mine, I would be informed in the hymnals, in addition to the date of birth, correctly given, "died in 1870." This seems premature, for though a retired minister, I am still teaching an Old Folks' Bible Class, and have been for eighteen years past.

[This was written in September, 1916.]   Bishop McCabe said that my hymn, "Let Me Go," written in 1862, was my best, while Mr. Sankey said "I Hear Thy Welcome Voice" was my best. It was written in 1872. I have heard it sung in several different languages, and last month a publisher, asking for it, said "I Am Coming, Lord" is often sung in the trenches of war-cursed Europe.

It was in 1851 that Mr. Hartsough joined the Oneida Conference of the Methodist Episcopal Church in New York. After holding several appointments his health failed, and he was sent into the Rocky Mountain district, where under his influence the Utah Mission was organized, and he was made its first superintendent. He continued to live in the West, residing at Mount Vernon, Iowa, when he answered the call of the "Welcome Voice," January 1, 1919.

The large part that the musical editor had in the preparation of *The Revivalist* will be realized from the following statistics: In one edition there are twelve hymns, that is, words, written by him; fourteen of the tunes were his, and thirty were arranged for this book by him. Of these, only one, "I Am Coming, Lord," has survived in the hymnals of the present day.

JOSEPH HILLMAN

Joseph Hillman, the compiler of *The Revivalist*, was born in 1833 in Schoharie County, New York. He joined the Methodist Episcopal Church in Troy when only thirteen years old, and became, and continued, an active member throughout his life. He was superintendent of the Congress Street Methodist Episcopal Church for fifteen years. He organized the Troy Praying Band in 1858, and ten years later selected the ground at Round Lake and became the president of an association for conducting a camp meeting there. He became interested in the union of the various branches of Methodism, and in 1874 personally conveyed to the General Conference of the Methodist Episcopal Church, South, an invitation to hold a fraternal camp meeting at Round Lake. At this meeting, held in July, representatives of ten branches of this denomination were present and a commission was appointed which later met at Cape May, N. J. This was perhaps the beginning of the movement for the union of that denomination, which is now well on its way toward accomplishment. Two other fraternal meetings were held at Round Lake in 1875 and 1876. Mr. Hillman died in 1890 as the result of an accident with the electric cars.

Mr. Hillman compiled three hymn books: *Sunday School Hymns, Sacred Hymns*, and *The Revivalist*. In regard to the origin of *The Revivalist* he tells us in his *History of Methodism in Troy*:

In 1866 the writer projected the publication of the popular hymn and tune book, *The Revivalist*. He proposed to expend one thousand dollars in the preparation and publication of the work. It was undertaken and completed. The rapid sale of the highly commended book compelled the printing of successive editions which numbered in all about 150,000 copies. The large amount of money arising from this unexpected popularity of *The Revivalist* not only paid the cost of its compilation and publication but afforded a sum sufficient to build a church and to repair many other churches.

Early in his evangelistic career Joseph Hillman went to Utica, where he labored in the church where

Lewis Hartsough was the pastor, and the latter was soon engaged as musical editor for the new hymn book. Most of the matter was selected by Mr. Hillman, but the work of putting it into proper form was left to the musical editor. As both the persons named were Methodists, and as the book was prepared especially for revival meetings, then almost entirely restricted to that denomination, a large number of the contributors were ministers of that connection. Among those who furnished hymns or tunes were John W. Dadmun, Hiram Mattison, the Rev. William Hunter, Abraham S. Jenks, and many others. Some of these we will mention more at length.

John W. Dadmun

"Rest for the Weary" is one of the tunes found in *The Revivalist*, very popular in those days, and occasionally found in present-day books. John William Dadmun was its composer. He was a Methodist minister, born in the country town of Hubbardston, Massachusetts, December 20, 1819. His preparation for his life-work, that of preaching, was begun in the denominational academy at Wilbraham, where he spent three years. He became a local preacher in 1841, and joined the New England Conference the following year. He began to preach in the town of Ludlow, serving appointments in several churches until the year 1868. During the last year of the war he was a member of the Christian Commission with the Army of the Potomac. In 1868 he became chaplain in the prison on Deer Island in Boston Harbor, where he continued for twenty years, and where he died May 6, 1890, at the age of seventy years.

He was the compiler of many collections of evangelical hymns. His first book was *Revival Melodies*, 1858, a pamphlet of thirty-two pages, which sold forty thousand copies during the first eight months. It was made up of some of the most popular hymns and tunes of the "Great Revival" of that year. Many of the tunes of Mr. Dadmun had been printed on sheets for the use of his meetings, but seeing the large sale of his first book he enlarged it to forty-eight pages and added many of his own compositions. Having discovered a new hymn writer, he announced it in these words:

Since publishing the first edition we have learned what we never knew before, that the Rev. W. Hunter, of the Pittsburgh Conference, is the author of some of the best hymns published in this work. They are "My Fatherland," "Joyfully," "A Home in Heaven," "My Heavenly Home." It is by permission of the author that we continue them in this edition.

Mr. Dadmun's later books were *The Melodeon*, 1860; *Army Melodies*, 1861; *Musical String of Pearls*, 1862; *The Sacred Harmonium*, 1864, with Lewis Hartsough; and *The New Melodeon*, 1866.

His most used tune is "Rest for the Weary," set to the words of Mr. Hunter, "In the Christians' Home in Glory." This has been included in many a book from the date of its composition until the present time. Another tune is called "Land of Beulah," and is used with words of the same writer, Mr.

Hunter, "I Am Dwelling On the Mountain." Another which was very popular in its day begins with the line, "Come, all ye saints to Pisgah's Mount." *The Revivalist* has nine tunes under his name.

Abraham D. Merrill

Abraham Down Merrill was also a country boy, born in Salem, New Hampshire, March 7, 1796. Making the best of the advantages that his State furnished for education, he seemed destined to a life on the farm, and at his marriage in 1816 settled down upon part of his father's land. On November 20, 1820, as he gives the date, he was converted at a revival, which was being conducted three miles from his home, and having told his parents and friends of his experience, which seemed to direct him toward the ministry, he was urged by them, and influenced by his wife, to begin the preparation for his future labors. He studied his Bible more thoroughly, and was soon preaching wherever a place was opened for him. In 1822 he joined the New Hampshire Conference of the Methodist Episcopal Church, and continued in its ministry until the close of his life, April 29, 1878, forty years of which were devoted to active work. His son, John M. Merrill, was also a minister, and together they gave to the church ninety-five years of service.

"Father" Merrill has been characterized as a revivalist, an indefatigable worker, and a sweet singer in Israel. He had a wealth of emotion, and his enthusiasm swept everything before him. Revivals were usual in his churches, and his songs did much to promote them. The one tune of his that has been used more than the others is called "Triumph" or "Joyfully Onward I Move," the latter name derived from the first words of the hymn that invariably accompanies it. This tune appeared as early as 1849 in *The American Vocalist*.

WILLIAM HUNTER

The hymn just referred to, "Joyfully, Joyfully, Onward I Move," was written by William Hunter. He was a Methodist, born in Ireland in 1811. When he was six years old his family emigrated to America and settled in York, Pennsylvania. Ten years later he was converted, joined the church, and soon entered Madison College at Uniontown. After a short period of teaching he was licensed to preach. In 1836 he began his work as an editor, and for three different periods, aggregating sixteen years, he was the editor of the Pittsburgh Conference Journal, afterward called the Pittsburgh Christian Advocate. In the intervals of his literary work he was presiding elder, pastor in the West Virginia Conference, and professor of Hebrew and biblical literature in Allegheny College. This last position he held for fifteen years. He compiled three collections of hymns, the last one issued in 1859, called *Songs of Devotion*, containing one hundred and twenty-five of his own composition. Some of these have come into common use. He was one of the committee for the revision of *The Methodist Hymnal*, known as the *Hymnal* of 1878, and two of his hymns are contained therein. These are "My Heavenly Home Is Bright and Fair," and "Joyfully, Joyfully, Onward I Move." *The Revivalist* has six of his pieces.

Hiram Mattison

Hiram Mattison, a member of the Black River Conference, furnished two tunes for the early edition of *The Revivalist*. Born in Herkimer County, New York, February 8, 1811, he served the Methodist Church in various relations, as pastor, professor in Falley Seminary, secretary of his Conference, delegate to three General Conferences, and secretary of the American and Foreign Christian Union. He died in Jersey City, November 24, 1868. He too compiled a book of *Sacred Melodies for Social Worship* in 1859, and assisted Isaac B. Woodbury in preparing his *Lute of Zion*, in 1853. His two tunes are "Go, Let the Angels in" and "Heaven at Last."

George A. Hall

George A. Hall is mentioned because he was one of the Troy Praying Band, whose religious activities called *The Revivalist* into being. He was a member of Troy University from 1858 to 1863, and belonged to the only class that was graduated from that institution, which was later absorbed by Middletown College and removed to Connecticut. He was secretary of the Young Men's Christian Association in Washington, D. C., from 1870 until 1875. He died in Montclair, New Jersey, on Washington's Birthday, 1904.

The Revivalist was largely the product of the camp meetings which were so popular at the time it was issued, and many of the persons who contributed either words or music were leaders in such meetings. Search has been made in many possible sources, and a few facts have been gathered regarding the persons whose names follow.

B. M. ADAMS

B. M. Adams, who contributed the hymn with the chorus, "All I Have I Leave With Jesus," was a Methodist minister of Brooklyn, New York, and was present and assisted at the opening of the camp meeting at Vineland, New Jersey, in 1867, and at Hamilton, Massachusetts, in July, 1870. He died about 1903.

B. W. GORHAM

The Rev. B. W. Gorham, who furnished four hymns, was a member of the Wyoming (Methodist) Conference, Pennsylvania, the author of a camp-meeting manual, published in Boston in 1854, and a hymn book, *Choral Echoes from the Church of God*, printed ten years later.

GEORGE C. WELLS

Of the Wells family three members were musical. The Rev. George C. Wells was born in 1819 at Colchester, Connecticut, united with the Troy (Methodist) Conference in 1845, was transferred to the Wisconsin Conference and later to the Minnesota Conference, and died at Minneapolis May 31, 1873, after a service of twenty-eight years in the ministry. Six pieces in *The Revivalist* have his name attached to them—the words of one, the tunes of two, and three were arranged as he sang them. His wife, Elvenah Raymond Wells, wrote three hymns for this book, one of them being "Tenting Again," a paraphrase on a popular song of the Civil War. Besides her hymns, Mrs. Wells was a writer of considerable prose and poetry, which was edited by her husband, and published posthumously under the title *Lingering Sounds From a Broken Harp*. One tune in *The Revivalist* was harmonized by their daughter, Miss Eva L. Wells.

ALVIN C. ROSE

Nine pieces were arranged for *The Revivalist* by Alvin C. Rose. He was a Methodist minister, a member of the Troy Conference, and a leader at Holiness camp meetings, his presence being noted at Round Lake in 1869, and at Hamilton, Massachusetts, in 1870.

BENONI I. IVES

Benoni I. Ives was another Methodist minister, and a fine singer of *The Revivalist* group, two pieces in this book making reference to his singing. He was born in 1822, was stationed at various places in New York State, and was for ten years chaplain of the prison at Auburn. He was also a delegate to three General Conferences of his church. He was frequently called upon to assist in the dedication of churches and to solicit funds for their erection, and is said to have attended twenty-five hundred such occasions and to have raised a total of more than twelve million dollars. He died December 9, 1912, at Auburn, New York, at the age of ninety-one, having spent sixty-seven years in the ministry.

WILLIAM McDONALD ·

William McDonald was perhaps the most facile

writer of the group of writers for this book. Two of the tunes were arranged by this musician, but only one of the hymns bears his name, yet this hymn has been in common use ever since that date. The first line is, "I Am Coming to the Cross." From his own statement the following facts are gained regarding his career: He was born March 1, 1820, at Belmont, Maine. His great-grandfather came to this country from Scotland. He became a local preacher in the Methodist Church in 1839, joined the Maine Conference in 1843, was transferred to the Wisconsin Conference in 1855, and to the New England Conference in 1859. For fifteen years he was the editor of the Advocate of Christian Holiness. He wrote a number of books on religious subjects and several biographies, besides compiling or assisting in the compilation of at least six music books. His *Western Minstrel* appeared in 1840, and his *Beulah Songs* in 1870. He died September 11, 1901.

WILLIAM G. FISCHER

William G. Fischer was the composer of the tune set to the hymn of William McDonald in *The Revivalist*. He also composed the music set to, and always sung with, Katherine Hankey's hymn, "I Love to Tell the Story." This latter music is said to have been written expressly for Bishop Charles C. McCabe. Mr. Fischer composed over two hundred tunes. Besides the ones already mentioned he wrote "Whiter Than Snow," which had a long popularity, "I Am Trusting, Lord, in Thee," and "A Little Talk With Jesus." He was born in Baltimore October 14, 1835, and at the age of eight was chosen to lead

the singing in a church of that city.   For the ten
years from 1858 to 1868 he was professor of music
in Girard College in Philadelphia.   He was very
successful in the leadership of large choruses.   During the Moody and Sankey meetings in the Quaker
City he directed a choir of one thousand persons,
and at the bicentennial of the landing of William
Penn he led a large chorus of Welsh voices.   He was
a teacher of harmony and piano for many years,
and also a dealer in musical instruments.   His membership was with the Christ Methodist Episcopal
Church during his residence in Philadelphia, and
while active in its religious work, refused to hold
any office.   He died August 12, 1912, at the age of
seventy years.

Mrs. Mary D. James

There were several female writers whose hymns
and tunes in *The Revivalist* have become famous.
One hymn, beginning "My body, soul, and spirit,"
was by Mrs. Mary D. James, and she tells us that
it was written July 10, 1869, at Round Lake camp
meeting, inspired by a sermon of Bishop Simpson,
and penciled impromptu.   A few minutes later the
author met Mrs. Phebe Knapp, daughter of her
friends, Mr. and Mrs. Walter C. Palmer, and showed
her what she had written.   Mrs. Knapp sat down at
her organ, and soon had a tune just adapted to its
words and sentiment.   During all the years since
that time, this hymn, with Mrs. Knapp's music, has
been one of the battle hymns of God's consecrated
hosts.   Another one of her hymns, perhaps the most
widely known of her sacred songs, is "All for Jesus,"

1871. At least three different tunes have been arranged for it by as many composers. Mrs. James was born August 10, 1810. In early life she was converted, and wherever she happened to be she threw her whole soul into Christian work. Her first experience at a camp meeting was the opening of a series of such occasions, and she came to think that no other place was quite so near heaven for her. In 1840 she made the acquaintance of Mrs. Phebe Palmer, who was to be so closely associated with her in religious work till death parted them. Much might be said of the contributions made by Mrs. James to the religious papers of the day, including the "Guide to Holiness"; of her help to the poor by her songs and her presence, of her patriotism during the war, and her temperance work preceding the passage of the Maine Law. But we must refer any who wish to know more about her to the interesting memoir written by her son. Suffice it to say that more than fifty of her hymns have been set to music and published in various collections of sacred songs for Sunday schools and social services. Her consecration hymn appeared in *Notes of Joy*, published by Mrs. Knapp in 1869. The music in this book was largely the product of Mrs. Knapp's brain, more than ninety being marked as her compositions. *The Revivalist* has two hymns by Mrs. Phebe Palmer, "Cleansing Wave," and "Welcome to Glory," both set to music by her daughter, Mrs. Knapp.

Mrs. Phebe Palmer Knapp

The subject of this sketch was born in New York

city March 8, 1839, and was the daughter of Dr. Walter C. and Phebe Palmer. She began at an early age to show her talent for music, both in singing and composition. In 1855 she married Joseph F. Knapp, who was successively superintendent of two Sunday schools in Brooklyn, and under their united labors these schools became famous. It is interesting to know that Mr. Knapp was for a time president of the Lithographers' Union of New York city, that he was the founder of the Metropolitan Life Insurance Company, and a successful business man, as well as an active worker in the church. After his death Mrs. Knapp devoted most of her time and income to works of charity, benevolence, and piety.

Few hymn books have had a larger sale, or a more extended use than *The Revivalist* of Joseph Hillman.

CAMP MEETING MUSIC[1]

CAMP meetings were first held by the Presbyterians, though the Methodists were not far behind them in adopting this method of extending their influence. In a letter written by John McGee in 1820, and recorded in the first volume of the Methodist Magazine in 1821, he tells how he and his brother William, though born and reared in a Presbyterian home, were converted and joined the church —William preferring the followers of Calvin, while John followed Wesley. In 1799 they had agreed to make a trip through Kentucky toward Ohio, and

[1] From The Choir Herald.

had attended a sacramental service with the congregation of the Rev. Mr. McGready, a Presbyterian, on the Red River. This was the beginning of a glorious revival of religion, and from this gathering camp meetings took their rise. The next popular meeting was on Muddy River, and Mr. McGee goes on to state that "perhaps the greatest meeting ever witnessed took place on Desha's Creek, near the Cumberland River. Many thousands of people attended. Here John A. Granade, the Western poet who composed the Pilgrim Songs, found mercy and pardon from God, and began to preach a risen Jesus."

The date of the birth of Granade is not known to the writer, though he says in one of his letters that it was May 9; but he fails to state the year. In early life he was a successful teacher of schools. He was converted at three different times, the last time so thoroughly that he gave up teaching and began to preach. Lorenzo Dow, in his account of certain camp meetings, says, "Some choice hymns, used in the early times of this revival at such meetings in the West, were mostly composed by J. A. G., called the Wild Man of the Woods." In the biography of Lorenzo Dow there are also a number of hymns, one stanza of which corresponds so closely with the one following, which is quoted from Finney's *History of Western Methodism*, as to indicate almost conclusively that the initials J. A. G. refer to John A. Granade.

"One evening, as I pensive lay
Alone upon the ground,
As I to God began to pray,
A light shone all around.

> Glory to God! I loudly cried,
>   My sins are all forgiven;
> For me, for me, the Saviour died;
>   My peace is made with heaven."

Two of the hymns of Granade were "The Bold
Pilgrim" and "Apollyon's Lions." The latter hymn
he says he composed while riding through a heavy
rain to attend an appointment where some wicked
men had sworn to meet him and beat him to death
because he had spoken plainly to them about their
sins. They accosted him, cursed and abused him
shamefully, but did not lay hands upon him; while
he told his trembling, weeping brethren that it was
his glory thus to suffer for Christ. He further tells
that while composing his songs, such perhaps as
"Sweet Rivers of Redeeming Love," he often had
to stop writing and praise God for his poetic gift,
for which he would not have taken ten thousand
worlds.

The following description is taken from Bang's
History of Methodism, and refers to a meeting held
on Desha's Creek:

Among others who were brought to a knowledge of the truth
at this meeting was John Alexander Granade, who after an
exercise of mind for a considerable time bordering on despair,
came forth a burning and a shining light as a public advocate
for the cause of Christ. He soon became distinguished among
his brethren as the Western poet, and the Pilgrim Songs
were the most popular hymns which were sung at those camp
meetings, and perhaps became the most fruitful source whence
sprang the numerous ditties with which the church was for a
long time deluged. These songs, though they possessed very
little of the spirit of poetry, and therefore added nothing
to true intellectual taste, served to excite the feelings of devotion and keep alive that spirit of excitement which characterized the worshipers in those assemblies. Granade contributed

much by his energetic labors to fan the flame of piety which had been kindled up in the hearts of the people in that country.

The extract given here is from Finney:

I have said Granade was a poet. His poetry was characteristic of the man and his style as a preacher—bold, towering, often tinctured with the awfully sublime, yet flowing with ease and naturalness, and sometimes extremely tender and pathetic. In my childhood I memorized many of his *Spiritual Songs*, but have forgotten most of them. I have not seen any of them in their natural dress for many years, and fear they are out of print. Some vestiges of them, occasionally found in compilations, are so mangled and distorted that the author, if living, would hardly recognize them. Mr. Granade labored but three years as an itinerant. His zeal carried him beyond his strength and under his indefatigable labors his health failed, and he located. My last information about him was that he was practicing medicine somewhere in southwestern Tennessee.

Granade became a Methodist minister in 1802, but located two years later, so that his labors as an itinerant were of short duration. He moved from the lower part of the State of North Carolina into Tennessee, was married in 1805, and died December 6, 1807.

WILLIAM HANBY

William Hanby compiled *The Church Harp* in 1841, and within eighteen months two editions had been sold and a third was issued in 1843 "suitable for private prayer, sanctuary, revival, and anniversary meetings, designed for the sweet singers of Israel of every denomination." This book is without music, has the Indian hymn, "In de Dark Wood," also a hymn for the close of camp meetings, a feet-washing hymn, and a number of choruses, several of which begin "O halle—, hallelujah." These choruses were a characteristic feature of the camp-meeting music of the early days, and several of the books prepared for such occasions had two or three pages at the end made up of choruses alone which could be sung after any of the hymns.

The Rev. William Hanby, the fifteenth bishop of the church of the United Brethren in Christ, was born April 8, 1808, in Washington County, Pennsylvania. At the age of sixteen he decided he would be a saddler, and apprenticed himself to a mechanic of that trade. On account of the bad treatment he received he ran away to Ohio, where he found a good home and a place to follow his chosen occupation. In 1830 he was converted, married, and the following year was licensed to preach. He traveled circuits, was presiding elder, and in 1836 was elected treasurer of the church paper, The Telescope, at Circleville, Ohio. He was editor of this same paper from 1839 to 1845, and again for another period at a later date. His Circleville home was a station of the underground railway, which conveyed its passengers from slavery to liberty, and it was also while there that he began his hymnological work. This consisted of *Hymns for the Sunday School*, 1842; *The Church Harp*, already referred to, a revised edition of which was issued in 1856, and a *Hymnal*. He was elected a bishop in 1845, and died May 17, 1880. His oldest son was

Benjamin R. Hanby

Benjamin R. Hanby was born July 12, 1833, and died March 16, 1867. He was the author of the once famous and familiar song, "Darling Nellie Gray." During the last years of his life he worked for the firm of Root and Cady in Chicago, assisting in the compilation of *Our Song Birds* and *Chapel Gems*, the latter appearing in 1868. Some who read these pages may remember these pieces that were contained therein: "Weaver John," "Down From the Skies," "Santa Claus," "Who Is He in Yonder Stall?" and the temperance song, "Crowding Awfully."

MOSES L. SCUDDER

Most of the camp meeting books contained the words only, and were of the pocket size. The earliest one I have found, containing the tunes, was copyrighted in 1842, and compiled by Moses L. Scudder of the New England Methodist Conference. This was *The Wesleyan Psalmist, or Songs of Canaan*, "a collection of hymns and tunes designed to be used at camp meetings." It was a small book of only 108 pages, was very widely used, and within four years 20,000 copies had been sold.

Mr. Scudder was born November 13, 1814, at Huntington Harbor, Long Island, and after graduating from Wesleyan University, Middletown, Connecticut, in 1837, joined the New England Conference, serving churches in Worcester and in Boston, Massachusetts; he was then transferred to the Troy Conference, the New York Conference, and later to the New York East Conference. His later years were spent in retirement from the active ministry, with his son in Washington, D. C., where he died June 7, 1891.

The tune commonly known by the name "Webb" appears in this book as "Millennial Dawn," with the remark that "the very extended use of this tune for the past year is the best evidence of its value." It was composed upon the ocean in 1830, and printed in James George Webb's *Odeon* in 1837, with the secular words, " 'Tis dawn, the lark is singing." Its setting in Scudder's book to the words, "The morning light is breaking," is, so far as I am able to discover, its first use with these words. It appeared in Mason and Webb's *Cantica Laudis*, 1850, under the name "Goodwin," set to these same words of the Rev. Samuel F. Smith.

ORANGE SCOTT

Orange Scott claims our attention because of a *New and Improved Camp Meeting Hymn Book*, of one hundred and ninety-two pages, copyrighted in 1829 and printed by E. & G. Merriam at Brookfield, Massachusetts. A fourth edition, increased to two hundred and twenty-four pages, was copyrighted in 1833 and printed by the same firm, then located in Springfield, Massachusetts. It will be noted that this is the firm that first issued *Webster's Dictionary*. Orange Scott was born February 3, 1800, at Brookfield, Vermont. He was converted at a camp meeting in 1820, and joined the New England Conference of the Methodist Episcopal Church in 1822. He held several pastorates in New England, was a delegate to three General Conferences, became interested in the anti-slavery movement, and tried to bring the leaders of the church to his way of thinking. His plans were voted down, and he felt compelled to withdraw from the church he had served for two decades, and with others in Michigan and Ohio, who were strong advocates of an anti-slavery church, organized the Wesleyan Methodist Connection at Utica, New York, in 1842, two years before the division which brought into being the Methodist Episcopal Church, South. Mr. Scott became the first president of the new organization, also served as its book agent, and continued his labors against slavery up to the time of his death, July 31, 1847, at Newark, New Jersey. His little book has no music and the names of the writers of the hymns are not given, so it is not known whether or not any of them were written by him.

ENOCH MUDGE

Enoch Mudge was the first native Methodist from New England. He was born in Lynn, Massachusetts, June 21, 1776, was converted and joined the New England Conference in 1793, continuing his work in the ministry until his death April 2, 1850. He served for two terms in the Legislature of his native State, and during the last thirteen years of his life he preached to the seamen of New Bedford. In 1818 he published *The American Camp Meeting Hymn Book*.

ABRAHAM S. JENKS

Devotional Melodies, dated 1859, brings to our attention a number of new names. A year or two before this date Abraham S. Jenks had issued a *Choral Hymn Book*, containing words only. *Devotional Melodies*, copyrighted in 1859, was a collec-

tion of original and selected hymns and tunes.   His
third book, issued in 1865, was called *Heart and
Voice*, and was intended especially for the use of
the Methodist Episcopal Church.   To the *Devotional Melodies* there were three principal contributors.   William J. Kirkpatrick did most of the editorial work, and eighty-six of the tunes have his name
attached.   Josiah Lowe composed thirteen tunes,
and J. H. Van Nardroff, twelve.   The following
information, received from Mr. Kirkpatrick, is
quoted from his letter:

I have no knowledge whatever concerning Mr. Josiah Lowe.
He was an acquaintance of Mr. Jenks, and I think had no
notoriety as a musician. J. H. Van Nardroff, however, was a
professional musician of New York and for several years
played the old organ in the Ocean Grove Auditorium.

Abraham S. Jenks was born and brought up as a Quaker,
but being converted in the Methodist Church, became a musical enthusiast. When I became acquainted with him in 1855-
56 he taught a most successful Bible class of young ladies in
the Wharton Street Methodist Episcopal Church of Philadelphia, and I became the occasional leader of his class singing, especially upon anniversary days. He was the first to
secure a cabinet organ (that I know of) for his class. He
had two sons, Daniel and James, and a daughter, who were
at that time well up in their teens. The daughter had a
fine piano. I gave one of the sons violin lessons. Mr. Jenks
himself had taken vocal lessons, and his fine, large house was
turned into a regular musical academy, so to speak. He had
a grand piano and an immense Peloubet pedal reed organ in
his parlor, a fine reed organ in his library, and a small reed
organ in his bedroom. His property contained a large lot
with fruit trees and flowers, and it was open every Sunday
afternoon to the members of his class or to his favorite
musical friends of the choir and congregation; and we had
royal good times there for an hour or two during the summers.

Mr. Jenks was then in the dry-goods business with Harper
and Jenks on Market street. He met Mr. Van Nardroff on

his purchasing trips to New York and before he took any notice or interest in my efforts. Previous to my acquaintance with him he published a little camp meeting singing book *The Choral Hymn Book,* words only, and as it had an immense sale he determined to have a music book on the same lines. In order to obtain the melodies for the hymns he and I visited the leading singers in and around Philadelphia who would sing them over while I wrote the tune down and subsequently harmonized it. Mr. Van Nardroff did the same work in New York. In 1865 he issued *The Heart and Voice,* practically a Methodist hymn and tune book, for it contained every hymn in the Methodist hymn book, though differently arranged. This book would have had a large sale but for the fact that Mr. Jenks refused to sell it to The Methodist Book Concern, and they hurried and issued one of their own, and, of course, the churches bought the official one.

Mr. Kirkpatrick did the musical work and compiling of this last-named collection. It contains three tunes by Mr. Jenks and there are two hymns in it written by Mrs. Jenks. Our informant goes on to say:

Mr. Jenks subsequently went into the insurance business with the Equitable Company, and lived to be well up in the seventies. His estimable wife was a fine hostess and enjoyed the entertainment of all his friends. After her death, his children all having homes and families of their own, he married a young woman and died within a year. Mr. Jenks had radically advanced ideas in church work, and as he did not hesitate to express them he was not popular among church officials.

The introduction to his *Heart and Voice* was written by John F. Chaplain who was in 1865 the pastor of the Wharton Street Church in Philadelphia. Mr. Jenks was a member of the Board of Education in Philadelphia from 1867 till the time of his death. He died on Sunday, September 22, 1895, at the age of seventy-five.

AN INDIAN HYMN

From *The Youth's Magazine*, London, November, 1814.   In possession of the author

Poetry.

AN INDIAN HYMN.

IN de dark woods, no Indian nigh,
Den me look heb'n, and send up cry
    Upon my knee so low;
Dat God on high, in shiny place,
See me in night wid teary face,
    My Priest he tell me so.

God send he angel take me care,
Him come heselp and hear um prayer
    If Indian heart do pray:
He see me now—He know me here;
He say,—Poor Indian, neber fear,
    Me wid you night and day.

So me lub God wid inside heart,
He fight for me—He take um part,
    And save um life before:
Yes,—God lub Indian in de wood,
So me lub He, and dat be good;
    Me pray him two* times more.

                                    T. D. C.

JESUS FULL OF TRUTH AND GRACE.

JESUS is rais'd that grace to give
Thro' which alone the dead can live,
    The guilty be forgiven:
That grace which purifies the soul,
Begins and carries on the whole,
    And brings at last to Heaven.

                                    Thus

        * Twice as much.

An Indian Hymn

The hymn beginning "In de dark wood, no Indian nigh," was one of the common hymns used in the early camp meetings from about 1815 to 1860, and it is found in many of the books of that period prepared for such occasions.   The name of the author is not known, though Hezekiah Butterworth in his *Story of the Hymns* states that it was written by William Apes, one of the best educated and most prominent of the Pequod tribe of Massachusetts Indians.   The only evidence of his authorship appears to be the fact that the hymn was printed at the end of the second edition of his autobiography in 1831.   The first edition, 1829, does not have it. It seems more probable that it was merely a favorite of his, and for that reason he added it at the end of his book.   The hymn with music is found in print as early as 1814, when it appeared in *The Youth's Magazine* or *Evangelical Miscellany*, published in London in November of that year.   William Apes tells us that he was born in Colraine, Massachusetts, January 31, 1798.   If this is correct, and if it is true that this hymn was his, it must have been written when he was not more than sixteen years of age. At that time he had not been converted, and during the year 1814 he was a soldier in the army of the Continentals, serving most of the time at Plattsburg, where he was when peace was declared at the close of the war.   It is therefore very unlikely that he should have written these stanzas at that age.

The title to the music in the *Youth's Magazine* is "An Indian Hymn, the air and sentiment from a

North American Indian," and the hymn has at its end the initials T. D. C. This music is doubtless that originally set to the hymn, for the melody is almost the same as that which I learned from my father years ago, and is very similar to the tune "Ganges," to which it was later set. This latter tune, called "Hull" in English hymnals, is said to be the composition of an American, S. Chandler. Not much has been found about this musician, though he is reported to have lived in and around Troy, New York, both before and after the year 1800. James Love, in his *Scottish Church Music,* says that the earliest copy of the tune which he had seen was in John Wyeth's *Repository of Sacred Music,* 1812. In a collection of sacred music published by Ananias Davisson in July, 1825, the tune is named "Indian Philosopher," and is set to a hymn by the Indian preacher, Samson Occum.

WASHINGTON HYMNODY AND PSALMODY[1]

WASHINGTON CITY has always been the gathering place for politicians, diplomats, and statesmen, because it is the seat of the government. Inventors and scientists are attracted here by the hopes for assistance from the nation. The early models of the first steamboat, the Clermont, built by Robert Fulton, and financially encouraged by Joel Barlow of Kalorama, were floated in the waters of Rock Creek. The first successful trains for passengers were run into this city from Baltimore in August,

[1] Read before the Abracadabra Club in Washington, D. C.

1835. The first long-distance telegraph message
was received May 24, 1844, from Baltimore by
Samuel F. B. Morse in the old Indian Office building
at Seventh and E Streets. The early tests of the
airplane were made at Fort Myer by the Wrights
in 1907, and an unsuccessful attempt at flying had
been made by Professor Langley, of the Smithsonian
Institution, several years earlier not far from the
Capital City. The first telephone message from one
house to another was sent by Alexander Graham
Bell while he was a professor in Boston University,
but Washington was the home of this inventor for
many years before his death.

The Capital City has had a long and honorable
history with its Choral Society, its Oratorio Section,
and other less ambitious organizations such as the
Moody Choir, the Inaugural Choruses, and the more
recent Billy Sunday singers. But when we seek the
names of those who have contributed to sacred music
either hymns or hymn tunes, there is no single source
of information. Many denominations have had a
share in this work. The Baptists appear to have
made larger gifts than any other, for the reason,
perhaps, that they had established here the Columbian College as early as 1820. Methodists, Congregationalists, Swedenborgians, Reformed, Presbyterians, Christians, Catholics, and no doubt others
have accomplished their part.

JOEL BARLOW

The career of Joel Barlow is very interesting
aside from his *Version of the Psalms*, and would
furnish material for a long article, but a hasty

review of his life must suffice to allow for consideration of his hymn work. Joel Barlow was a native
of Connecticut, graduated from Yale in 1778, and
after the Revolutionary War settled in Hartford
for the practice of law. Watts' psalms had been
used for many years in the churches of the General
Association of Connecticut, but after the peace of
1783 and the founding of the national government
there were many local passages in them that it
was thought should be changed to comport more
accurately with the new conditions; furthermore,
there were twelve psalms that Watts had failed to
put into meter. By vote of the General Association
Barlow was authorized to make the desired alterations and add a version of the omitted psalms. This
book was issued in 1785, and immediately took the
place of the version of Watts previously used. For
awhile Barlow was a bookseller in Hartford, where,
in company with Babcock, he devoted his time to
printing his version and placing it upon the market.
Two editions were issued the first year, distinguished
by the word "Watts" upon the title page. In the
one copy the title reads, "Dr. Watts' Imitation of
the Psalms of David, corrected and enlarged by
Joel Barlow," while the other one reads, "Dr.
Watts's Imitation . . ." This version was adopted
by the Synod of New York and Philadelphia May
24, 1787, and an edition was put out with a somewhat changed title, as "The Psalms, carefully suited
to the Christian worship in the United States of
America, being an improvement of the Old Version
of the Psalms of David."

Mr. Barlow's first public poetry was presented at

his graduation from Yale.   His masterpiece was an epic poem called "The Columbiad," written in 1808 and dedicated to Robert Fulton.   "The Columbiad" was reprinted a number of times with successive corrections by the author, and the last edition was printed in Washington City, June 1, 1825, though it was published by Joseph Milligan of Georgetown. A copy of this very rare edition may be seen in the Library of Congress.

Our mention of Robert Fulton introduces us to a number of local allusions, and so we turn aside for a moment to mention them.   Barlow spent a number of years in Paris, but in 1805 returned to America, purchased an estate in Washington, which he called Calorama—though later invariably spelled with a K—and settled down to a quiet literary life.   This is a description of the place as given in a letter to a nephew:

I have here a most beautiful situation; it only wants the improvements that we contemplate to make it a little paradise. It is a beautiful hill about a mile from the Potomac and two hundred feet in elevation above tidewater with Washington and Georgetown under my eye and Alexandria eight miles below still in view, the Potomac reflecting back the sun in a million forms and losing itself among the hills that try on each side to shove him from his course. If you have a plan of the city, I can show you my very spot. Look at the stream called Rock Creek that divides Washington from Georgetown. I am just outside of the city on the Washington side of the creek, just above where it takes its last bend and begins its straight short course to the Potomac. My hill is that white circular spot. I find that the name "Belair" has been already given to many places in Maryland and Virginia, so by the advice of friends we have changed it for one that is quite new—Calorama—from the Greek signifying "fine view," and this place presents one of the finest views in America.

Fulton's friendship with Barlow began in 1797, when he had crossed over from England to France for the purpose of advancing his projects for marine navigation. In Paris the two men met, and during the seven years the inventor remained there, a room in the poet's house and a seat at his fireside were always reserved for him. Barlow assisted financially in the projects for the marine torpedo, and later upon their return to America, he had a part in the experiments with the steamboat, the early models for which were tested in Rock Creek, where it skirted the base of Kalorama. There is on exhibition in the halls of the Library of Congress a letter dated June 8, 1810, at Kalorama written by Robert Fulton to a member of Congress relative to his invention of the torpedo.

Mr. Barlow died December 24, 1812, in Poland, whither he had gone to have an audience with Napoleon relative to a treaty with the United States, and he was buried in that foreign land. In 1890 a bill was introduced into Congress providing for the return of his body to his native land, but nothing came of it.

Ephraim M. Whitaker

Another Washingtonian, who may have been a Presbyterian, was Ephraim Mallory Whitaker, who was born in 1816 and died in 1880. After his marriage he lived in Ann Arbor, Michigan, but was appointed in 1865 from the State of New York as a clerk in the Department of Agriculture, continuing till into the seventies. From 1879 he was in the book and stationery business with his son, Greenville

A. In 1872 he furnished one tune for the *Church Hymn Book*, compiled by Edwin F. Hatfield, and the complimentary copy sent him by the publishers is now in my library.

The Baptist Hymn Book

This book introduces us to the Baptist writers, and is itself a Washington product. It was compiled by two North Carolina pastors, William P. Biddle and William J. Newborn; printed in 1825 in Washington, D. C., by John S. Meehan, who served later for thirty years as the librarian of Congress; recommended by Obadiah B. Brown, pastor of the First Baptist Church, and by Luther Rice, who was the virtual founder of Columbian College, now George Washington University.

William Staughton

The first president of Columbian College was William Staughton, a native of England, where he was born January 4, 1770. He came to America in 1793, and after moving from South Carolina to New York, and to Philadelphia, was secured by Luther Rice as president for the new college; and he directed its destinies for eight years. He had resigned in 1829 to accept the presidency of a new college in Kentucky, but died in Washington before reaching his new field of labor. Doctor Staughton began to write poems at an early age, and had published a volume when he was only seventeen years old. When the fourth American edition of John Rippon's *Hymns* was printed in 1819 in Philadelphia, it contained additional hymns by William Staughton.

Another edition in 1826 also had some hymns of his, and *The Baptist Hymn Book*, already referred to, has five under his name. He was intensely patriotic and composed words to be sung to the French "Marseillaise," and in 1812, when music by an Italian composer was received in Philadelphia, he was asked to furnish English words, and wrote "Strike the Cymbal," which is commonly sung at old folks' concerts.

BARON STOW

Baron Stow was one of the first members of the new Columbian College. Born June 16, 1801, at Croyden, New Hampshire, he graduated in 1825 from college, was pastor successively of two Baptist churches in Boston for thirty-five years, and died December 27, 1869. On account of his delicate health he decided not to attend college in the Northern climes of his birth, so came to Washington in September, 1822, and entered Columbian. His studies were so far advanced that he passed to the sophomore class before the end of his first year. He took a part in the first graduation in December, 1824, and completed his own course in December of the following year, carrying off first honors as valedictorian of his class. His activities in Washington may be judged from the fact that during his junior year he was vice-president of the Sunday School Union of the District of Columbia, and later served as editor of the Columbian Star, a Baptist paper, secretary of the board of trustees of the college, secretary of Sabbath School No. 1, and director of the Seaman's Friend Society.

In 1843 he edited, in conjunction with the Rev.
Samuel F. Smith, a hymn book called *The Psalmist*,
intended for Baptist churches, and to take the place
of the editions of Watts that were then in common
use.   A revised and enlarged edition of this book
was copyrighted in 1854.   A smaller book intended
for use of prayer and conference meetings was prepared in 1848 by these same compilers.

Percy Semple Foster

The musical abilities of Percy S. Foster, as a
leader of large choirs, are well known to most Washington people.   He was in business here for at least
twenty-five years, and has conducted most of the
large nonprofessional choruses during that time.
Born in Richmond, Virginia, September 15, 1863,
he removed to Baltimore at an early age, where he
began his business career as an expert stenographer.
In 1895 he became manager of the Washington office
of the Baltimore firm of Sanders and Stayman, dealers in musical instruments and supplies.   Later he
conducted business along the same lines in his own
name.   When Dwight L. Moody held revival services
in Washington in 1894, Mr. Foster organized and
directed the choir which sang at the meetings; and
for a number of years subsequently the organization
was continued with occasional rehearsals, and it
formed the nucleus of the inaugural choruses which
took part in the concerts during the inaugurations
of McKinley in 1897 and 1901, and of Roosevelt in
1905.   Mr. Foster is a member of Immanuel Baptist
Church, was superintendent of its Sunday school for
a number of years, and has served as president of

the Christian Endeavor Union of the District for two years. As a successful leader of large bodies of singers he has directed the choruses at the Christian Endeavor Conventions at Cleveland, Ohio, in 1894; Boston, 1895; Washington, 1896; Nashville, 1898; Detroit, 1899; Cincinnati, 1901; Boston, 1902; and others. He has written a number of tunes which have appeared in the *Northfield Hymnal*, 1904, and the *Christian Endeavor Hymnal*, 1901. His "Loyal Soldiers," written in 1895, was dedicated to the Christian Endeavor Union of the District of Columbia, and was inserted in the official program of the Convention of 1896. At a large assembly held on the east front of the capitol this piece was sung by a choir of five thousand voices led by the composer. The words of this inspiring hymn were written by John D. Morgan, who was in that year living in Washington as a clerk in the office of the adjutant-general, and who was secretary of the local committee which had the arrangements of the convention in charge.

E. Hez. Swem

E. Hez. Swem, one of the best-known of the Baptist clergymen of the city, is also a musician. His church, Centennial Baptist Church at Seventh and I Streets N. E., is in a new building and has a large choir and a fine new pipe organ. The church has been using a special edition of *The Gospel Message*, printed in 1912 by the Hall-Mack Company, and having at the beginning a picture of Doctor Swem, and thirty-three of his compositions, both words and music. Recently the church has purchased a new hymn book, *The Baptist Hymnal,* by **W. H. Doane** and **E. H.** Johnson, 1883, in which there have been bound as a supplement thirty-nine of the pastor's compositions.

Doctor Swem is a native of Indiana, and received his education at DePauw University and at the Southern Baptist Theological School at Louisville, Kentucky. He was ordained in 1881, and held two pastorates before coming to Washington in August, 1884, where he has served the same church for nearly forty years. He has been moderator of the Columbia Association of Baptist Churches for several terms.

Jeremiah Minter

In 1818 there was printed for the author, Jeremiah Minter, in Washington City, *A Book of Hymns and Spiritual Songs* for the use of all Christians, never before published, containing two hundred and sixteen pages. He tells us that he had already issued about one hundred and seventy hymns and songs in three different small publications, and also a volume of psalms, all of his own composition, but I have not been able to find a trace of any one of them. He was a preacher in Virginia, and we learn from his book a few facts about him. In the preface of his book he says:

There have been many collections of hymns and spiritual songs published in our country but none that can claim the merit and attention of being all new or by one man that I have met with or heard of, to the amount of one half the number of this volume. There is great diversity in these compositions, many and far the most suiting any sincere Christian in devotion, but some of them can be fully understood by such Christians as have passed through very great afflictions and tribulations and oppressions both of body and of mind with God's special aid to triumph through.

Of himself he writes:

I stand in the ministry of the gospel as an independent, calling myself by no name but a Christian and wish for no other.

He then adds this experience, which may indicate that he inclined toward the Baptists:

I am very credibly informed that an old Baptist preacher by the name of John Courtney, has so far disgraced himself in trying to disgrace me or in the aim of raising his fame upon my shame or at the expense of my reputation as a Christian as to tell different persons, how many I know not, a positive lie against me, namely, that when I first embraced religion I offered myself to him to baptize me and that he refused me. Now, that I asked him his principles upon predestination and told him a little of my religious experience, I by no means deny. But I said not one word about baptism or joining him at all.

A sample verse from one of his hymns is added:

"My God is true, I know he is,
   His ways are just and meet;
I'll trust his love, his goodness prove
   Or perish at his feet."

The following quotation from *The Recollections of a Long Life*, by Jeremiah Bell Jeter, 1891, adds a few interesting items about Mr. Minter:

In my boyhood I saw another man who, if less gifted and less distinguished than (Lorenzo) Dow, was certainly not less eccentric. This was Jeremiah Minter. He was a tall, spare man, probably sixty years old when I saw him. His residence was, I think, in Mecklenburg County, Virginia. He was an independent, itinerant evangelist—probably an imitator of Dow. He had been a Methodist but either from choice or necessity, had been dissevered from that communion. He wrote and published several small volumes which he sold, probably for his support, in his religious ramblings. He interpreted Matthew XIX, 12 literally, and showed his faith by his works. His error can scarcely be considered so strange, as it is that the same operation should be performed to secure for the Pope's choir at Rome fine alto voices. It made Minter, however, an object of curiosity and wonder, and caused him to be viewed with mingled emotions of contempt and amazement.

Whether he was a monomaniac I am not qualified to say. His appearance, manners, and conversation, so far as I can remember them, furnished no proof of his insanity. A statement contained in one of his books seemed to evince that he was laboring under a hallucination. In one of his journeys among the Alleghany mountains he affirms, with great confidence, that he saw the ghost of Bishop Asbury (I think that is the name), and that he was in torment. He appeared in an old field, on the roadside, in the form of a white horse. That Minter saw the horse is quite likely, but how he identified him with the good bishop he does not state. If the white horse was really a spirit from the invisible world, it might more reasonably be inferred from his color that he was an "angel of light" than a lost spirit from the region of "the blackness of darkness." To all ages and among all peoples white has been the symbol of purity and black of guilt and error.

Unitarian Hymn Books

In 1821 the Unitarian Church in Washington was on the northeast corner of Sixth and D Streets N. W. The pastor, the Rev. Robert Little, lived near by on the north side of Pennsylvania Avenue, between Second and Third Streets. On the east side of Ninth Street, between D and E, was the printing office of William Cooper, Jr. During this year the printer named issued a book of two hundred and twelve pages of *Hymns for the Use of the Unitarian Church in Washington*. No compiler is named, but there is a notice of recommendation from the pastor of the church, the Rev. Robert Little.

The following has been taken mostly from the life of Jared Sparks. Mr. Little, the Unitarian candidate in charge of the Washington Society, was an Englishman, born in London, who had been six years a Calvinist preacher in Perth, Scotland, and for two or three years a Unitarian preacher in Gainesborough, Lincolnshire. He had removed to America with his family and had brought a letter of introduction to Mr. Sparks from the Rev. Mr. Belsham, of London, in the fall of 1819. He soon took up his residence in Washington, and, assisted by Mr. Sparks, began to develop a Unitarian society. He served as the chaplain of the House of Representatives for five months in 1821. He died in August, 1827, in Harrisburg, Pennsylvania, from inflammation of the brain, contracted by traveling in the intense heat on his journey thither.

Stephen Greenleaf Bulfinch

Another graduate from Columbian College was Stephen Greenleaf Bulfinch. He was born in Boston June 18, 1809, but at the age of nine was taken to Washington, where his father, Charles Bulfinch, had been engaged as architect for the rebuilding of the capitol, burned by the British in August, 1814. Mr. Bulfinch was educated in Washington, graduated from Columbian College in 1827, and from the Harvard Divinity School in Cambridge, Massachusetts, in 1830. The following year he was ordained in the Unitarian ministry at Charlestown, South Carolina, by Dr. Samuel Gilman, a New England preacher, whose father-in-law was one of the "Indians" who took part in the Boston tea party. From 1837 to

1845 this young clergyman was pastor of the Unitarian church in the capital city, whence he had come from a church in Pittsburgh. He continued to serve several churches till his death, October 12, 1870.

Mr. Bulfinch wrote many hymns which have been in common use in various hymnals, mostly in those intended for Unitarians. His first ones were contained in his book, *Contemplations of the Saviour,* issued in 1832 at Boston when he was only twenty-one years old. This book consisted of fifty selections from the Scriptures followed by reflections and a hymn. Twenty-eight of these hymns were original. In 1857 he put forth a selection of hymns called *The Harp and Cross.* His most popular hymn begins:

> "Hail to the Sabbath day!
>   The day divinely given,
> When men to God their homage pay,
>   And earth draws near to heaven."

JOHN QUINCY ADAMS

Few think of John Quincy Adams as a hymn writer, or know that he made a complete metrical version of the psalms. This was never printed, but when his pastor in Quincy, the Rev. William P. Lunt, was preparing a hymn book, *The Christian Psalter,* in 1841, he selected seventeen of these psalms and five of the other poetical compositions of the former President, and placed them in his book. His version of the nineteenth psalm is in three stanzas and is very close to the original as will appear from the first one, which is here quoted.

"Turn to the stars of heaven thine eyes,
  And God shall meet thee there;
Exalt thy vision to the skies,
  His glory they declare,
Day speaks to day, night teaches night,
  The wonders of their frame,
And all in harmony unite
  Their maker to proclaim."

Mr. Adams lived in Washington four years as President, and then seventeen as representative from the Bay State, dying here at his post of duty February 21, 1848.

JOHN W. BISCHOFF

Of the three musicians from the First Congregational Church, Doctor Bischoff comes first to mind. Most of us knew him, at least by sight, and all who heard him play the organ were charmed by the beauty and the resources of his execution. He was born in 1849, became blind at the age of two years, came to the Congregational Church as organist and choir-director at the age of twenty-five, and remained for thirty-five years up to the date of his death on Memorial Day, May 30, 1909. He was a prolific composer, most of his work being of the lyric style. In his first book, *Crystal Songs*, compiled in 1877 with the assistance of Otis F. Presbrey, there are thirty-two tunes of his composition. During many years of his service here he provided music lovers with a series of monthly concerts, at which a high grade of music was rendered.

OTIS F. PRESBREY

Otis F. Presbrey (1820–1900) was educated for a

physician and followed that profession for four years. Later he became connected with the Internal Revenue Department at Buffalo, and then in Richmond. He came to Washington in 1870 as attorney for the claims made against that department. From this city he went to New York city, and was for a time publisher of the New York Evangelist. During the twenty-one years that he lived in Washington he was a trustee of Howard University. He was also a trustee of the Congregational Church, and for five years the superintendent of its Sunday school. In *Gospel Bells* there are several pieces of music of his composition.

JEREMIAH EAMES RANKIN

Three years after the issue of *Crystal Songs*, the organist and superintendent were assisted by their pastor in the preparation of another book called *Gospel Bells*, bearing date of 1880, which is noteworthy as containing the first appearance in print of the farewell song, now so popular, "God Be With You Till We Meet Again." About forty of the hymns in this book were contributed by Doctor Rankin, and half a dozen were set to his own music. One tune bears the name of Walter N. Rankin, a son of the minister, of whom we are told by the records of the Congregational Church that he joined there January 5, 1873, and that he died May 11, 1877.

Jeremiah E. Rankin is so well known to Washingtonians that it will suffice to say that he became a native of New Hampshire, January 2, 1828, and closed his earthly labors in Cleveland, Ohio, November 28, 1904. Nineteen years of his life were spent in the capital city—fifteen as pastor of the Congregational church and four as president of Howard University.

WILLIAM GOULD TOMER

The hymn "God Be With You Till We Meet Again" introduces us to a Methodist composer, for it was William G. Tomer's music which has been wedded to this hymn since it was first used in public. During the nine months of his war service as a member of the One Hundred and Fifty-third Pennsylvania Infantry, he was detailed at the headquarters of General O. O. Howard, the founder of Howard University, and at the close of the war he came to Washington, where he spent nearly twenty years in the employ of the government, most of the time in the office of the third auditor, but later in the office of the adjutant-general. At the time of writing this music I am told he was leading the choir in the Grace Methodist Episcopal Church. Both he and Doctor Bischoff submitted a tune for the words, but Mr. Tomer's was selected and adopted for use in *Gospel Bells*. After leaving Washington Mr. Tomer taught school for a number of years in New Jersey, where he died in 1897.

HARRIET EUGENIA PECK BUELL

Mrs. Buell was born Sunday, November 2, 1834, near Cazenovia, New York, and died on Sunday, February 6, 1910, at Washington, D. C. The hymn "Child of a King" was suggested to her during a Sunday-morning service which she was attending in 1878 at Thousand Island Park, New York, and the stanzas were largely composed while she was walking home to her cottage after the service. She had no thought of its ever being used as a hymn. She was a constant contributor for something like fifty years to the Northern Christian Advocate, published at Syracuse, New York, and the poem was sent, as were most of her writings, to that paper. It was first published in 1878, and she received, much to her surprise, a copy of the hymn and music in the autumn of that year, from the Rev. John B. Sumner, a total stranger to her. He found it in the Advocate. Another surprise came to her shortly afterward, when she first heard it sung in public. She had returned from her summer home at Thousand Island Park to her home at Manlius, New York, and the pastor of the Manlius Methodist Church, of which she was for many years an enthusiastic member, had asked her to read a paper at the Sunday-evening service. At its conclusion he announced as a solo by the church soprano, Miss May Williams, now Mrs. Amasa Scoville, of Chicago, the hymn, "Child of a King." This hymn has become very popular, has been copied into many books, and has been translated into a number of languages. A few of her other poems have been set to music, but are not now in use. Mrs. Buell lived in Washington during the winters from 1898 to the time of her death, but always spending her summers at her loved cottage at Thousand Island Park.

DAVID CREAMER

The first American Hymnology was based on *The Methodist Hymnal* of 1832 and was compiled by

David Creamer. Though a resident of Baltimore for the greater part of his life, he spent his last ten years as a clerk in the Post Office Department in this city. He died April 8, 1887. Mr. Creamer was one of the committee of seven appointed in 1848 to revise *The Methodist Hymnal*, being one of the two laymen of this committee. The other layman was

ROBERT ATHOW WEST.

Mr. West was then a resident of Brooklyn. But he too spent his last years in this city, residing in Georgetown, and employed in the office of the judge-advocate general. He died February 1, 1865, and is buried in Oak Hill Cemetery. He contributed two hymns to *The Methodist Hymnal* of 1849, one of them having the following as its first stanza:

> "Come, let us tune our loftiest song,
> And raise to Christ our joyful strain;
> Worship and thanks to him belong,
> Who reigns, and shall forever reign."

This hymn writer was the father of Henry Litchfield West, a former commissioner of the District of Columbia.

JOHN TURNER LAYTON

Washington has had one colored composer to whose efforts are due the compilation of the hymn book now used by the African Methodist Episcopal Church. This book was prepared under the direction of a committee of that church, but most of the work was done in this city at the home of John T. Layton, his wife and Bishop Embry assisting. Mr. Layton was born of free parents in 1849, and had

ROBERT ATHOW WEST
From picture furnished by his son,
Henry Litchfield West

an exceptional training for his life-work as a musician, beginning at Round Lake, New York, then a course at Northwestern University, Evanston, Illinois, followed by special courses under Doctor Kimball and Ernest Lent, of this city. After coming to Washington he served a few years on the police force, and in 1883 entered the public schools as a teacher of music. In a short time he was selected as the first male director of music in the colored schools, and retained this position up to the time of his death, February 14, 1916. For forty-three years he sang in and directed the choir in the Metropolitan Methodist Episcopal Church, and as conductor of the Samuel Coleridge-Taylor Choral Society secured the presence of that composer when the society rendered his masterpiece, "Hiawatha." His compilation already referred to contains a dozen tunes by Mr. Layton, and at the end of the book are a number of pieces for special occasions, written mostly by colored authors. Among these is one by Miss Mary E. Church, who after becoming the wife of Robert H. Terrell, a judge of the municipal court, served as a member of the School Board for several years. This book also contains two tunes by Henry F. Grant, a colored teacher of music in this city.

Frank Sewall

Frank Sewall, of the Swedenborgian Church, has compiled more hymn books than any other Washingtonian that I know of. He was born in Bath, Maine, September 24, 1837, graduated from Bowdoin College in 1858 as A. B., received the degree of

Master of Arts in 1862, and S. T. D. in 1902. He was ordained in the New Church in 1863, and held two pastorates before coming to this city. He was president of Urbana University for sixteen years, came to Washington in 1890 to become pastor of the Swedenborgian Church, and was president of the Swedenborgian Scientific Association from 1898 up to the time of his death. He died December 7, 1915. Someone has divided his life into three periods of twenty-six years each—the first in preparation, the second in pastoral work before coming to Washington, and the last twenty-six years was spent in this city.

He began his hymnological work in 1867 with the issue of *The Christian Hymnal*, to which he contributed twenty-two tunes, there printed for the first time. During the same year he prepared *A Prayer Book* for the use of the New Church. A book of hymns, songs and lessons for the children of the New Church, called *The Welcome*, and having eighty pages, was published in New York in 1868. The preface is signed F. S., Glendale, Ohio. Doctor Sewall was a member of the committee which prepared the *Book of Worship* for the New Church in 1912, a hymn book in which there are two anthems and seventeen tunes credited to him.

In 1884 he edited *A Daily Psalter and Hymnal*, with tunes for schools and households, and the same year prepared *A Manual of Daily Devotions* containing the Litany, Psalter, Gospels, and Companion to the Altar. In *The Hosanna*, published in 1878, there are twelve pieces attributed to him. His latest work was perhaps as chairman of the committee in 1912 which reported a tentative edition of the *Book of Worship* for the use of the New Church. This book has one of his chants.

THE REV. JOHN M. SCHICK

The Rev. John M. Schick was born in Richmond, Virginia, November 8, 1848, was educated at Mercerburg College, Franklin County, Pennsylvania, and had served three churches before coming to Washington in 1900. He came here from Tiffin, Ohio, one of the university towns of the Reformed Church, where he had among the members of his congregation professors from the faculties of both Heidelberg College and the Theological Seminary. It is from this institution that he received his degree of Doctor of Divinity in 1891. During his pastorate in this city President Roosevelt was an attendant at his church. Doctor Schick wrote much for the publications of his church, was for ten years stated clerk for the Pittsburgh Synod, and held an important position on many of the church boards.

At a meeting of the General Synod of the Reformed Church in the United States, held in Akron, Ohio, June, 1887, Doctor Schick was appointed one of the committee to prepare such a collection of hymns as should be best adapted to the needs of the church. This book was issued in 1900. A copy in my possession is filled with his corrections as to spelling, capitalization, and punctuation.

FATHER SIDNEY S. HURLBUT

The most recent book of sacred music by a former

resident of Washington is *A Treasury of Catholic Song,* issued in 1815 for the compiler, Sidney S. Hurlbut, by S. Fischer & Brother in New York city. There were some errors in this book, as shown by a page of errata, and in the following year, with a double copyright, 1915 and 1916, a second edition was published under the auspices of the Saint Mary's Auxiliary of Hagerstown, Maryland. The book contains 236 pages of words and music, and is, the compiler says, the fruit of many years' careful critical selective editorial labor.

Here and there a verse translated from Latin, in one instance a carol from the German, and some five musical settings the joint work of Father Hurlbut and Mr. George Herbert Wells, the latter a music teacher residing in this city. Father Hurlbut was a native of Wisconsin, born in 1858 of New England Protestant parents, and was engaged in secular activity until a period of very discreet manhood in the city of Chicago, with the exception of two years, 1885–86, when he held a position in the Treasury Department at the capital. His studies for the priesthood were made among the Passionists in the Balkan countries and his ordination was received in Bucharest, Rumania, in 1898. Continuing his theological studies for one year in Rome he returned to America in poor health, and after a year or more of convalescence in Washington, the time being spent at the University and at Saint Paul's Church on V Street, he was adopted into the Baltimore Archdiocese and given pastoral work in Rockville, 1900, Clarksville, Maryland, 1900–11, and in 1911 he removed to Saint Mary's Church in

Hagerstown, where he remained up to the time of his death in the year 1921.

Perhaps the most interesting book published in Washington, D. C., for the Roman Church was "*A Collection of Psalms, Hymns, etc.* (with the evening office), for the use of the Catholic Church throughout the United States." It was printed by J. F. Haliday in 1830, and contained 289 pages. Besides the Catholic hymns, many of which were in Latin, there were some from Watts, Wesley, Doddridge, and Pope, as well as from some lesser known Protestant writers.

Thoro Harris

Thoro Harris is a native of Washington, having been born there March 31, 1874. He lived there for most of the time up to 1903, when he removed to Chicago, and since that time he has been engaged in composing and arranging music and in editing and publishing hymn books. He is the owner of the Windsor Music Company, which published almost every class of music, his works of sacred music numbering more than a score. His tune in *The Methodist Hymnal* is called "Crimea." In other books he has shown his familiarity with this vicinity by using such names as "Takoma," "Sligo," "Anacostia," "Vienna," "Benning," and "Berwyn."

John Luckey McCreery

The hymn of Mr. McCreery, "There Is No Death," is one of the most frequently asked for in the columns of the Notes and Queries in various newspapers and magazines. It is a long poem, but four of its stanzas were used as a hymn in *The Spiritual Harp* of 1868, and it is also to be found in another and later hymnal for the use of Spiritualists. It is popular not only on account of the human interest that it has for everyone, but from the fact that it was for a long time attributed to Bulwer Lytton. The story of the manner in which it came to be connected with the name of Lord Lytton is a strange one.

The poem was first printed in Arthur's Home Magazine for July, 1863. The author at that time was living in Delhi, Iowa, and publishing the Delaware County Journal. After the appearance of his poem in the Philadelphia paper he copied it into his own, crediting it to the Home Magazine instead of signing his own name to it. A marked copy was sent to a friend in Illinois, where Mr. McCreery had learned the printer's trade, and this friend reprinted the poem in the paper on which he was then working. Someone named Eugene Bulmer wrote an article for a Chicago paper on immortality and closed with these verses without attributing them to the source from which taken. From this paper the verses only were copied and ascribed to the author of the article on immortality, but instead of using the whole of the given name the verses were signed, E. Bulmer. Now some wise body, who knew more about Edward Bulwer than of E. Bulmer, thought he had discovered a typographical error, and having changed the "m" to "w" the evolution was nearly complete. One more change and the poem became the composition of Bulwer-Lytton.

John Luckey McCreery was born December 31, 1835, in Sweden, Monroe County, New York.

Luckey was his mother's maiden name. His father was a Methodist minister. His brother was prepared for his father's calling, but John did not incline in that direction. He began to learn shorthand when he was fifteen years old, thus preparing for his life-work as a newspaper man. He learned the printer's trade in the office of the Telegraph at Dixon, Illinois. In 1856 he removed with his father's family to Iowa, and grew up with the country. He founded the Delaware County Journal at Delhi, and conducted it for four years. Later he served for a number of years as superintendent of the schools of Delaware County, and for fifteen years he was connected with papers in Dubuque as editorial writer. He came to Washington in 1880, and served with the Congressional committee that went to the South to investigate the election frauds there. He also served with several other congressional committees, held a position in the Post Office Department, and during the last years of his life he was an assistant attorney in the Interior Department. He died September 8, 1906, from the effects of an operation for appendicitis.

> "There is no death. The stars go down
>   To rise upon some fairer shore;
> And bright in Heaven's jeweled crown
>   They shine forevermore.
>
> "There is no death. The dust we tread
>   Shall change beneath the summer showers,
> To golden grain or mellowed fruit
>   Or rainbow-tinted flowers.
>
> "There is no death. The leaves may fall,
>   The flowers may fade and pass away—
> They only wait through wintry hours,
>   The warm sweet breath of May."

MATHIAS KELLER

1813–1875

THE AMERICAN HYMN

(THE HYMN THAT COST A HOUSE)

AFTER a description of the writers who have lived and produced hymns or music in our national capital, what more appropriate subject to close these sketches than Mathias Keller and his "American Hymn"? It may seem rather incongruous that a foreign-born German should write a national hymn that has been as popular as Keller's American Hymn. Yet for over sixty years it has held a place side by side with the other patriotic compositions such as "Hail Columbia," and "The Star-Spangled Banner." Mathias Keller, the writer of both words and music referred to, was born at Ulm, in Wurtemburg, Germany, March 20, 1813. When very young his musical aptitude showed itself, and this was encouraged by his parents, who sent him to study at Stuttgart. At the age of sixteen he began his public career as first violinist in the Royal Chapel, retaining this position for five years. It was during this period that he began to compose. Next he studied harmony and counterpoint at Vienna, and three years later became bandmaster of the third Royal Brigade, which position he held for seven years. He was a republican in politics, and quite free in the expression of his views. So it is not strange to find that his superior officers should have occasion to criticize him, and that he should become

unpopular. Thoughts of leaving the Fatherland
had already come to him when he attended a Fourth
of July celebration and dinner with a Mr. Thorn-
dyke, a New Englander from Boston, Massachusetts,
and it was not long before he had made up his mind
to emigrate to that New World, where every man
could have an opinion, and need not fear to express
it. March 20, 1846, was his thirty-third birthday,
and it was also the day that he started for his new
home, taking passage from Havre. Among the
passengers upon the boat was a family named Ravel,
and the polka which he composed on the trip he
called the "Ravel Polka." For this piece he received
one dollar and a half.

Once on American soil, he sought out a friend in
Philadelphia, by whose assistance he secured a
position as player of first viol in the Walnut Street
Theater. Later he was leader for Miss Jean
Davenport at the Chestnut Street Theater, after
which he removed to New York. It was while
here that he saw an offer of five hundred dollars for an "American Hymn," and determined
to enter the competition. The financial part of the
offer was not the chief incentive so much as the
popularity which would come to him if he should be
successful. Both the words and the music were of
his own composition, and they won the prize. The
words begin, "Speed our republic, O Father on
high!"

Having won the prize, it now remained to introduce the hymn to the public at a grand concert.
Of this concert he says:

The piece was privately rehearsed by my orchestra, meeting with a hearty approval, and it was resolved that the hymn should be brought before the public at a concert to be given at the Academy of Music in New York, the project of which involved an outlay of about six hundred dollars, which I had not at hand. My brother at that time had laid aside between three and four hundred dollars for the payment of an installment on his house, which then was used, together with a borrowed sum of two hundred dollars to give a grand Union Concert, which brought on a loss of about five hundred dollars, the total receipt of the concert having been only forty-two dollars. The consequence was that my brother lost his house, and there was yet to pay the two hundred dollars borrowed from a friend.

In Boston he was more successful in having his hymn taken up by the bands and made a part of many of their programs. For several successive years it was played by the bands on the Common on Independence Day, and at the surrender of the Regimental Flags to the State at the close of the war this piece was played by Gilmore's Band at the special request of Governor Andrew.

At the beginning of the war a song by W. W. Story, "Up With the Flag of the Stripes and the Stars," was arranged for four male voices by Mathias Keller, and among the music which was used at the First Peace Jubilee in Boston in 1869, there were three pieces by him. The music of the Invocation Hymn was his, the "American Hymn" was used as a setting for the "Ode of Peace," written by Dr. Oliver Wendell Holmes for the occasion, and the "German Union Hymn," written especially for this Jubilee. The latter was dedicated to Emperor Wilhelm, and drew from the Kaiser an autographic letter of acknowledgment and a small gift of money, which later Mr. Keller, with his char-

acteristic generosity, sent home for the benefit of
the German soldiers who had suffered in the war
with France. At the Second Peace Jubilee, held in
Boston in 1872, Mr. Keller conducted his "German
Union Hymn" on the third day, and a newspaper
account of it comments as follows: "It is effective
and is constructed on the true model of national
music, being broad, simple, and imposing."   He
wrote over one hundred songs, including many of a
sacred nature, such as "A Christmas Carol," and
"The Babe of Bethlehem." About fifty of his compositions were settings to words by Dexter Smith,
the publisher of a musical magazine for many years.
For much of his music he wrote the words himself,
and a year before he died he collected his literary
work and published a collection under the title,
Keller's Poems.   One has said of his pieces, "None
poor, many are remarkable for their grace, tender-
ness and beauty."

"Possessed of a genial sunny nature, which shone
through his music as well as through his kindly eyes,
he was a general favorite among his circle of professional and other acquaintances. Even a long
series of reverses did not seem to sour his disposition
or dampen his spirits, and he was philosopher
enough to discern even the humorous side of misfor-
tune. His venerable, patriotic form was for many
years familiar on the streets of Boston, and many
who did not even know his name nor his music missed
him when he had gone." His last days were spent
with a married daughter. He suffered much from
rheumatism, but the direct cause of his death was
paralysis. He died October 13, 1875, leaving as his

most popular contribution to the music of his adopted country the "American Hymn," which bears his name, and which, as he had requested, was sung at his funeral, rendered by a Swedish quartet. He was buried in the Dorchester District beside his wife, who had died several years before him.

KELLER'S AMERICAN HYMN

"Speed our republic, O Father on high!
    Lead us in pathways of justice and right;
Rulers as well as the ruled, one and all,
    Girdle with virtue, the armor of might!
        Hail, three times hail, to our country and flag!

"Foremost in battle, for freedom to stand,
    We rush to arms when aroused by its call;
Still as of yore when George Washington led,
    Thunders our war-cry, we conquer or fall!
        Hail, three times hail, to our country and flag!

"Rise up, proud eagle, rise up to the clouds,
    Spread thy broad wings o'er this fair Western world;
Fling from thy beak our dear banner of old!
    Show that it still is for freedom unfurled!
        Hail, three times hail, to our country and flag!"

ERRATA

The following page numbers for the subjects named should be noted instead of those appearing in the Index:

The first sentence under "Amos Doolittle," page 89, should begin: Amos Doolittle, the partner of Simeon Jocelyn (see page 64),

INDEX

(Titles of articles are in capitals and small capitals)